DAYS OF *Awe*, DAYS OF *joy*

Divrei Torah on Elul, Rosh Hashana, Yom Kippur, and Sukkos from 1999-2017 on TorahWeb.org

With contributions by

**RABBI HERSHEL SCHACHTER, RABBI DR. ABRAHAM J. TWERSKI,
RABBI YAKOV HABER, RABBI ELIAKIM KOENIGSBERG,
RABBI YAAKOV NEUBURGER, RABBI MICHAEL ROSENSWEIG,
RABBI YONASON SACKS, RABBI ZVI SOBOLOFSKY,
RABBI DANIEL STEIN, RABBI MAYER TWERSKY,
RABBI MORDECHAI WILLIG & RABBI BENJAMIN YUDIN**

Copyright © 2018 The TorahWeb Foundation

No part of this publication may be translated, reproduced, stored in a retrieval system, or transmitted in any form or by any means, electronic, mechanical, photocopying, recording, or otherwise, without prior permission in writing from both the copyright holder and the publisher.

Please send any suggestions, comments, or questions to TorahWeb@TorahWeb.org

All rights reserved
ISBN: 978-0-69215-026-9

Also available from TorahWeb

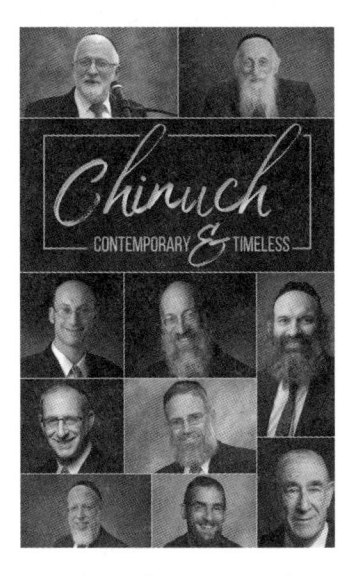

More information about
"Chinuch: Contemporary and Timeless"
can be found in the appendix of this *Sefer*

Distributed by Menucha Publishers

Rav Hershel Schachter's notes from
Rav Yosef Dov Soloveitchik zt"l's *gemara* shiurim

ו' חלקים יצאו לאור:

- מס' גיטין
- מס' קידושין, פרקים א' - ב'
- מס' שבת
- מס' פסחים, ר"ה, יומא, ומגילה
- הלכות נדה
- עניני ציצית, עניני תפילין, והלכות קריאת התורה

Distributed by Rabbi Yaakov Levitz

About TorahWeb.org and this book

The *yomim tovim* are not merely "holidays", i.e. times to break from the routine of daily life and celebrate some past event, group of people, or societal institution. Rather, each *yom tov* is distinctively, intrinsically holy, and it is the unique *kedushas ha-yom* of each *yom tov* which generates the *mitzvos* which Hakadosh Baruch Hu commands us to keep that day. Each *yom tov*, if properly appreciated and taken advantage of, can be a time of unique spiritual growth.

The exceptional nature of *yomim tovim* is perhaps most obvious and pronounced during the *Yomim Noraim* and in their aftermath, on *Sukkos*. This volume collects nineteen years (1999-2017) of *divrei* Torah that provide insight and guidance regarding the obligations and opportunities that we each have every Elul and Tishrei. We hope that making them available in a *sefer* will, b'ezras Hashem, help each of us take maximal advantage of the unique opportunities intrinsic to the *Yomim Noraim* and *Sukkos*.

The *divrei* Torah contained herein were originally written by our *rebbeim* for TorahWeb.org. The realities of the time pressures with which these Torah leaders function on a daily basis result in the *divrei* Torah on the web site often not being properly edited, missing *mareh mekomos*, etc. These shortcomings were addressed for the version of the *divrei* Torah included in this volume.

The TorahWeb Foundation, a 501(c)(3) not-for-profit organization, was founded in 1999 at the initiative of members of our community. Its goal is to disseminate *divrei* Torah and *hashkafa*, with special attention to contemporary religious and social issues. TorahWeb's board consists of Rav Hershel Schachter, Rav Michael Rosensweig, Rav Mayer Twersky, and Rav Mordechai Willig. TorahWeb's primary projects have been publishing weekly divrei Torah written by our *rebbeim* on www.TorahWeb.org as well as on our email list and arranging for *leilei iyun* a number of times a year in various communities, the audio and video of which is available on TorahWeb.org as well. Neither the *rebbeim* nor other individuals involved in TorahWeb receive any financial compensation. In addition, shuls receive the *leil iyun* programming free of charge.

Please send any suggestions, comments, or questions to TorahWeb@TorahWeb.org.

לז"נ

הרב דוב זאב
בן הרב יהושע

מח"ס שמן הטוב

*Hyman & Ann
Arbesfeld*

DEDICATED BY
RABBI STEVEN PRUZANSKY

Congregation Bnai Yeshurun

TEANECK, NEW JERSEY

Young Israel of Woodmere

**IS PROUD TO HONOR
THE
Y.U. ROSHEI YESHIVA**

IN GRATITUDE TO TORAHWEB
AND ALL THE WONDERFUL
REBBEIM WHO ARE SPREADING
AND SHARING THEIR
INSPIRATIONAL TORAH
RABBI EFREM GOLDBERG
Boca Raton Synagogue

Congregation Beth Aaron

TEANECK, N.J.

RABBI LARRY ROTHWACHS
JOSH KLAVAN, PRESIDENT

Congregation Beth Abraham
BERGENFIELD, N.J.

RABBI YAAKOV NEUBURGER,
RABBI
RABBI TANCHUM COHEN,
ASSISTANT RABBI
RABBI MOSHE TZVI WEINBERG,
MASHPIA

IN HONOR OF THE MEMBERS OF THE *Beis Haknesses of North Woodmere*

IN DEDICATION TO OUR RAV AND REBBETZIN

RAV ZVI & DR. EFRAT SOBOLOFSKY

WITH TREMENDOUS HAKARAS HATOV FOR THE LEADERSHIP, DEDICATION, SHIURIM AND CHESED YOU PROVIDE TO OUR SHUL, THE TEANECK/ BERGENFIELD COMMUNITY, AND KLAL YISRAEL.

MAY HASHEM PROVIDE YOU WITH GOOD HEALTH AND STRENGTH TO CONTINUE TO LEAD, GUIDE AND INSPIRE OUR SHUL AND THE COMMUNITY FOR MANY YEARS TO COME.

Congregation Ohr HaTorah

Table of Contents
Elul

In the Pursuit of Happiness
Rabbi Hershel Schachter...3

The Elul Shofar
Rabbi Yaakov Neuburger 7

LeDovid Hashem: Planning and Praying for the Right Things
Rabbi Yaakov Neuburger 10

Deep Faith and Deep Love
Rabbi Yaakov Neuburger 13

Temptations and Triumphs: Ki Savo, the Parasha of Private Moments
Rabbi Yaakov Neuburger 16

The Significance of Rosh Chodesh and the Month of Elul
Rabbi Michael Rosensweig 19

Ahavas Hashem: The Teshuva of Chodesh Elul
Rabbi Michael Rosensweig 23

*Rambam's View of Ahavas Hashem as the Telos of Teshuva,
an Indispensable Manifestation of Avodas Hashem*
Rabbi Michael Rosensweig 27

Interpersonal Teshuva
Rabbi Dr. Abraham J. Twerski..31

Glatt Kosher Is Not Enough
Rabbi Dr. Abraham J. Twerski..34

Teshuva: In Your Mouth and in Your Heart
Rabbi Mayer Twersky...39

Transforming Attitude into Gratitude
Rabbi Benjamin Yudin..42

Rosh Hashana

An Attitude of Confidence
Rabbi Hershel Schachter..49

Malchuyos
Rabbi Hershel Schachter..51

Remembering the Beginning
Rabbi Hershel Schachter..54

The Light of Torah
Rabbi Hershel Schachter..57

Recommitting Ourselves to the Torah Shebe'al Peh
Rabbi Hershel Schachter..60

The Shofar: External and Internal
Rabbi Yakov Haber..66

Approaching Rosh Hashana: How to Earn His Patience and Tolerance
Rabbi Yaakov Neuburger 69

A Blueprint for Teshuva
Rabbi Michael Rosensweig..72

Yom Terua and Zichron Terua:
The Centrality of Mitzvas Shofar Even on Shabbos Rosh Hashana
Rabbi Michael Rosensweig..79

Zichron Terua: Perspectives on Tekias Shofar
Rabbi Yonason Sacks..84

Creating the Mood for Rosh Hashana
Rabbi Zvi Sobolofsky 89

A Cry from the Soul
Rabbi Zvi Sobolofsky 92

A Good and Sweet Year
Rabbi Zvi Sobolofsky 95

Wrong Way!
Rabbi Daniel Stein..98

Malchus: The Theme of Rosh Hashana
Rabbi Dr. Abraham J. Twerski 102

Fear and Love, Truth and Peace
Rabbi Mordechai Willig..106

The Months, Divine Attributes and Purpose of Creation
Rabbi Mordechai Willig..111

Praying for What?
Rabbi Benjamin Yudin 115

On the Edge
Rabbi Benjamin Yudin 118

If at First You Don't Succeed
Rabbi Benjamin Yudin 122

Going "Sho-Far" for Hashem
Rabbi Benjamin Yudin 126

Group Coverage
Rabbi Benjamin Yudin 129

Be Basket-like
Rabbi Benjamin Yudin 132

Aseres Yemei Teshuva

Bechira Chofshis
Rabbi Hershel Schachter 137

Shabbos and Teshuva: Remaking the World, Remaking the Self
Rabbi Yakov Haber 139

Becoming Bound to Each Other and to Hashem
Rabbi Yaakov Neuburger 141

Reaching Our Destination
Rabbi Zvi Sobolofsky 143

Remember Your Creator
Rabbi Mayer Twersky 146

Teshuva: A Mandate for Change
Rabbi Mayer Twersky 148

Haughtiness, Humility and Din
Rabbi Mordechai Willig 150

Reuven's Teshuva: A Model for Life-Long Growth
Rabbi Mordechai Willig 154

Yom Kippur

Yom Kippur, the Yom Tov of Torah Shebe'al Peh
Rabbi Hershel Schachter 159

The Torah of Chesed and the Day of Chesed
Rabbi Hershel Schachter 164

And Rejoice in Trembling: The Mitzva of Seudas Erev Yom Kippur
Rabbi Yakov Haber 167

The Two Goats and the True Self
Rabbi Yakov Haber 170

The Torah's Song; the Song of Torah
Rabbi Yakov Haber 173

Teshuva on Yom Kippur
Rabbi Michael Rosensweig 179

Yom Kippur: The Day of the Kohen Gadol
Rabbi Michael Rosensweig 183

Angels or Sinners: Who Are We?
Rabbi Zvi Sobolofsky 187

Torah and Chesed: The Secrets of Kappara
Rabbi Zvi Sobolofsky 190

Atonement on Yom Kippur
Rabbi Mordechai Willig 193

Communal Atonement
Rabbi Mordechai Willig 199

Sukkos

Shemini Atzeres and Simchas Torah: One Simcha
Rabbi Hershel Schachter 207

One Continuum of Jewish History
Rabbi Hershel Schachter 210

Lashon Hara in the Sukkah
Rabbi Hershel Schachter 213

Active Prayer
Rabbi Yaakov Haber 216

Sukkos: Universal Holiday?
Rabbi Yaakov Haber 220

Chag HaSukkos: The Festival of Divine Providence
Rabbi Yaakov Haber 224

Chag HaSukkos: The Tishrei Connection
Rabbi Yaakov Haber 228

Kerias Shema and the Festivals of Tishrei
Rabbi Yaakov Haber 231

Sukkos: Two Types of Divine Providence
Rabbi Yaakov Haber 234

The Sukkah: The Key to True Happiness
Rabbi Eliakim Koenigsberg 240

Sukkos and Shemini Atzeres: Hashem's Expression of Love
Rabbi Eliakim Koenigsberg 243

Shemini Atzeres: Living in Hashem's Presence
Rabbi Eliakim Koenigsberg 247

Simchas Torah: In Anticipation
Rabbi Yaakov Neuburger 251

Bezos Ani Boteach
Rabbi Yaakov Neuburger 253

Grass-Roots Ownership of the Torah
Rabbi Yaakov Neuburger 256

The Majesty at Hand: The Torah Readings of Yom Kippur and Sukkos
Rabbi Yaakov Neuburger 259

The Link between Yom Kippur and Sukkos
Rabbi Michael Rosensweig 263

Vehayisa Ach Sameach: The Joy of Shemini Atzeres
Rabbi Michael Rosensweig 267

Shemini Atzeres: The Contrast, Complement and Culmination of Sukkos
Rabbi Michael Rosensweig 271

Chag HaSukkos: Avodas Hashem in the Aftermath of the Yomim Noraim
Rabbi Michael Rosensweig 275

Simchas Sukkos: An Expression of Avoda and Hashra'as HaShechina
Rabbi Michael Rosensweig 279

The Song of Life
Rabbi Zvi Sobolofsky 285

The Secret of Shemini Atzeres
Rabbi Zvi Sobolofsky 287

The Harvest Festival: A Spiritual Perspective
Rabbi Zvi Sobolofsky 289

The Unity of the Sukkah and the Daled Minim
Rabbi Daniel Stein 291

Sukkos: A Time for Teshuva
Rabbi Mayer Twersky 295

Sukkos: A Call to Teshuva
Rabbi Mayer Twersky 297

Seeing Straight
Rabbi Mordechai Willig 299

Success Is in the Palm of Your Hand
Rabbi Benjamin Yudin 302

Weather Forecast for Sukkos: Cloudy
Rabbi Benjamin Yudin 305

Resolving the Sukkah Paradox
Rabbi Benjamin Yudin 309

Appendix

Excerpt from "Chinuch: Contemporary & Timeless" 313

Elul

In the Pursuit of Happiness

RABBI HERSHEL SCHACHTER

Everyone is searching for happiness. Even in the tradition of the American founding fathers, all men are entitled to "the pursuit of happiness." Exactly what constitutes happiness? To some it means money; to others, *kavod*. To others it means a yacht; and yet to others, a cigarette.

The *pasuk* in *Koheles* states (6:7) that whatever man acquires will neither satisfy him nor make him happy. The *Midrash* explains by way of a parable that if a farmer marries a princess, he will never be able to satisfy her. Even if he buys her items that would be considered "luxurious" for a farmer – the most fancy dungarees with the most colorful patches, and a lot of straw to sleep on – it will not make her happy, since she is used to royal clothing and the most beautiful furniture. Similarly, Jewish souls come *mitachas kissei hakavod* ("from below the throne of *Hashem*"), and are used to being close to the *Shechina*. All the money, yachts and cigarettes in the world will not bring a Jewish soul satisfaction.

From *Rosh Chodesh Elul* until the end of *Sukkos*, it is customary in many communities to recite the twenty-seventh *perek* of *Tehillim* at the

---

Originally published on TorahWeb.org in 2007

conclusion of the *tefilla*. In that *perek*, Dovid *Hamelech* points out that he has only one real request of *Hashem*: "to be able to stay in the House of *Hashem* for the rest of [his] life." The one and only thing that people are searching for is happiness, and Dovid *Hamelech* defines happiness as being "in the presence of *Hashem*." The *pasuk* tells us (*Divrei Hayamim I* 16:27) that in the presence of *Hashem* there is always joy. The Talmud comments (*Chagiga* 5b) based on this *pasuk* that there is no sadness when one is in the presence of *Hashem*. Jewish *neshamos* are used to being close to the *Shechina* (before they were born), and the only way for them to attain happiness and comfort is to return to that state.

The Torah often writes that we should "rejoice in the presence on *Hashem*." (See, for example, *Parashas Re'eh* 16:11.) The Talmud understands that the state of being "in the presence of *Hashem*" causes one to rejoice. Because the *Kohen Gadol* must always be in the *Beis Hamikdash* ("in the presence of *Hashem*")[1], it follows that he has a *mitzva* of *simcha* all year long. The rest of *Klal Yisrael* has a *mitzva* of *simcha* on the *Shalosh Regalim* because at those times we all have an obligation to visit the *Beis Hamikdash* to enter into the state of "*lifnei Hashem*." (See *Moed Katan* 14b and *Nefesh HaRav*, p. 314.)

There is a dispute among the *Tanaim* as to whether there is a *mitzva* of *simcha* on *Rosh Hashana* and *Yom Kippur*. (See *Moed Katan* 19a.) The accepted opinion is that there is such a *mitzva*. Rav Soloveitchik explained that the prophets compare sins to a *mechitza* that separates a person from *Hashem*. Only when one does *teshuva* can one return to his original state of *lifnei Hashem*. Because on *Yom HaKippurim* there is a special *mitzva* of *teshuva* (over and above the *mitzva* of *teshuva* of all year round), and an obligation to come *lifnei Hashem*, we have a special *mitzva* of *simcha* on *Yom HaKippurim*.

---

[1] Rambam, *Hilchos Klei Hamikdash*, 5:7

The Talmud points out that because the purpose of blowing the *shofar* on *Rosh Hashana* is "to bring before *Hashem* the remembrance of the Jewish people," (i.e., blowing of the *shofar* constitutes a form of *tefilla*), when we blow the *shofar* it is considered as though we were in the *Kodesh Hakodashim*, in the presence of *Hashem* (*Rosh Hashana* 26a). This state, in turn, engenders the *mitzva* of *simcha*.

When Kayin killed his brother Hevel, he realized on his own that he would be punished. He assumed that his punishment would be that he would no longer be permitted to be "in the presence of *Hashem*" (*Bereishis* 4:14). And indeed, the *Chumash* states that that was his punishment – he had to leave "the presence of *Hashem*" (*Bereishis* 4:16). What does this mean? How can one possibly leave the presence of *Hashem*, who is omnipresent and omniscient!? The Ramban (*Parashas Bereishis*) explains that "to be in the presence of *Hashem*" means that one has the ability to *daven* and has the right to offer *korbanos*, and it was these rights that Kayin was denied.

When the serpent was punished for having caused Chava to sin and eat from the *eitz hada'as*, the Torah records that part of his punishment was that from then on he would eat sand and dust (*Bereishis* 3:14). The *Midrash* there comments that when *Hakadosh Baruch Hu* punishes, He doesn't utterly destroy the sinner, but rather gives him a lighter punishment which is less horrible. Although the serpent will no longer eat delicious foods, and whatever he eats will always taste like sand, there is still a positive side to this punishment: that he will never have to worry about food. Sand is available all over. From now on, the serpent will never have *da'agas haparnasa*.

At first glance, the comment of the *Midrash* seems very strange. It would appear that for the serpent, his *aveira* paid off. How can it be "that the sinner is being rewarded"?! A famous explanation was offered by one of the great Chasidic *Rebbes*, Reb Itzele Surker. Because the serpent would never be lacking anything, he would have no right to pray. *Tefilla* is only permitted when one perceives that he is lacking some of his needs. By giving the serpent *parnasa* for the rest of his life, *Hashem* was actually punishing him, just as Kayin was punished with never again being allowed to pray.

The Talmud (*Berachos* 8a) points out that since the destruction of the *Beis Hamikdash*, the only way to enter into the presence of *Hakadosh Baruch Hu* is by learning Torah. We believe that the Torah is a description of *Hashem*'s essence, and when one engages in Torah study, he gets a better understanding of what God is all about and thereby becomes closer to Him. (See the introduction to my most recent *sefer*, Ginas Egoz.) "When one learns Torah at night, the *Shechina* will be there in front of him" (*Tamid* 32b).

Happiness can be attained. We all have the opportunity and the privilege to *daven* and to learn. "I rejoice when they tell me, 'Let us go to the home of *Hashem*'" (*Tehillim* 122:1). It's all up to us!

The Elul Shofar
RABBI YAAKOV NEUBURGER

Is there a more sobering and even disquieting sound in our tradition than the *Elul shofar*, announcing that *Rosh Hashana* is upon us once again and marking the march of time as we get closer and closer? It is in this two-step fashion that the Rosh (at the end of *Maseches Rosh Hashana*) presents the history and observance of the *Elul shofar*. The earliest source of this practice presents it as a rabbinic legislation but sees it limited to blowing the *shofar* on *Rosh Chodesh Elul* alone. A *midrash* (*Pirkei DeRabi Eliezer*, chapter 46) records that on our very first *Rosh Chodesh Elul*, a few months after *matan Torah* and the calamitous *cheit ha'eigel*, we were, understandably, a shaken and spiritually diminished people. As Moshe was invited to ascend *Har Sinai* to accept the *luchos* one more time, we grew concerned that we would err once again in calculating Moshe's return and despair over his absence. Therefore we decided to sound the *shofar* as Moshe left us. The *midrash* concludes that as the Rabbis realized that *Hashem* was greatly honored by this *shofar* sound, they legislated its re-enactment every *Rosh Chodesh Elul*. The Rosh further comments that we continue to sound the *shofar* every morning of the month to remind us to do *teshuva*.

Originally published on TorahWeb.org in 2010

What impressed our Sages so about that one sounding of the *shofar* of *Rosh Chodesh* that they decided to memorialize it? Moreover, did the Rosh record a second and independent practice of blowing the *shofar* throughout the month which happens to dovetail with the rabbinic enactment of *Rosh Chodesh*? Or are we to continue memorializing the *shofar* at *Har Sinai* throughout *Elul*, and if so, why?

I would suggest that the *shofar* of *Elul* reminds us of the *avoda* of *Elul*, the spiritual responsibilities and challenges that we face throughout our preparation for the *Yamim Tovim*. I believe that the decision to sound the *shofar* as Moshe ascended added a voluntary but oftentimes indispensable dimension to the *teshuva* process. Perhaps that is why *Hashem* himself was honored in an unparalleled fashion at that moment. Let me explain.

It is well known that the *mitzva* of *teshuva* prescribes that we must respond to our flaws and errors through admission of our lapses, expressions of regret and shame at our lack of compliance to *Hashem*, and articulation our further commitment to do better going forward. The Rambam teaches that our thought process must be earnest enough to win the nod of *Hashem* himself, and further teaches that the process is completed once we are tested and we do not err again (*Hilchos Teshuva* chapter 2).

However, Moshe's generation adopted a new behavior to bolster their pledge for the future and thus introduced a new concept to the *teshuva* process. The *halachos* of *teshuva* are fully satisfied by a genuine and deep *cheshbon hanefesh* – soul-searching introspection and commitment. Yet we know that we often have trouble following through, especially if we are repeat offenders and have unsuccessfully tried, with all the seriousness we can muster, to improve. Many of us find ourselves honestly mentioning the same misstep in the *al cheit*s year after year.

The *shofar* reminds us of a technique that we established long ago when we experienced deep remorse about the past and profound fear of our frailty in the future. Sometimes even deep-seated regret may simply not be enough. Action may be required. In *halacha* and in the *musar sefarim* it is called making a *geder* (fence), a protective measure.

In practice, the person who has trouble arousing himself for *minyan* makes a *geder* to learn with someone else before *davening*, adding extra pressure on himself when he is still half asleep. The person who finds the days roll by without learning will establish the *geder* of setting his time to learn immediately after dinner or *Ma'ariv*. Similar *gedarim* may aid the individual who never finds the time to exercise or to make the all-important phone calls. Self-awareness and creativity will help one find a protective move or act that will forestall compromising another's privacy or dignity, and maintaining the standards of interpersonal conduct for which we strive.

The decision to sound the *shofar* that *Rosh Chodesh Elul* at *Har Sinai* signaled the deepest remorse, as well as the insightful realization of human weakness. It launched a form of *tikkun* that deserves eternal observance. Later generations understood this and established the daily *shofar* so that we would consider this *tikkun* over and over again as part of our *avoda* throughout the month of *Elul*.

LeDovid Hashem: Planning and Praying for the Right Things
RABBI YAAKOV NEUBURGER

The first six *pesukim* of לדוד ה' אורי וישעי ("For David, *Hashem* is my light and my salvation," the *perek* of *Tehillim* repeated daily throughout this season) describe a level of confidence and trust that we recite rather longingly. For almost a month we say:

> *Hashem* is my light and my salvation, whom shall I fear? *Hashem* is the stronghold of my life, from whom shall I be frightened? ... My enemies ... stumbled and fell ... If a war should rise ... in this I trust ... and now, my head will be raised over my enemies ... I will sacrifice ... sacrifices with joyous song, I will sing to and praise *Hashem* ... (*Tehillim* 27:1-6).

In the seventh *pasuk*, that uplifting faith suddenly gives way to an impassioned expression of helplessness and despair. Without a textual clue to allude to any calamitous event, we continue:

Originally published on TorahWeb.org in 2012

Listen *Hashem* to my voice when I call out, and favor me and answer me ... do not hide your presence from me, do not turn me away with anger ... do not forsake me and do not abandon me.

What happened? What impending calamity confronted Dovid *Hamelech*?

Imagine yourself feeling that all is wonderful and that all your physical needs are amply addressed, but one aspiration in life is unfulfilled: you are unable to spend countless hours in the *beis hamidrash* from morning to night, and you do not understand *Hashem* and His ways. Of course, in such a situation we would pray genuinely and sincerely to *Hashem* that He complete our lives with *beis hamidrash* time. But would this disappointment motivate us to scream out as one facing the ravages of a disease, begging *Hashem* not to abandon us? Would we plead as one who has been deserted by one's parents and has no one to whom to turn? Perhaps that is exactly the intent of the centuries-old custom to have this *perek* carry us through each day of this introspective *Elul* and *Yom Tov* season.

Indeed, Rav Samson Raphael Hirsch understands that the intensity of Dovid *Hamelech*'s focus is born of the supreme importance he places on his spiritual quests. In the very center of this *perek*, Dovid's heart shouts out to *Hashem* upon realizing that only his physical safety and comfort have been amply satisfied, but the sacred quests of his life have yet to be achieved. To Dovid *Hamelech*, disappointing his spiritual ambitions is far more devastating than any other shortcoming.

Interestingly, in the *perek* that we say before *Pisukei DeZimra*, מזמור שיר חנוכת הבית ("A psalm, a song of dedication of the house"; *Tehillim* 30), Dovid also cries out like someone in dreadful pain or frightened of an irreversible illness: "Of what value will I be if I were to die ... please listen to my voice ..." after saying that *Hashem* has given him every reason to feel secure in His protection! Here, Rav Elyashiv *zt"l* points out that according to *Chazal*, Dovid *Hamelech* was praying to be allowed to build the *Beis Hamikdash*. Once again Dovid felt that should his service of *Hashem* not live up to his expectations, his military and administrative achievements would not be meaningful at all.

Perhaps this is why *Klal Yisrael* adopted *LeDovid Hashem* to be the "*shir shel yom*" of *Elul* and *Tishrei*. It is during these days that we are appropriately focused on the blessings that we will hopefully earn through our *teshuva* and prayer. The health, prosperity and companionship that we ask for are all well-articulated pursuits and prayers. Have we taken time, however, to articulate our aspirations as a friend, as a family member, and as one who has a place in the sacred mission of *Bnei Yisrael*? Have we given time to consider a plan of how will we grow the spiritual parts of our lives as we focus on plans to grow so many other parts of life?

The passion of Dovid *Hamelech* in his unrelenting quest to simply be in close proximity to *Hashem*, even after he has achieved far more than a rare few, encourages us to ponder and articulate our spiritual quests, to plan for them, and to pray for them during the months of *Elul* and *Tishrei*.

Deep Faith and Deep Love

RABBI YAAKOV NEUBURGER

"...We should now contemplate how to live with people whose ideas are distant from us, to engage them with love and brotherliness, even as we firmly distance our opinions and intuitions from their positions."[2]

That this quote comes from the correspondence of one the leading figures of the *musar* tradition, describing one of the goals of the annual *Elul* spiritual journey, came as a surprise to me. It was penned by none other than Rav Simcha Zissel Ziv *zt"l* (1824–1898), known as "the *Alter* of Kelm." He accepted this title "the elder member of the group" because he felt unworthy of being known as a *talmid* of his *rebbe*, Rav Yisrael Salanter. Needless to say, he was one of the greatest students of Rav Yisrael, and in turn shaped his own students, Rav Yerucham Levovitz of Mir, Rav Eliyahu Dessler, Rav Yechezkel Levenstein and Rav Elia Lopian, all of whom impacted their generation immeasurably. Rav Simcha Zissel's piety was otherworldly and his *yiras Shamayim* was apparently entirely all-embracing, mesmerizing and frightening all at once.

---

[2] Quoted in Rav Wolbe's BeEmunaso Yichyeh, p. 93. Loosely translated.

Originally published on TorahWeb.org in 2016

Indeed, it is this profound and practical awareness of *Hashem* which produces a person who can be totally true to all the nuances of the truths that shape his life, and at the same time love the brother who disagrees. According to Rav Wolbe *zt"l*, the influential and thought-provoking *mashgiach* of Mir, it is only the profound awareness of how much we all mean to our Creator that can produce the balance that the *Alter* of Kelm strove to achieve. That is why this balance has its place among the spiritual heights to be sought during *Elul*.

As I was studying this quote and Rav Wolbe's interpretation that it speaks to the depth of one's *emuna*, it occurred to me that it also sheds light on the juxtapositions and flow of ideas in this week's *parasha*. We first study about the aggressive evangelical idolater (*meisis*) who does not receive the routinely mandated judicial patience and assumptions of innocence. Then we learn the *parasha* of the *ir hanidachas*, the theoretical city in Israel that is inundated with belligerent idolaters and is to be destroyed. Following all that, we read: "You are the children of *Hashem* – lo sisgodedu…" What a jarring non sequitur!

The literal reading of "*lo sisgodedu*" (*Devarim* 14:1) bans the early Semitic practice of cutting oneself and views that as an overreaction, or at least as a poorly directed reaction, to loss. According to Ibn Ezra this is the meaning of the introductory phrase of the *pasuk*, "You are children of *Hashem*," i.e., our belief in His concern for us should blunt the depth of our reaction to tragedy. However, the *mesora* teaches that "*lo sisgodedu*" also rules against establishing "*agudos agudos*," factions and walls within a community.[3]

---
[3] That means that whereas we are all encouraged to maintain authentic and well-based customs and practices, we must refrain from doing so within a community that has a decidedly different observance. Refraining from putting on tefillin on Chol Hamoed in a beis hamidrash in Yerushalyim, despite one's personal practice, is the classic modern illustration of the mesorah's principle. Clearly, maintaining one's practice of putting on tefillin on Chol Hamoed when it does not set one apart from the community is mandated. Yet even a firmly-based communal legacy must be set aside if it would create the image of two groups distinguishing themselves in their observance.

After reading about the obligation to confront and remove those who aggressively and programmatically seek to destroy the very core of our faith, we are forcefully reminded to see all who do not cross that line as *Hashem*'s offspring. In turn, *Hashem* asks that we all subscribe to the unity of our people and subject ourselves to its requirements.

It is the attitude of "'בנים אתם לה' – you are children of *Hashem*," that according to Rav Wolbe determines that one's deeply-felt faith and religiosity will be empathetic and engaging, rather than fierce, threatening and self-righteous. He argues that the *mitzva* of *ahavas Shamayim* – to love *Hashem* – assures that our beliefs must be accompanied with that love and that it spills over to all that *Hashem* loves, all of his children.

Studying the *parasha* of the cities and the well-planted spies that attempt to undermine our entire enterprise reminds us of how uncompromisingly protective we must be of the greatest gifts and challenges given to us. It is palpable faith naturally coupled with a robust *ahavas Shamayim* that in turn assures that we are as protective and as loving of Jews as we can possibly be.

Temptations and Triumphs: Ki Savo, the Parasha of Private Moments

RABBI YAAKOV NEUBURGER

It seems like it was a great feel-good event for the Jewish people. Though the curses are boldly recorded, the blessings are softly referenced, waiting for Rashi to make sure we do not miss them. While there would be some who sadly were terribly censured, would not the vast majority earn the blessings of the *Leviyim* and *Kohanim* as they looked up at us from their station in between the mountains? Here is how it seems to have sounded:

"Blessed be you who did not fashion an idol. Blessed be you who did not curse your father or your mother. Blessed be you who did not stealthily and illegally move the fence between you and your neighbor...who did not willfully give bad advice...who did not commit various forms of incest...who did not twist the judgments of the orphans and the widows..."

Originally published on TorahWeb.org in 2017

Would we not do quite well? Maybe we would not earn the blessing for those who never speak ill of others or the *beracha* for those who observe the entirety of Torah. Yet nine of eleven seem QED. Can it be that easy to earn His blessings?

Not at all; don't count your blessings yet! The prolific *Yerushalmi* sage, *Harav* Moshe Shternbuch, explains why the blessings are only detailed through the explicit censures and otherwise cannot be found. He suggests that this presentation teaches us that the blessings and curses addressed only polar opposites and no one else. Just as the curses censured those who struggled and failed, so too, the *Leviyim* blessed only those who were tempted and triumphed. That means that the blessings were reserved for the one who was overcome with a powerful persuasive force and compelling reason to serve idolatry, or to take advantage of a vulnerable relative, or to cravenly steal away one's neighbor's backyard. Only that Jew who nevertheless summoned the inner strength, like Yosef of old in the home of Potifar, will enjoy the blessings of *Har Gerizim*.

Allow me to complete the picture with the observation of another personality from Yerushalayim, the venerable *maggid*, *Harav* Mordecahi Druk *zt"l*. Whereas it is clear that some of the blessings are reserved for the *mitzvos* that are observed privately, Rav Druk believes that the entire *parasha* only projects a curse on those who fail in the privacy of their own homes and a blessing on similar triumphs. In other words, special blessing is reserved for the quiet struggle, unnoticed by the public eye, gaining no strength from disapproving friends and not expecting the praise of anyone watching.

Putting it all together, the *Leviyim* at the foot of *Har Gerizim* blessed that genuine Jew and that genuine Jewishness that knows temptation and perseverance, draws singularly on inner strength, and relishes the triumph that he will share with *Hashem* alone.

This leaves us with an impressive *parasha* for our *Elul* preparations. *Davening, shiurim, Selichos, shofar,* parlor meetings, *kumsitzen* and *seuda shlishis* are all crucial for our preparation for *Yamim Noraim* and are powerful moments for our spiritual growth. However, *teshuva*, as described by the Rambam, consists of the private moments that one experiences with *Hashem*. It is introspection and self-assessment. It is, as the Rambam says, "*bifnei Hashem.*" It is for the most part uncelebrated by our fellow Jew and gets no public validation.

But it soars to the top of *Har Gerizim* and receives magnificent blessings.

The Significance of Rosh Chodesh and the Month of Elul

RABBI MICHAEL ROSENSWEIG

"דרשו ה' בהמצאו קראהו בהיותו קרוב" –Seek the Lord where He is found; call Him when He is near" (*Yeshayahu* 55:6). This *pasuk*, which plays such a central role in times of crisis and contemplation as the introduction to the *haftara* on fast days, implores us to seek out *Hashem* and cultivate a more profound relationship with Him precisely when His presence is near. While the *Gemara* in *Rosh Hashana* 18b interprets this as a reference to *Aseres Yemei Teshuva*, the *midrash* in *Vayikra*, as understood by Meiri (*Chibur Hateshuva*, p. 250), seems to characterize the entire month of *Elul* as "*bihyoso karov*," an opportune time and propitious opportunity in which *Hashem*'s presence is particularly accessible. It is on this basis that he reports the geonic view that one should say *Selichos* every Monday and Thursday throughout the month. However, it is apparent from his formulation "כדאי שיכנס לראש השנה בטהרת הלב - it is proper that he enter *Rosh Hashana* with purity of heart," that Meiri apparently perceives the primary significance of *Elul* as a means of preparing for *Rosh Hashana* in such a way as to ensure that one enters into *Rosh Hashana* al-

---

Originally published on TorahWeb.org in 2000

ready in a state of purity with a clean slate, so that he can better capitalize on the opportunities presented by that unique day. Thus, the exigency of *teshuva* and *tefilla* during *Elul* constitutes nothing more than a lengthier preparation for the *Yamim Noraim*. From this perspective, there is no fundamental difference between the thirty-day period that precedes *Rosh Hashana* and those that introduce other *chagim*.

It is, however, conceivable that *Elul* represents "*bihyoso karov*" in its own right, distinguishing it from other thirty-day preludes. Undoubtedly, this would qualify it still further as the most effective vehicle through which to prepare for the *Yamim Noraim*. It would also accent that the *din* and *kappara* generated by these transcendent days cannot take place in a vacuum, but constitute the culmination of a rigorous process of introspection and spiritual reinvention.

The *Tur* (no. 581) introduces the laws of *Rosh Hashana* by citing the *Pirkei DeRabi Eliezer*'s explanation of the origin of *shofar* on *Rosh Chodesh* and the month of *Elul*. It is reported that Moshe's ascension to the mountain to receive the second *luchos* was marked by the blowing of the *shofar*, signifying the abandonment of idolatry, which had doomed the first *luchos*. We are informed that *Hashem* Himself was elevated by this *shofar* blast (based on *Tehillim* 47:6 "עלה א-לוקים בתרועה ה' בקול שופר – God shall be exalted with the trumpet blast; the Lord with the sound of the *shofar*"). The Tur proceeds to explain that the *minhag* to blow the *shofar* during the entire *Elul* in order to inspire *teshuva* was based upon the verse in *Amos* (3:6) which establishes that the sound of the *shofar* has the capacity to inspire fear and awe. The *Beis Yosef* speculates why two distinct sources (the anniversary of Moshe's ascension and the verse in *Amos*) are required to ground the practice of *shofar* in *Elul*. A close reading of the text, however, may indicate that the *Tur* distinguishes between the *shofar* on *Rosh Hashana* that commemorates Moshe's renewed mission, and the verse in *Amos* that conveys the role of the *shofar* in inspiring *teshuva*, serving as the foundation for the *minhag* during the entire month. (The Bach and *Perisha* seem to allude to this distinction, as well.) In light of this analysis, it is noteworthy that *Hashem's* remarkable reaction coincides with Moshe's ascension on *Rosh Chodesh Elul*. Indeed, the Bach argues that *Hashem* was twice elevated by means of *Klal Yisrael's* initiative of *tekias shofar*. He projects that while "*alah Elokim beterua*" refers to *Hashem's* response to the *shofar* of *Rosh Hashana*, "*Hashem bekol shofar*" occured on *Rosh Chodesh Elul*!

What emerges from these sources is that the events of *Rosh Chodesh Elul* are marked independently both with respect to Moshe's and *Klal Yisrael's* initiative, as well as *Hashem's* reciprocal response! Moshe's *Rosh Chodesh* mission actually signified a renewed and changed relationship between *Hashem* and *Klal Yisrael*. According to *Chazal*, the sin of the *eigel* forever changed Jewish history and the nature of the relationship between *Hashem* and His people. Much evidence, including the *pesukim* that characterize the two sets of *luchos*, points to the fact that the renewed relationship would be one in which the nation would be required to invest more obvious effort and initiative and responsibility, and which would accent a more evidently reciprocal relationship, one in which man would also have greater input within prescribed limits. The explicit renunciation of idolatry and, symbolically, significant dimensions of their spiritual profile that characterized the pre-*eigel* period, and *Hashem's* elevation by virtue of *Klal Yisrael's shofar* initiative perhaps reflected the imminent change, capturing the essence of Moshe's renewed mission to reconstitute *Yahadus*. The momentous events of *Rosh Chodesh Elul*, then, constituting as they did a watershed in the reciprocal relationship between *Hashem* and *Klal Yisrael*, surely demand commemoration and generate anew yearly the obligation of contemplation and introspection.

Of course, Moshe's dramatic and ambitious mission, initiated on *Rosh Chodesh Elul*, encompassed that whole month and did not conclude until *Yom Kippur*. Notwithstanding the independent significance and theme of *Rosh Chodesh Elul*, the link to the *Yamim Noraim* is undeniable. Indeed, as alluded to previously, the themes represented by *Rosh Chodesh Elul* and by the *Yamim Noraim* are interconnected and mutually enhancing.

Consequently, one can and should relate to the entire month of *Elul* both as the aftermath and continuation of the *Rosh Chodesh Elul* initiative of old that produced the second and normative *luchos*, and as the necessary and conducive vehicle of preparation for the upcoming *Yamim Noraim*. Indeed, the reassessment of personal religious status generated by the anniversary of Moshe's mission to reinvent the relationship between *Klal Yisrael* and *Hashem* establishes *Elul* as the ideal precursor to *Rosh Hashana* and *Yom Kippur*.

The *Perisha* speculates why *shofar* and not *divrei hisorerus* emerged as the visible symbol of *Elul* if preparation for the *Yamim Noraim* is the primary goal of this period. Perhaps, however, the motif of *Rosh Chodesh Elul* and the renewed reciprocal relationship that developed through the second *luchos* accounts for this phenomenon. It was precisely the dual impact and implication of that *kol shofar* on *Rosh Chodesh* that dramatically encapsulated this new spiritual foundation.

This idea can be highlighted by the fact that the Abudraham and others invoke "אני לדודי ודודי לי - I am my beloved's and my beloved is mine" (*Shir Hashirim* 6:3), the *pasuk* that particularly underscores the close and reciprocal relationship with *Hashem*, as an acronym that conveys the special role of *Elul*. It is precisely a reassessment of that intimate relationship in its broadest strokes (alongside an evaluation of individual actions and transgressions), which characterizes the unique agenda of this month. *Elul*, in all of its dimensions – independent, preparatory and integrated – truly affords the opportunity of "*kerauhu bihyoso karov.*"

Ahavas Hashem: The Teshuva of Chodesh Elul

RABBI MICHAEL ROSENSWEIG

The month of *Elul* ushers in a period of intensive introspection and urgent repentance that culminates with the *Yamim Noraim* (days of awe), *Rosh Hashana* and *Yom Kippur*. The fact that we sound the *shofar* until *Rosh Hashana* and cap our prayers with Psalm 27, "דוד ה' אורי וישעי" - For David, *Hashem* is my light and my salvation," during this period highlights the broader effort to stimulate a meaningful awakening to repentance (see Rambam, *Hilchos Teshuva* 3:4, "עורו ישנים משנתכם" - awaken, sleepers, from your slumber").

We have noted elsewhere ("The Significance of *Rosh Chodesh* and the Month of *Elul*,") the view cited by the Meiri (*Chibur Hateshuva*, p. 250) that דרשו ה' בהמצאו קראוהו בהיותו קרוב – Seek the Lord where He is found; call Him when He is near" (*Yeshayahu* 55:6), alluding to *Hashem*'s increased accessibility, refers not only to the period between *Rosh Hashana* and *Yom Kippur* (*Rosh Hashana* 18b), but to the entire month of *Elul*. We have suggested that the relationship between *Elul* and the *Yamim Noraim* is a dialectical one. While *Elul* necessarily focuses on preparation for the *Ya-*

Originally published on TorahWeb.org in 2008

mim Noraim, the proximity of *Yom Hazikaron* and *Yom Hadin* and the history of *Elul* during the aftermath of the *eigel hazahav* transgression provide an incentive and climate particularly conducive to developing certain facets of *avodas Hashem* that are also integral to *teshuva*.

The special emphasis of *Elul* is perhaps reflected in the primary motif of the ubiquitous "לדוד ה' אורי וישעי" - For David, *Hashem* is my light and my salvation." The Malbim (*Tehillim* 27:1, 4, 7, 12) notes that this psalm exclusively accentuates the desire for an enduring and deeper connection to *Hashem*. It conveys the theme that *devekus baHashem* (clinging to the Divine) is the ultimate goal rather than a means to some other end. Achieving a genuine relationship with *Hashem* eclipses all other interests; all other requests are significant only to the extent that they facilitate the enhancement of this relationship. "אחת שאלתי מאת ד' אותה אבקש - One [thing] I ask of the Lord, that I seek: that I may dwell in the house of the Lord all the days of my life," encapsulates the simple but profound ambition to attain that relationship. Perhaps this theme is underscored repeatedly during *Elul* because *Elul* is the time in which the relationship between *Hashem* and *Klal Yisrael* was reinstated and also refashioned in the aftermath of the sin of the *eigel*, as Moshe ascended the heavens to receive the reworked second *luchos*. The Tur (581) explains that "עלה א-לוקים בתרועה - God shall be exalted with the trumpet blast" (Psalm 47) refers to *Hashem*'s elevation in response to *Klal Yisrael*'s formal renunciation of the idolatry that doomed the first *luchos* and jeopardized the entire relationship.

Against this background, we can better appreciate the Abudraham's thesis that *Elul* is an acronym that conveys the reciprocal love of *Hashem* and the Jewish people ("אני לדודי ודודי לי" - I am my beloved's and my beloved is mine") that is at the core of this relationship. The entire thrust of *Shir Hashirim* is based upon the premise of mutual love and affection between *Hashem* and his nation. *Chazal* consistently develop this theme. *Matan Torah* is perceived as a kind of marriage contract. The twenty four books that comprise the canon of *Torah Shebichsav* are compared to the jewels that adorn a bride (*kekalla hamekushetes*). Moreover, this intense bond transcends marriage, as it is irrevocable (See Rav Soloveitchik, *Family Redeemed*, p. 63). The verse in Hoshea (2:21) attests to the permanence of the marriage: "וארשתיך לי לעולם - And I will betroth you to Me forever." In *Eichah* (1:1), the abandonment of Yerushalayim and the rejection of the nation is compared to the state of a widow, not a divorcee, and even that comparison is imprecise ("*ke'almanah*" – see Rashi). The prophet Isaiah (50:1) remonstrates with the nation, reminding them that *Hashem* never divorced/rejected the nation; it was their improper behavior that alienated them from Him.

Elul focuses particularly on reasserting and refining the relationship between *Hashem* and *Klal Yisrael* founded upon intense *ahavas Hashem* and rooted in reciprocity. The perspective of irrevocable mutual love and reciprocal commitment implied by "*ani ledodi vedodi li*," reinforced by the "*achas sha'alti mei'eis Hashem*" of *LeDovid Hashem ori*, and the reformulated contract of the second *luchos* evoked by the daily *shofar* also contribute significantly to the effectiveness of repentance in preparation for the *Yomim Noraim*. Authentic repentance requires sincere regret (*charata*), heartfelt embarrassment, and a future commitment (Rambam, *Hilchos Teshuva* 1:1, 2:2). The capacity to achieve these three requirements is immeasurably enhanced by the framework of the irrevocable relationship that is reinforced during *Elul*. One can only truly muster deep regret and embarrassment when the relationship that is damaged is one that is indispensable to one's very existence and when the alienated party is an integral part of both one's past and future.

The *Gemara* in *Yoma* (86a) distinguishes between *teshuva mei-ahava* (repentance flowing from love) and *teshuva miyira* (repentance motivated by fear). While the Rambam does not formally and explicitly register this distinction, he does reflect the centrality of *ahavas Hashem* in repentance in a more subtle but perhaps more profound way. The culminating chapter of *Hilchos Teshuva* (ch. 10) is devoted to *ahavas Hashem* as a goal distinct from any functional benefit. The Rambam focuses on the method of achieving this telos and how this affects the performance of *mitzvos* and the study of Torah. Clearly, he intends to convey that achieving this level in the relationship with *Hashem* is the ultimate purpose of repentance, though it also transcends repentance. Indeed, the final chapter of repentance transitions into the Rambam's next volume, entitled *Sefer Ahava* (Book of Divine Love), which is dedicated to expressing *ahavas Hashem* through the performance of *mitzvos*. It is noteworthy that the Rambam (*Hilchos Teshuva* 10:3) compares the intensity and single-minded focus of *ahavas Hashem* to that of an all-consuming marital relationship, invoking *Shir Hashirim*. The *ani ledodi vedodi li* theme of *Elul* emerges clearly.

Rav Chaim of Volozhin postulates in *Nefesh HaChaim* that *teshuva mei-ahava* is most effectively attained by increased Torah study. This idea confirms our analysis, as Torah study is the primary mechanism to engage and enhance the relationship with *Hashem*. The *haftara* of *Shabbos Shuva* emphasizes this as well "'קחו עמכם דברים ושובו אל ה' – , "take with you words, and return to *Hashem*" (see the *midrash* link to *ya'arof kamatar likchi* etc.). Our obligations and opportunities in the month of *Elul* should inspire us to ever greater spiritual aspirations that will jointly advance our *ahavas Hashem* and facilitate a *teshuva sheleima* (complete repentance).

Rambam's View of Ahavas Hashem as the Telos of Teshuva, an Indispensable Manifestation of Avodas Hashem

RABBI MICHAEL ROSENSWEIG

In a celebrated passage in *Masseches Yoma* (86b) the *Gemara* declares that *teshuva meiahava* (repentance out of love) has the almost miraculous capacity to transform *zedonos* into *zechuyos* (intentional halachic infractions into spiritual credits or merits). Much has been written and many different explanations have been posited in an effort to comprehend and explicate this astonishing facility of *teshuva* to redeem and even revise the past. *Teshuva meiahava* is typically understood as referring either to the motivation or to the methodology of this ambitious, reality-changing repentance.

However, it is striking that the great codifier Jewish law, the Ram-

Originally published on TorahWeb.org in 2015

bam, apparently omitted any mention of this most singular and far-reaching manifestation of *teshuva*. This is particularly surprising considering that he devised and devoted an independent ten-chapter section to the laws of *teshuva* (though strewn throughout the Talmud without any cohesion) as the culmination of the first of the fourteen books of *Yad HaChazakah* (*Sefer HaMadda*, which also accentuates the integration of philosophy and law, a critical linchpin theme for the Rambam!), his comprehensive and masterful halachic magnum opus. Ignoring an incredibly consequential though unusual dimension of repentance law is totally inconsistent with the fact that the Rambam particularly expanded, reorganized, and invested pioneering effort in the formulation of these laws. The neglect of this puzzling yet singular and pivotal concept in the Rambam's extensive framework is both extraordinary and astounding. While it is conceivable that the Rambam perceived this rabbinic statement as aggadic hyperbole, it is noteworthy that he includes numerous other midrashic assessments of the consequential impact of repentance in these chapters.

Yet, a closer scrutiny of *Hilchos Teshuva* provides a compelling solution to this riddle. Without explanation, the Rambam devotes the entire final chapter, the climax, of *Hilchos Teshuva* to the principle of *avodas Hashem mei'ahava* (religious observance and growth through love of Hashem). Indeed, this chapter, which completes the first book of Jewish law, *Sefer HaMadda*, seamlessly transitions into the second book, entitled *Sefer Ahava* and dominated by the theme of *avodas Hashem mei'ahava*, pithily captured by the introductory citation that also emphasizes the comprehensiveness of this foundation and perspective of *avodas Hashem*: "מה אהבתי תורתך, כל היום היא שיחתי -How I love Your Torah! All day it is my conversation!" It cannot be a coincidence that the Rambam chose the culmination of *Hilchos Teshuva* to ruminate about the motivation and ambition of religious commitment that is suffused with and engenders *ahavas Hashem*. We may confidently speculate that the Rambam's unusual presentation reflects his profound if singular comprehension of the *Gemara Yoma*'s ambitious formulation of *teshuva mei'ahava*. Evidently, *ahavas Hashem*, a doctrine that the Rambam projects centrally at the very outset of *Sefer Hamitzvos* (*aseh* no. 3, immediately following only the theological axioms of Divine Belief and Divine Unity), that is the focus and title of his second section of halachic law, and which he revisits again and again (see also *Hilchos Yesodei Hatorah* 2:1–2; 5:7, 11 [*Yoma* 86a]), is not merely the methodology or motivation for *teshuva*, but its ultimate telos.

By focusing attention on *ahavas Hashem* as the climax of *teshuva*, the Rambam expands and elevates the role of *teshuva* and redefines its character as well, thereby also justifying its presentation in and as the culmination of *Sefer HaMadda*. The Rambam depicts the idealism of *avoda mei'ahava* that eschews any ulterior motive (*Hilchos Teshuva* 10:2: "לא מפני יראת הרעה, ולא כדי לירש הטובה, אלא עושה את האמת מפני שהוא אמת וסוף הטובה לבוא בכלל – moved neither by fear of calamity nor by the desire to obtain material benefits – rather, he does what is truly right because it is truly right, and ultimately, happiness comes to him as a result of his conduct"). He dramatically formulates the required intensity of this all-encompassing relationship by comparing it with a passionate and comprehensive marital bond and by noting that *Shir Hashirim* aspires to capture this interaction. The implication of this subtle yet effective perspective-presentation is that *teshuva* is not merely an instrument for change or a mechanism for renewal or the neutralization of sin, but a manifestation and dimension of *avodas Hashem* itself. Moreover, the capacity of the *teshuva* process to neutralize transgression itself stems from its broader character and agenda.

The transition to daily *mitzvos*, *Sefer Ahava*, reinforces these broader themes and accentuates the broader relationship that is also addressed in the process of *teshuva*. The initiation of *Sefer Ahava* on the heels of the culmination of *teshuva-ahava* with the laws of *kerias Shema* that encapsulate the comprehensiveness of *ahavas Hashem* – בכל לבבך, בכל נפשך, ובכל מאודך "with all your heart, with all your soul, and withyou're your resources," infused with the mission of total religious and halachic commitment –, קבלת עול מלכות שמים acceptance of the yoke of Heaven, further broadens the motif of *teshuva* and integrates it with the other primary institutions of *avodas Hashem*.

The Rambam's perspective on *teshuva* explains why he integrated these *halachos* specifically into *Sefer HaMadda*, in conjunction with other tenets – *Yesodei Hatorah, De'os, Talmud Torah* etc., rather than assign these laws to a narrower if more obvious classification, like *Hilchos Shegagos*, or *Sefer Zemanim*. His doctrine of *ahavas Hashem* as the goal of *teshuva* and his implied stance that *teshuva* is itself an expression of *avodas Hashem* is particularly meaningful in connection with the *teshuva* of *Elul*, whose acronym (Avudraham – *ani ledodi vedodi li*) underscores the love relationship between *Hashem* and *Am Yisrael*. As we have noted elsewhere (see "*Ahavas Hashem*: The *Teshuva* of *Chodesh Elul*"), the repentance of *Elul* and the *Yomim Noraim* particularly employ and facilitate *teshuva mei'ahava*. Indeed, the Rambam's unique, subtle, but compelling perspective on the profound and dynamic relationship between *teshuva* and *ahavas Hashem* fully justifies the *Gemara*'s seemingly radical conclusion that the *teshuva* process and perspective is constructively transformative and spiritually beneficial and meritorious (turning *zedonos* into *zechuyos*).

Interpersonal Teshuva
RABBI DR. ABRAHAM J. TWERSKI

The season of heightened *teshuva* is before us. The daily sounding of the *shofar* in the month of *Elul*, the early morning *Selichos*, *Rosh Hashana*, the Ten Days of Penitence culminated by *Yom Kippur*, the Day of Forgiveness. It is of interest that *Yom Kippur* is generally translated as the "Day of Atonement" rather than the "Day of Forgiveness," although the term *kappara* generally refers to forgiveness. It is unknown who coined the term "Day of Atonement," but perhaps there is something to be learned from it.

In contrast to forgiveness, atonement connotes making restitution and compensation. This concept is not really relevant to sins of *bein adam leMakom*, between man and *Hashem*, because we cause *Hashem* no harm when we sin, as Elihu said, "Were you to have transgressed, how would you have affected Him, and if your rebellions were numerous, what would you have done to Him?" (*Iyov* 35:6). " חנון המרבה לסלוח -Gracious One, who forgives abundantly," *Hashem*'s mercy is infinite and His forgiveness is abundant, but that is only for sins between man and *Hashem*. If one has sinned against another person, *Hashem* does not forgive those sins until one has appeased whomever one has offended. The *Chasam Sofer* said, "I am worried much more about sins *bein adam lechavero* than *bein adam*

Originally published on TorahWeb.org in 2009

leMakom. I trust *Hashem's* forgiveness, but I cannot be sure about people."

So for there to be forgiveness on *Yom Kippur*, there must be atonement, restitution, and that is not always easy to achieve. Ironically, easiest of all is if you were a *goniff* (thief) and stole something, because then all that is required is that you make monetary compensation. It is much more difficult if you maligned someone by speaking disparagingly of him. Here you may be in a quandary, because if you were to ask the person to forgive you for having spoken badly about him, you may cause him to agonize, "I wonder what he said about me and to whom." Rabbi Yisrael of Salant said that in this case it is better not to tell the person that you spoke badly about him, hence there is no way to ask for forgiveness. In addition, if you spread a false rumor about him, *halacha* does not require that he forgive you.

Whereas one can make restitution by returning the money one stole, there is no way of making restitution if you "stole" someone's time, i.e., if you promised to meet someone at a certain time and you kept him waiting for twenty minutes. You deprived him of time, a commodity which cannot be replaced.

Perhaps you mistreated your child with improper discipline. You might have come from work having had a very difficult day and were very irritable, and were unjustly harsh to your child. That is an offense against another person which requires that person's forgiveness. However, inasmuch as a child is legally incompetent, he cannot grant forgiveness, and *Yom Kippur* cannot erase that sin!

Bein adam lechavero applies to husbands and wives vis-à-vis one another. An abusive spouse incurs a sin when he or she mistreats one's partner, and the aggrieved spouse may not forgive wholeheartedly.

Suppose someone asked your advice, and you told him what you thought would be best, but it turned out that your advice was misguided, and the person sustained a loss because of your advice. Although your intentions were good, you did inadvertently cause him damage, for which you are just as responsible as if you accidentally broke his window. The Steipler Gaon, in the very last moments of his life, cried bitterly, saying "I am afraid that perhaps I may have given someone bad advice."

What can we do about those situations in which restitution is not feasible? One of the students of the Vilna Gaon felt that he had offended someone by sarcastically rejecting the latter's explanation of a difficult Talmudic passage. He went from *shul* to *shul* throughout Vilna, looking for the man to ask his forgiveness, but did not find him and was heartbroken. The Gaon told him, "If you have truly done everything within your power to ask his forgiveness, you can be sure that *Hashem* will put it in his heart to forgive you."

That is the solution for those incidents for which one cannot atone. If one makes serious effort to make restitution and appease the offended people, then *Hashem* will put it in their hearts to forgive. But one must be thorough in making restitution and asking forgiveness wherever possible, and that includes your spouse and your children if you have offended them, because only then will one merit *Hashem*'s intervention on one's behalf.

Glatt Kosher Is Not Enough

RABBI DR. ABRAHAM J. TWERSKI

"Who is a wise person? One who learns from everyone" (*Pirkei Avos* 4:1). In the hope that I may become wise, I try to learn from everyone. For over forty years, my practice involved treating alcoholics, and I would like to share what I learned from them.

Some alcoholics consult a psychiatrist or a psychologist for help. However, not even the most excellent therapy can accomplish anything if the client is still drinking. No therapy can make an impression on a brain that is suffused with alcohol. The person must first abstain from all alcohol, and only then can therapy be effective.

But, you might ask, if the person is abstaining from alcohol, what need is there for therapy? The answer is that if all an alcoholic has done is to stop drinking but has made no significant character changes, he is what we call a "dry drunk." That is, although he is indeed "dry," his behavior is little different than when he was drinking. He is still the same self-centered, inconsiderate, stubborn, self-righteous, intolerant, and impatient person he was when he drank. So abstaining from alcohol is indeed a crucial first step, but it is only a first step. The "dry drunk" must

---

Originally published on TorahWeb.org in 2009

proceed to improve his character and abandon the behaviors that led him to alcohol in the first place.

This progression applies to *Yiddishkeit* as well. A person who is in violation of the *mitzvos* is like the alcoholic who is drinking, and he cannot implement *Yiddishkeit*. If one goes through the motions of observing all the *mitzvos*, one has indeed taken the first crucial step, but it is only the first step. Such a person is a spiritual "dry drunk," not yet internalizing and fully implementing *Yiddishkeit*.

What, then, does a complete implementation of *Yiddishkeit* entail? Listen to the words of Rebbe Chaim Vital, the foremost disciple of the Arizal: "Bad character traits (*middos*) are much worse than sin, and we can understand why the Talmud says that a person who goes into a rage is as if he worshipped idols, and that a vain, arrogant person is equivalent to one who denies God. A person should therefore be more meticulous about eliminating bad character traits than fulfilling the positive *mitzvos* and the prohibitions. If one will have good *middos* one can easily fulfill all the *mitzvos*" (*Shaarei Kedusha* 1:2). Just like the alcoholic must improve his character to become sober, a person wishing to become an *oveid Hashem* must improve his *middos*. Let us remember, of course, that just as an alcoholic cannot alter his character while drinking, neither can a person improve one's *middos* if one is in violation of *halacha*. Transgressions of Torah are toxins which render one incapable of addressing one's *middos*.

The *baalei musar* (ethicists) explain that although committing a sin is indeed grave, it does not become part of one's personality, and one can do *teshuva*. A bad character trait, however, becomes part of one's personality, and is much more difficult to uproot.

But this is not the way we think. If a *frum* person loses his temper, we are likely to still consider him a *frum* person, but if we found that he ate a ham sandwich, we would not consider him *frum*. Rebbe Chaim Vital says that the person who goes into a rage is no different than the person who eats *treif*.

Moshe says, "Now, O Israel, what does *Hashem* ask of you? Only to fear *Hashem*, to go in all His ways and to love Him, and to serve *Hashem* with all your heart and with all your soul, to observe the commandments of *Hashem* and His decrees" (*Devaim* 10:12-13). Notice that Moshe places *yiras Shamayim*, (fear of *Hashem*), emulating *Hashem*'s attributes and love of *Hashem*, ahead of observing the mitzvos.

"*Yiras Shamayim*" is not referring only to fear of being punished for committing sins. Such fear is juvenile but is necessary as a beginning. A two-year-old who runs into the street cannot understand a lecture on the dangers of traffic, and he must be discouraged by a *putsch*. However, a *putsch* need not hurt the child. I remember when my little brother climbed out the window onto the roof. My father called him back gently, then took the child's hand in his own, and delivered a firm *putsch to his own hand*, not to the child's. No pain was inflicted on the child. It is the *action* of the *putsch*, not the pain, which delivers the discipline. The action shows the father's disapproval, and the child does not have to be hurt to get the message. Once the child reaches the age of reason, even this kind of punishment should be unnecessary. The parent should earn the respect of the child to the degree that the child would not act contrary to the parent's wishes.

As mature as we may be, we are all juvenile, if not infantile, relative to *Hashem*, and therefore it is essential that we know that there is reward for *mitzvos* and punishment for sins. But we must go beyond that. Elemental *yiras Shamayim* means to be in awe of *Hashem*'s majesty, so that one would not act inappropriately in His presence. This is the very first *halacha* in the *Shulchan Aruch*, to always behave with the awareness that we are in the presence of *Hashem*. Elemental *yiras Shamayim* is essential to *Yid*-

dishkeit. Without *yiras Shamayim*, even the most meticulous *glatt* kosher observance is not *Yiddishkeit*.

But how far we are from that! The Talmud relates that before his death, Rebbe Yochanan ben Zakai told his disciples that their *yiras Shamayim* should be no less than their awe of humans. "A person often will not do something improper if another person sees him, but is not afraid to do so if the only one that sees him is *Hashem*" (*Berachos* 28b).

There is unfortunately a plague of internet pornography that has infected some *"frum"* people, younger and older, men and women, and people are asking what the antidote to this is. When I say, "*Yiras Shamayim*," they say, "That is not enough." Of course it is enough; it is just that it is not there. As Rebbe Yochanan ben Zakai said, these people would not be seen entering a shop that peddles pornography and other indecent things. They are afraid and ashamed of someone seeing them there. But they are not afraid and ashamed of indulging in pornography in the privacy of their home or office, where they are seen only by *Hashem*.

I am told, "You can't expect that level of *yiras Shamayim* from people. It is unrealistic to expect them to be a *Chafetz Chaim*." Does one have to be a *Chafetz Chaim* to avoid eating pork? Without awareness that one is in the presence of *Hashem*, and if one is not ashamed to do things that one would not do if others were watching, one has not begun the first paragraph of the *Shulchan Aruch*, and one has not even begun *Yiddishkeit*.

It is not uncommon that children do not follow in their parents' footsteps. Some may become more *frum*, others may stray from Torah observance. Parents wonder, "Where did we go wrong? Why are our children deviating from the way we raised them?"

Make no mistake about it. Our children are very sensitive and can detect whether our *Yiddishkeit* is genuine or superficial. Genuine *Yiddishkeit* begins with "to fear *Hashem*, to go in all His ways," i.e., *yiras Shamayim*, as defined above, and proper *middos*: controlling anger, ridding ourselves of grudges, dishonesty, envy, *lashon hara*, inconsiderateness, and developing the *middos* of *chesed*, truth, *ahavas Yisrael*, respect, and consideration of others. We want our children to adhere to *Yiddishkeit*, and not go off the *derech*. Only genuine *Yiddishkeit* will keep them close to us.

Teshuva: In Your Mouth and in Your Heart

RABBI MAYER TWERSKY

"כי המצוה הזאת אשר אנכי מצוך היום לא נפלאת היא ממך ולא רחוקה היא ... כי קרוב אליך הדבר מאד בפיך ובלבבך לעשתו" – For the commandment that I command you today is not hidden from you and it is not distant. . . . Rather the matter is very near to you – in your mouth and your heart – to perform it" (*Devarim* 30:11, 14; Artscroll Stone Edition translation).

According to the Ramban, the *mitzva* depicted in these verses is the *mitzva* of *teshuva* (repentance). The Torah emphasizes our capacity and ability to repent. It is "in your mouth and your heart" to repent.

Let us focus on the Torah's choice of words – "in your mouth and your heart." Clearly, the Torah is conveying that *teshuva* is very doable, but that has already been conveyed by the first half of the verse, "[it] is very near to you." What is added by the phrase "in your mouth and your heart"?[4]

This terse, rich phrase anticipates the myriad excuses that we of-

---

[4] Ramban, ad locum, provides a *peshat* interpretation that "in your mouth" refers to *viduy* (confession) and "in your heart" adds that, the indispensability of *viduy* notwithstanding, the essence of *teshuva* is an inner experience, a *kiyum shebalev*. What ensues is a homiletical interpretation.

Originally published on TorahWeb.org in 2006

fer for our failures to do *teshuva*. Our first line of defense is that we do not need to do *teshuva*. We are not at fault. After all, we are only human. And to be human is to sin. Alternatively, we silence our consciences by reasoning that our sins are not our fault. Our sins are due to our upbringing, society, genetics, etc. In a word, we do not assume responsibility for our sins. The Torah utterly rejects such moral escapism. "Free will is bestowed on every human being … the human species had become unique in the world … there is none who can prevent him from doing that which is good or that which is evil" (Rambam *Hilchos Teshuva* 5:1). Being human is not a source of extenuation, but rather moral responsibility. "Thus Yirmiyahu [Jeremiah] said 'out of the mouth of the Most High not evil and good'; that is to say, the Creator does not decree either that a man shall be good or that he shall be wicked" (ibid, *halacha* 2).

The primordial ploy of shifting the blame – "The woman whom you gave to be with me – she gave me of the tree, and I ate"; "The serpent deceived me, and I ate" (*Bereishis* 3:12, 13 Artscroll translation) – was rejected by *Hakadosh Baruch Hu* in time immemorial. The modern equivalents – my upbringing is responsible, society is to blame, there is no overcoming genetic tendencies – will share the same fate.

Thus the Torah exhorts us that *teshuva* is "in your mouth … to perform." The *teshuva* process begins "in your mouth," by confessing and thereby accepting responsibility for our sins.

When our first line of defense for not doing *teshuva* fails, we seek other justifications for our inaction. One common excuse appeals to age. "I am too old; my habits are too deeply entrenched. After all, you cannot teach an old dog new tricks." What is the Torah's response to this hackneyed excuse? "For You do not wish the death of one deserving death, but that he repent from his way and live. Until the day of his death You wait for him; if he repents You will accept him immediately" (*Musaf, Yamim*

Noraim, Artscroll translation).

At times, we attribute our failures to repent to the magnitude of our sins. "I have sinned too egregiously; I am too mired in sin. How can you expect me to do *teshuva*?" The Rambam (*Hilchos Teshuva* 2:1) paraphrases the Torah's response, "Even if he transgressed throughout his life but repented on the day of his death and died as a penitent, all his sins are forgiven." Even a lifelong sinner can, and therefore must, repent.

And, finally, another favorite excuse: "If only someone would help me. If only my Rebbeim *z"l* were still alive…" The *Gemara* (*Avoda Zara* 17a) debunks this excuse by depicting the *teshuva* of Rabi Elazar ben Durdia. Rabi Elazar had led a life of wanton promiscuity; he had "consorted with every harlot in the world." Finally impelled to seek forgiveness, he petitioned the mountains and hills to implore on his behalf. They declined, citing their need to pray on their own behalf. Next, he addressed himself to heaven and earth, seeking their intervention on his behalf. Their response was identical to that of the mountains and hills. Then Rabi Elazar appealed to the sun and moon with the same negative results. Finally, he said, "It (i.e., attaining forgiveness) is entirely dependent upon me." He rested his head between his knees and burst out crying until his soul departed. A heavenly voice emerged and proclaimed, "Rabi Elazar ben Durdia is prepared and deserving of the world to come." The "if only" excuse is just that, a shallow, hollow excuse אין הדבר תלוי אלא בנו. – *Ein hadavar talui ela banu*; repentance depends entirely upon us.

The Torah rejects our second line of defense – "I am only human," "I am too old," "If only …. " *Teshuva* "is in your heart to perform." If only we inwardly resolve and strive, we can, with *Hakadosh Baruch Hu*'s help, repent, *vechein yehi ratzon*.

Transforming Attitude into Gratitude
RABBI BENJAMIN YUDIN

The Ashkenazic practice is to begin the recitation of *Selichos* on a *Motzei Shabbos*, minimally four days before *Rosh Hashana*. A popular source (*Mishna Berura* 581:6, citing *Eliyahu Rabba*) for this is the fact that in conjunction with every *Yom Tov* the Torah introduces the *korban musaf* in *Parashas Pinchas* using the word "והקרבתם" "*vehikravtem*" – and you shall offer – the particular additional sacrifice. In contrast, regarding *Rosh Hashana*, the Torah mandates (*Bemidbar* 29:2) "*va'asisem* – and you shall make an offering," understood by the rabbis to infer that man should make himself worthy of an offering. As an animal in the *Beis Hamikdash* required a ביקור מום "*bikur mum*" – physical inspection – over a period of 4 days assuring and insuring that the animal is blemish-free and fit to be offered, so too is man to introspect and examine his ways, thoughts, and actions that they are worthy and appropriate for the service of *Hashem*.

At first glance the particular *kerias HaTorah* that is read on the *Shabbos* before *Selichos* need not be related to *Selichos*. At the same time, this year *Parashas Ki Savo* is read, and I believe that a careful understanding of the opening *mitzva* of *bikkurim* can shed light and enhance our appreciation of *Selichos*.

Originally published on TorahWeb.org in 2015

There are two *mitzvos* out of the 613 that deal with *bikkurim*. In *Mishpatim* (23:19) the Torah legislates the *mitzva* of bringing the first fruits to the *Beis Hamikdash*, and in *Ki Savo* (26:5-10) the Torah provides an exact text of a declaration, *mikreh bikkurim*, that the farmer is to recite upon presenting his first fruits to the *kohen* in the *Beis Hamikdash*. The essence of this declaration is thanksgiving to *Hashem* for the produce, for the land of Israel, and for His directing history and redeeming the enslaved Jewish nation from Egypt and bringing them to the Promised Land. Upon completion of the declaration, the farmer prostrates himself before *Hashem*.

Dovid *Hamelech* (*Tehillim* 50:23) says, "זבח תודה יכבדנני - one who slaughters a *toda* honors Me," which can be understood in one of two ways. One way is: the one who offers a thanksgiving offering honors *Hashem*. The Talmud (*Berachos* 54b) teaches that individuals who underwent challenging and dangerous situations are obligated to bring a thanksgiving offering, including seafarers, those who have gone through the wilderness, one who was ill and recovered, and one who was incarcerated in prison and came out. Their offering, the prescribed *korban toda*, is a recognition of *Hashem*'s divine providence, and thereby honors *Hashem*. Today, when we do not yet have the third *Beis Hamikdash*, we recite the *Birkas Hagomel* instead.

Rashi, however, understands the word "*toda*" not as thanksgiving but as an admission and confession. Thus the verse is to be understood as: the one who brings an offering of repentance and confesses his sins is truly honoring *Hashem*. It is interesting to note that the root of the word "*toda*" means both to admit and to offer thanks. Indeed, Rav Hutner *zt"l* noted that the two understandings complement each other in the *beracha* of *Modim*, which is the theme of the final section of every *Shemoneh Esrei*. The Jew acknowledges and admits something (as in "*modeh bemiktzas*," when one admits to part of a financial claim against him). Here too the worshipper admits that he could not do it alone, that he needed the assistance of another.

Indeed, every time we say thank you we are first stating that we have needed something, and that we could not do it all on our own. Subsequently, having admitted this reality, the second meaning of "*toda*" – thanks – emerges, and one expresses appreciation for the good they have received.

The Torah mandates that upon completion of the recitation of *mikreh bikkurim*, the farmer prostrates himself before the *mizbeach* – the altar of *Hashem*. The act of *hachnaa*, of total submission to *Hashem*, follows naturally the detailed declaration of *hakaras hatov* – thanksgiving. The more one realizes that they have been the beneficiary of His bounty, the more grateful and humbled they become and the more they desire to reciprocate in kind, fulfilling His every wish.

The *talmidei* HaGra share, in the name of their teacher, a related insight into the *Shema*. The opening line of *Shema* expresses the sovereignty of *Hashem*, and *Shema* continues to tell us to love God with **all** our hearts, **all** our souls, and **all** our might. Why the threefold repetition of "*bechol*" – "with all"? It is teaching us not only the existence and uniqueness of *Hashem*, but that **all** emanates from Him. Thus our *hakaras hatov* –gratitude – is directed to one Source only, hence the three "**all**"s concretizing this idea.

There is an interesting difference of opinion about the ideal time to recite the opening *Selichos*. Rav Elyashiv *zt"l* opined that it is best to say *Selichos* early Sunday morning. This is based on the words of the *Shulchan Aruch* (*Orach Chaim* 581:1) that the practice is to rise early to recite *Selichos*. The very rousing of one's self from sleep and slumber sets the tone for acknowledging one's sins. The motivation is one of *toda* –*viduy* – admission of guilt, i.e., not having actualized one's full potential.

The *Leket Yosher* (a student of the *Terumas Hadeshen*) taught that we recite *Selichos* on Saturday night, going from the joy of *Shabbos* to the joy of *Selichos*. The joy of *Shabbos* emanates from the spiritual effect of greater and more meaningful studying of Torah on *Shabbos*, and the physical *oneg*, the delight of *Shabbos*. The positive mood and delight of *Shabbos* are the ideal prerequisites for *Selichos*. This is the *toda* of thanksgiving leading to the *toda* of admission. Namely, in view of the excessive bounty that *Hashem* gives each and every one of us – *be'ezras Hashem* our health, our family, our environment, our sustenance – one realizes that we can never sufficiently repay Him, and therefore we come to *Selichos* with a happy countenance, wanting to improve ourselves to give Him *nachas*.

The *Midrash Rabba* explains the opening words of the Torah, "*Bereishis bara Elokim*," to mean, "for *reishis* – the first – *Hashem* created" the world, and that "*reishis*" refers to the Torah, *Bnei Yisrael* (see Rashi on the opening verse of Torah), and *bikkurim* (which are called "*reishis*" in *Shemos* 23:19.) Now we understand why the world was created for *bikkurim*. Its declaration of *hakaras hatov* sets the tone and foundation for man to serve *Hashem*. The attitude that it's all **me** is transformed to appreciate and recognize that everything comes from **Him**.

Thus, the *Midrash Rabba* (*Bereishis* 22) teaches that when Adam asked Cain what occurred after his horrific act of fratricide and Cain said, "I did *teshuva* and was pardoned," Adam responded with, "'טוב להודות לה - *tov lehodos Lashem* – it is good to thank the Lord." The *Chasam Sofer* cites the *midrash* which explains *tov lehodos Lashem* to mean "it is good to confess and accept total submission to *Hashem*." His beneficence leads to our character development. May we be ever aware and *makir tov* of His constant showering us with goodness, and be thereby prompted to reciprocate and be worthy thereof.

Rosh Hashana

An Attitude of Confidence

RABBI HERSHEL SCHACHTER

In anticipation of *Rosh Hashana*, we take haircuts and dress as we do for *Yom Tov* to demonstrate that we are confident that God will be kind to us and judge us favorably on the Day of Judgment. Likewise, just after the close of the *Yom HaKippurim*, we celebrate by having a festive feast, to demonstrate again that we are confident that the judgment was a favorable one.

How can we be so confident? Every year tragedies do occur. Some young people die prematurely; others become impoverished. There is a lot of suffering in the world that would seem to contradict such confidence.

The *Chazon Ish* explains in his essay on *emuna* and *bitachon* that when we ask a sick person to have *bitachon*, it does not mean that he should be convinced that he will recover. That would be ridiculous; one cannot be sure that he will not die. *Bitachon* simply means to live by *emuna*, and *emuna* means believing that God has complete control over everything in the world. If God wants me to live and be healthy and happy, then there is nothing anyone can do to negate that. If for some reason, God wants me to suffer, then as that is His will, we should accept it with joy, with the knowl-

---

Originally published on TorahWeb.org in 1999

edge that anything that God does is for the good (*Berachos* 60b.)

When someone harms another, one should not think that were it not for that individual, the other person would not have suffered. We believe that *bechira* is always limited. No one has the ability to harm another person unless there was a *gezeira* from heaven decreeing that the victim should be harmed. "No one will injure his finger on this earth unless it was so ordained from above" (*Chullin* 7b). Once such a *gezeira* is decreed, God gives everyone the ability to use his or her *bechira*, even to the extent of harming another individual.

We are all expected to lead our lives in accordance with these principles of *emuna*, and living by the principles of *emuna* is what it means to have *bitachon*. We are not confident that our judgment on *Rosh Hashana* and *Yom HaKippurim* will be in our favor. Rather, our confidence consists of our belief that God is all-powerful, that His will shall prevail, and that whatever He does is always *letov*, even in the event that it is detrimental to us.

Malchuyos
RABBI HERSHEL SCHACHTER

According to the popular opinion in the *Midrash*, five of the *Aseres Hadibros* (Ten Commandments) were etched on one stone, and the other five on the other stone (as is commonly displayed in shuls). The *midrash* adds that the first of the *dibros* ("*Anochi Hashem* …" "I am the Lord …") is related to the sixth ("*lo sirtzach*" "do not murder"), which was parallel to it; the second is related to the seventh, which was parallel to it, etc.

Our religion believes in a kind God, who has created man in His image, *betzelem Elokim*. Because of this *tzelem Elokim* which was imparted to all people, our religion preaches the importance of *kavod haberiyos*. One who kills another human being, or even as much as acts disrespectfully towards others, obviously does not appreciate the other person's *tzelem Elokim*. This lack of appreciation of the concept of *tzelem Elokim* is often due to a lack of belief in *Elokim*, or a distorted perception thereof. Years and years of development of civilization can be overturned and destroyed by people who do not understand *Elokim*, and consequently do not appreciate the concept of *tzelem Elokim*.

One of the major themes of *Rosh Hashana*, which comes through the *Aseres Yemei Teshuva* until *Yom Kippur*, is the idea of *malchuyos*. God calls upon us to coronate Him, to try to get others to do the same, and God

Originally published on TorahWeb.org in 2001

has promised us that the day will come when all of mankind will accept Him as King. According to the interpretation of Rashi, this promise appears in the opening passage of *Shema Yisrael*: *Hashem*, who at present is only recognized as God by us ("*Hashem Elokeinu*") will ultimately be universally accepted as King ("*Hashem Echad*").

And this is the central theme of the *beracha* of *malchuyos*: we pray to *Hashem*: "מלוך על כל העולם כלו בכבודך -Reign over the entire world in Your glory," that He should see to it that His promise be fulfilled – that ultimately the day will come when His kingdom will be recognized by all people. And we further plead with God that it is not fair that just because a small group of people reject His Kingship, that the overwhelming majority of the people of the world should suffer. We pray on *Rosh Hashana* and *Yom Kippur*: "וכל הרשעה כולה כעשן תכלה - and all the wickedness should disappear like smoke," that *Hashem* eradicate that small group who refuses to accept His kingship, and who are thereby holding back the fulfillment of the promise of *malchuyos*.

On the night of *Pesach* we celebrate the redemption of *Klal Yisrael*. At the occasion of *Yetzias Mitzraim*, God promised Moshe *Rabbeinu* "(אהיה אשר אהיה -I will be what I will be") that just as He was redeeming *Bnei Yisrael* at that time, so too the day will come when He will redeem all of mankind. This is the biblical promise of *malchuyos*. It is for this reason that on *Pesach* night we recite "נשמת כל חי תברך את שמך ה' א-לוקינו - the soul of every living thing shall bless Your name, *Hashem* our God"; we pray to God that He see to it that all of mankind accept His kingship. And on *Pesach* night as well, we pray regarding the small group of people who simply refused to accept – don't allow them to hold up the fulfillment of your promise of *malchuyos*: שפוך חמתך אל הגוים אשר לא ידעוך – pour out your anger on that small group! תרדוף באף ותשמידם מתחת שמי ה' – chase with fury and destroy them from under God's sky.

God has declared that He personally will forever wage battle with Amalek; and He called upon us to participate in that battle. We should not assume that evil will disappear by itself. We must help fight against it. As long as Amalek, who are לא ירא א-לוקים , ("did not fear God") are still around, the kingship of *Hashem* is incomplete " - כי יד על כס קה – אין הכסא שלם For there is a hand on God's throne – the throne of God is not complete .... "

We still have backward barbarians around who refuse to recognize *malchus Hashem* (God's kingship). Their distorted perception of *Elokus* (Godliness) causes them to not appreciate the dignity of human life, which rests on the *tzelem Elokim* of each and every human.

When we blow the *shofar* at the conclusion of the *beracha* (blessing) of *malchuyos*, we are (a) coronating God, and accepting Him once again as King; and (b) enhancing the urgency of our request at the end of the *beracha* of *malchuyos* to see to it that His promise of *malchuyos* be fulfilled.

Remembering the Beginning

RABBI HERSHEL SCHACHTER

In the *tefillos* for *Rosh Hashana*, we mention that "today is the anniversary of the beginning of the world." This refers to the **sixth** day of creation, when Adam was formed. It is the anniversary of the first day of the history of mankind. The first five days of creation are considered "prehistoric," since there were no human beings around at that time.

In the *tefillos*, we also emphasize that on this day of *Rosh Hashana* we commemorate what happened so many centuries ago on that first day of human history.

On *Pesach* we commemorate the historical events connected with *Yetzias Mitzrayim* and are mindful of the lessons we learned from those events. On *Shavuos* we commemorate *Ma'amad Har Sinai* and all that it implies. So, too, on *Rosh Hashana* we commemorate the creation of Adam, and all that occurred on the first day of man's creation which is relevant for us today. This includes:

The Torah relates that man was created "*betzelem Elokim*," and the *Mishna* points out that because of His love for man, God made Adam

Originally published on TorahWeb.org in 2005

aware of this.[5] This concept of *tzelem Elokim* implies that man has tremendous potential to be original and creative, and to accomplish much in both a physical and a spiritual sense.

The *Midrash* relates that God showed Adam all the beautiful trees in *Gan Eden* and warned him that if he sins, he will be ruining God's beautiful world![6]

On that same day that man was created, God revealed Himself to him and communicated with him, commanding him regarding the Noahide *mitzvos*, which are binding throughout all generations, and regarding not eating from the *eitz hada'as*, which was only intended as a *hora'as sha'a*. Some philosophers who were not present to witness this communication find it logically impossible to conceive of such communication between the Infinite God and the finite human being. But our religion considers this one of the basic principles of faith, that however He accomplished it, God did reveal Himself to man and communicated with him, and will again reveal Himself to man in the future.

The Torah tells us that God did not cause the rain to fall until after Adam was on the scene to pray for the rain.[7] Not only do we believe that God can communicate with man, but we also believe that man has the power of *tefilla* and can communicate with God. From day number one, we already started to pray.

Chava sinned with the *eitz hada'as* because she fooled herself into believing the words of the *nachash*, that she "will become as great as God Himself." Many individuals are led to sin because they fool themselves into believing that they are someone other than whom they really are; they join groups of people where they don't really fit in. To fool others is a serious

---

[5] See Rambam's commentary to *Avos* 3:14.
[6] See *Mesillas Yesharim*, chapter 1.
[7] See Rashi to *Bereishis* 2:5.

sin; to fool oneself is a greater sin.[8]

The Torah describes **all** the trees in *Gan Eden* as being extremely delicious and pleasant-looking. And yet, the *nachash* convinced Chava to sin with the forbidden fruit because it was so pleasant-looking and delicious. Why was Chava tempted to partake of the forbidden fruit when all of the trees were equally appealing? That is human nature. We always imagine that "the stolen waters are sweeter," and the grass is greener on the other side. The real truth is that one can enjoy life just as much by keeping the Torah as by violating it.

The *Midrash* interprets the Torah to be telling us that Adam also ate from the forbidden fruit because Chava pressured him by her crying. Many people sin due to social pressures. People must do what is really correct and disregard what is politically correct. This indeed takes a lot of courage!

When God confronted Adam and questioned him regarding his sin, Adam responded (according to the *Midrash*), "Yes, I have eaten from the forbidden tree, and I will continue to eat!" Everyone who sins tends to rationalize his actions. Before sinning, man can properly distinguish between right and wrong. But after sinning, the *"tov vara"* become confused. Man finds it hard to admit that he did anything wrong.

These fundamental principles, and many others, are called to mind on *Rosh Hashana* when we commemorate the first day of the history of mankind.

---

[8] See *Yemei Zikaron* by Rav Yosef Dov Soloveitchik, p. 208.

The Light of Torah
RABBI HERSHEL SCHACHTER

In the *tefillos* of *Rosh Hashana* we assume that Adam *Harishon* was created on the first of *Tishrei*. That day at that time was a Friday, which today is impossible; according to the calendar that we use, *Rosh Hashana* can never fall out on a Friday. Even though that day was the sixth day of creation, we refer to *Rosh Hashana* as "זה היום תחילת מעשיך" – "the beginning of the creation of the world" – because the first five days were prehistoric since there was no human being there to notice anything.

In the *tefillos* of *Rosh Hashana*, we mention that on this day of *Rosh Hashana* we should all recall what happened on that very first *Rosh Hashana*. The *midrash* tells us, commenting on the *pasuk* in *Tehillim*, "Hashem ori veyishi" "God is my light and my salvation," that "*ori*" is a reference to *Rosh Hashana* and "*yishi*" is a reference to *Yom HaKippurim*. On that very day that *Hashem* created *Adam Harishon*, he granted him illumination by instructing him to observe the basic *mitzvos* that apply to all of mankind. The Talmud (*Bava Metzia* 83b) comments that the *pasuk* in *Borchi Nafshi*, " תשת חושך ויהי לילה- You make darkness, and it is night" (*Tehillim* 104:2) is a reference to *olam hazeh*. Many issues in this world are very unclear, just like in the middle of a dark night; there are *mitzvos* that people think are really *aveiros* and there are *aveiros* that people consider to be *mitzvos* (see the *hakdama* of *Mesillas Yesharim*). Without illumination

Originally published on TorahWeb.org in 2011

granted by *Hashem* through the laws of the Torah, we will remain "in the dark." *Rosh Hashana* for Adam *Harishon* was his day of *kabbalas haTorah*.

According to the tradition recorded in the *Midrash*, Adam *Harishon* sinned on that very same first day that he was created. He was judged and punished on the same day, and *Hashem* notified him that just as He judged Adam on this day, so too will He judge Adam's descendants in all future generations on this day. The fact that *Rosh Hashana* is the *yom hadin* is never mentioned in *Tanach*, but is an oral tradition from Adam *Harishon* (*Drashas HaRamban LeRosh Hashana*).

The story of the "original sin" does not really play a significant role in Jewish theology. It was recorded in the Torah, however, to teach us certain aspects about sin that are relevant to all of us today.

According to one *midrash*,[9] if Adam *Harishon* would have waited until *leil Shabbos*, he would have been permitted to eat the fruits of the *eitz hada'as*. He could not even contain himself for a few hours. We all have to train ourselves to realize that it is not that essential to have instant gratification. *Hashem* created us all to enjoy the world,[10] but it is not absolutely necessary to have pleasure all the time. The Jewish farmer plants a tree, and he does not eat of its fruits until a few years go by. The *shochet* slaughters an animal but he does not eat of the meat until he first checks the lungs.[11] It is not that terrible to postpone having pleasure from the world a little bit.

The reason Adam and Chava could not control themselves, and sinned by eating from the *eitz hada'as*, is that the fruit seemed so delicious and appealing. When we read the *pesukim* in *Parashas Bereishis*, the Torah gives the exact same description with respect to all the trees in *Gan Eden*. They were all delicious and appeared very appealing. But we always have

---

[9] Quoted by the Ramban in his sefer *Milchamos Hashem* at the begining of *Maseches Chullin*.
[10] See *Mesillas Yesharim* regarding *perishus*.
[11] As stated in the aforementioned *midrash*.

the attitude that the grass is greener on the other side. We always think that "stolen waters are sweeter" (*Mishlei* 19.) To the *reshaim*, who have violated *aveiros*, the *yetzer hara* appears like a strand of hair (*Sukkah* 52a). They realize that they did not get any more pleasure from doing the *aveiros* than they would have had doing the *mitzvos*. To the *tzaddikim* who never violated the *aveiros*, the *yetzer hara* appears as though it were a gigantic mountain. They conjure up in their mind an image of what tremendous pleasures one would certainly receive if he were to violate the *aveiros*.[12] But the truth of the matter is that any forbidden pleasure has a parallel in the realm of *heter* (*Chullin* 109b). One can enjoy *olam hazeh* by keeping *mitzvos* to the same extent that the *reshaim* enjoy doing *aveiros*.

When *Hashem* confronted Adam *Harishon* and told him that he would be punished for having sinned, He says, "שמעת לקול אשתך כי - because you listened to the voice of your wife." The *Midrash* understands that expression to mean that Chava coaxed her husband to eat along with her from the forbidden fruit by crying in front of him. Very often we sin because we give in to social pressure.

On *Rosh Hashana*, and all year long, we should take to heart the details of the original sin and realize that it simply does not make sense to violate the *mitzvos* of the Torah.

---

[12] This explanation is offered by the *Beis Halevi*.

Recommitting Ourselves to the Torah Shebe'al Peh

RABBI HERSHEL SCHACHTER

The Talmud (*Berachos* 47b) describes the process of becoming a *talmid chacham* as consisting of three parts: One must be (1) *kara* (2) *veshana* and (3) *veshimeish talmidei chachamim*.

Kara means that one must master *Tanach*, which we refer to as *Mikra*. *Shana* refers to mastering *Mishnayos*, which represent all of the *halachos* of the *Torah Shebe'al Peh*. However, just mastering *Tanach* and all of *Mishna* is not sufficient; one who is not *meshameish talmidei chachamim* is referred to by the *Gemara* (ibid.) as an *am ha'aretz*. *Torah Shebe'al Peh* does not consist only of a body of *halachos*; the *mesora* of the Oral Torah transmits attitudes as well, and this is the meaning of *shimush talmidei chachamim*. If one applies himself diligently, he can succeed in mastering the body of the *halachos* in the *Gemara* in a matter of several years. But the Talmud (*Avoda Zara* 5b) tells us that in order to absorb the attitudes that the *Torah Shebe'al Peh* transmits from generation to generation, one requires forty years.

After forty years of teaching *Am Yisrael* after *Matan Torah*, Moshe Rabbeinu states that after all of these years, *Bnei Yisrael* finally understood

---

Originally published on TorahWeb.org in 2013

Rosh Hashana

what he was driving at: "ולא נתן לכם ה' לב לדעת ועינים לראות ... עד היום הזה - Yet the Lord has not given you a heart to know and eyes to see ... until this day" (*Devarim* 29:3). The *Chachamim* derive from this *pasuk* that one does not really succeed in absorbing the attitudes transmitted within the *Torah Shebe'al Peh* until after forty years. The *dor hamidbar* did not have to work for a living and had the luxury of learning for forty years from Moshe Rabbeinu. In our generation, people learn from a *rebbe* for several years and then get married, get a job, and raise a family. Nonetheless, if they continue to learn for forty years according to the guidelines which they received from their *rebbe*, then they will understand this aspect of the *Torah Shebe'al Peh* as well. The Talmud (*Sotah* 22a with Rashi) refers to those who have mastered *Tanach* and *Mishna* but are lacking the *shimush talmidei chachamim*, and yet take it upon themselves to teach others, as a "*rasha arum*," since they have the ability to quote biblical and talmudic sources and fool the public into believing that they are *talmidei chachamim* even though they really are not.

In recent years, some people who claim to be *talmidei chachamim* have introduced new religious practices. Some have women read *Megillas Rus* on *Shavuos* or *Megillas Esther* on *Purim* for the whole community; others have women get some of the *aliyos*, and yet others have women recite *Kabbalas Shabbos* or *Pesukei deZimra*. On one occasion when Rav Soloveitchik was consulted about women's prayer groups, he did not want to say that it was prohibited. However, after pointing to the expression in the Talmud "אין רוח חכמים נוחה הימנו - the Sages are not pleased with him" (see *Kiddushin* 17b), he said that Orthodox Jews should understand that the displeasure of the great *talmidei chachamim* of a given generation with a practice indicates that the practice in question is against the attitudes transmitted as part of the *Torah Shebe'al Peh* (See *Sefer Mipeninei HaRav* p. 82, #1). When someone pointed out to the Rav that some of the *musmachim* who had introduced some of these practices seemed to know how to learn, the Rav responded in a sharp tone that one who is קרא ושנה ולא שימש תלמידי חכמים (learns *Tanach* and *Mishna* but does not serve *talmidei chachamim*) is considered an *am ha'aretz* (ibid., p. 208, #7.) The attitudes of the *Torah Shebe'al Peh* are not only an essential part of Torah which must be transmitted by a *rebbe* to his *talmidim*, but are also a litmus test for evaluating the correctness of any new practice.

On several occasions, the *Chazon Ish* would issue a *pesak* on a contemporary social issue, and people would ask him: where does it say this *pesak*? Where did you get that from? He would point with his index finger to his heart and respond, "It is written over here" (from *Pe'er Hador*, the biography of the *Chazon Ish*). Rashi in his commentary on the *Chumash* (*Shemos* 28:4) writes in one place, "*Libi omer li*" (see *Nefesh HaRav* p. 43). In Yiddish folklore the question is posed: How can Rashi follow what his heart dictates to him; isn't doing so a violation of "*velo sasuru acharei levavchem*" – "you may not stray after the dictates of your heart" (*Bemidbar* 15:39)? The traditional answer is that for one who has fulfilled the instructions of *Mishlei* (3:3), "כתבם על לוח ליבך - write them [the words of Torah] on your heart" there is nothing wrong with following one's heart. But this process of engraving the Torah on one's heart is what takes forty years of continued learning according to the guidelines of one's *rebbe*.

We often hear people asking, when one of the *rabbanim* of our generation issues a *pesak* on a sensitive *shaila* with social implications, "Where does it say that *pesak*?" Are we Karaites and as such require that everything has to be written down on parchment or in a book!? We have a *masora* of a tremendous *Torah Shebe'al Peh* which includes within it attitudes on everything. Honest *talmidei chachamim*, who have not only mastered *Mikra* and *Mishna* but have also been *meshamesh talmidei chachamim* and have absorbed these attitudes, are certainly entitled and obligated to express their opinion based on the *masora* that they have received and absorbed.

We believe, as it says in the Torah, that man was created betzelem Elokim. The Torah instructed all of us "ויכרדב תכלהו - walk in His ways" (Devarim 28:9), to preserve that tzelem Elokim by developing middos, i.e., developing the middos which the Tanach uses to describe Hakadosh Baruch Hu. The navi Yeshaya describes Hakadosh Baruch Hu as "א-ל מסתתר - God who conceals Himself" (Yeshaya 45:15. See "The Breaking of the Glass").[13] The Ribbono Shel Olam does such a good job at hiding and being inconspicuous that there are many atheists who think that He is not even there. The Rav pointed out that the middas hatzniyus of Hakadosh Baruch Hu, which comprises doing everything betzina (in an inconspicuous fashion), which we are expected to adopt in our personal lives as part of the mitzva of preserving our tzelem Elokim, is most difficult for Americans. In America people long for their "five minutes of fame" and to see their picture and name publicized; everybody goes for publicity and nothing is done betzina.

The Torah tells us that the difference between man and woman is not only physiological, rather there is also a difference in the *tzelem Elokim* (see *Bereishis* 1:27 and *Divrei HaRav* p. 244). The Torah tells us that on rare occasions, *Hakadosh Baruch Hu* felt it necessary to reveal Himself. We too are called upon, on occasion, to do things *befarhesiya*. For example, we have a *chazan* who *davens* at the *amud*, somebody gets an *aliya*, and we appoint a rabbi to lead our community. The *Chumash* tells us, "שום תשים עליך מלך - You shall set a king over you" (*Devarim* 17:15), and the *Torah Shebe'al Peh* comments, "מלך ולא מלכה - a king but not a queen." Even when it is necessary to compromise on our *middas hatzniyus*, the *Halacha* recommends that whenever possible a woman should not be called upon to be the one to compromise. True, strictly speaking, the *Mishna* tells us that a woman may get an *aliya*, but the Talmud points out that this would constitute a violation of *kavod hatzibbur*, since it would imply that there were not

---

[13] http://www.torahweb.org/torah/2005/parasha/rsch_yisro.html

enough literate men available to take care of the entire *kerias haTorah* and as such we felt compelled to ask a woman to compromise on her *tzniyus*. Getting an *aliya* or reading the *Megilla* in public is not, and should not be seen as, an entitlement, which one might then think that women should be equally entitled to. It is rather a necessary compromising of one's *tzelem Elokim*. As we mentioned above, this perspective is the diametric opposite of the attitude of contemporary American society.

The time of *Ma'amad Har Sinai* through the building of the second *Beis Hamikdash* was the period of *Torah Shebichsav*. The *Seder Olam* tells us that after the *nevi'im acharonim* passed away, the Jewish people no longer had any prophecy, and from then on we have had to pay close attention to what the *chachamim* tell us. This means that the end of *nevua* marked the beginning of the period of *Torah Shebe'al Peh*. Indeed the *Midrash* comments (*Vayikra Rabba* 7:3; see *Bava Basra* 8a), based on the *pasuk* in the *navi*, that the future *geula* will only take place in the *zechus* of the study of *Mishnayos*, i.e., the *Torah Shebe'al Peh*. During the entire period of the second *Beis Hamikdash*, there was trouble from the *Tzedukim* (see *Be'ikvei Hatzon* p. 139.) Ultimately, the *Tzedukim* disappeared and the traditions of the *Torah Shebe'al Peh* preserved the Jewish people.

Orthodox Judaism is a God-centric religion dedicated to fulfilling *Hakadosh Baruch Hu*'s will, not to injecting our own will into His Torah. There have been many groups over the course of Jewish history, from the Karaites and *Tzedukim* to today's deviationists, which were led by people who rejected the attitudes of the *Torah Shebe'al Peh* and catered to contemporary desires and fads. In each case these groups, with the passage of time, disappeared and their adherents were lost. By contrast, the Jews who absorbed and lived by the attitudes transmitted from generation to generation via *shimush talmidei chachamim* live on eternally through their

Torah-observant descendants.[14]

The *Shabbos* prior to *Rosh Hashana* is always *Parashas Nitzavim*. As the *parasha* says, we are called upon this time every year to enter anew into a covenant with *Hakadosh Baruch Hu*. We must recommit ourselves to the *bris* of the *Torah Shebe'al Peh*, with all that that implies, and in that merit may we be *zocheh* to the *geula*.

---

[14] Ed.: See "Straightening Out Our Priorities," http://www.torahweb.org/torah/2005/parsha/rsch_matos.html, where Rav Schachter further develops the idea of living on through our children.

The Shofar: External and Internal

RABBI YAKOV HABER

One of the major focal points of the prayer service on *Rosh Hashana* is the *Musaf Amida* containing blessings with the three themes of *malchuyos, zichronos,* and *shofaros*. The Talmud (*Rosh Hashana* 34b) tells us that *Hakadosh Baruch Hu* tells us: "Recite before Me *malchuyos, zichronos,* and *shofaros: Malchuyos* – so that you shall coronate me as your King. *Zichronos* – so that your remembrance comes before me for the good. And with what? With the *shofar*." Notably, even though each theme has its own *beracha*, the Talmud seems to explain the reason for the first two *berachos* directly. The third *beracha* is mentioned only in a secondary way: "With what? With the *shofar*." This seems to be an explanation of why we **blow** the *shofar*. Why isn't the purpose of the **beracha** of *shofaros* more explicitly stated?

Furthermore, when we analyze the text of the three *berachos*, we see that the first, concerning *malchuyos*, clearly focuses on coronating *Hashem* as our King. The second clearly focuses on God remembering our actions. The third, though, focuses on God revealing His presence in the world starting at *Har Sinai*. Why doesn't the *Gemara* spell out this theme

---

Originally published on TorahWeb.org in 2014

rather than just vaguely referencing the *shofar*?

In addition, each *beracha* contains three verses from the Torah, three from *Tehillim*, and three from *Nevi'im*. In the *beracha* of *shofaros*, which, as mentioned, focuses on Revelation, the first three *pesukim* from the Torah focus on the Revelation of Sinai punctuated by the sound of the *shofar*. The last three highlight the Revelation of the final redemption, also accentuated by *shofar* blasts. But the middle three *pesukim* from *Tehillim* do not seem to focus on Revelation. One verse speaks of the *shofar* on *Rosh Hashana*, "תקעו בחודש שופר בכסה ליום חגינו"- Blow the *shofar* at the moon's renewal, at the time appointed for our festive day" (*Tehillim* 81:4). One speaks of God being elevated with the *shofar*, "עלה א-לקים בתרועה, ה' בקול שופר- God has ascended with a blast, *Hashem* with the sound of the *shofar*" (*Tehillim* 47:6; translations from Artscroll). The final verses of this section, taken from the last psalm, speak of many musical instruments being used to praise *Hashem*, including the *shofar*. How are these verses related and how do they relate to the general theme of Revelation?

Rav Soloveitchik (*Yemei Zikaron*, "עלי תאנה וכותנות עור") beautifully explains that the *pesukim* from *Tehillim* focus on the revelation of *Hashem* on *Rosh Hashana* itself. God reveals Himself to the penitent, encouraging him, embracing him, awaiting his return. Elsewhere (seen in *Niflaos HaRav*), Rav Soloveitchik explains that the Torah's statement of "ושמחתם לפני ד' א-לקיכם - you shall rejoice before the Lord, your God" (*Vayikra* 23:40), indicates that true joy occurs only when in the presence of God. The fear of judgment of *Rosh Hashana* eliminates the ability to recite *Hallel* which would ordinarily reflect this joy (*Arachin* 10b). Nonetheless, a hidden *Hallel* is indeed recited through the verses from the last *mizmor* of *Tehillim*, indicating all the instruments including the *shofar* being used to praise *Hashem*. According to the Rav, then, all of the *pesukim* do indeed focus on the theme of Revelation.

Based on this idea, perhaps we can answer our other questions as well. The *Gemara* states *"Bameh? Bashofar!"* Perhaps the *Gemara* is referring to both the blessings of *malchuyos* and *zichronos*. How are we to coronate God? How are we to assure that *Hashem* remembers us *letova*? The *Gemara* answers: With the *shofar*! The *shofar* represents God's revelation to us. But this revelation was not only to be punctuated in the historical record at its endpoints – at *Har Sinai,* at the beginning of Jewish national history, and at the Final Redemption, the last stage of Jewish history. It is also a constant one on both the national and individual levels. God constantly reveals Himself to us in our lives by exercising His Divine providence over us. His constant knowledge of every aspect of our lives, even the most minute, His constant monitoring, modifying, and re-creating all of our life pathways reflect His constant intense connection to us. To be sure, the intensity of the connection to *Hakadosh Baruch Hu* depends on our spiritual level, but *Hashem's* connection to everyone is a given. How are we to coronate God, to recognize Him as the ruler of not only the world, but also to realize that the entire purpose of our existence is to connect to Him? How are we to ensure that we are remembered for the good before the heavenly court? *Bashofar* – through being aware of God's constant presence in our lives. To not get caught up in the *havlei hazeman*, which tend to numb us to this awareness of God's presence in our lives. The *shofar* wakes us up (Rambam, *Hilchos Teshuva*), breaks down the barriers (*Michtav MeEliyahu* as per the *shofar* of Yericho), and allows us to start on our journey to return.

The *haftara* for *Shabbos Shuva* begins, "שובה ישראל עד ה' א-לוקיך – Return, Israel, to *Hashem*, your God!" Rather than viewing the return as a journey **toward** God, perhaps we can characterize this as a return **inward** to that which is already there, to God's constant connection to us which we are not taking full advantage of. May we all "re-sign" on the *bris* with *Hakadosh Baruch Hu* on *Rosh Hashana*, and may the awareness of His constant presence carry us through a sweet new year!

Approaching Rosh Hashana: How to Earn His Patience and Tolerance

RABBI YAAKOV NEUBURGER

Some forty years ago, *Harav* Chaim Shmulevitz (*Sichos Musar* 5732:38) formulated an inspiring approach to these last days of the year, which has since been repeated countless times in various articles and speeches. Rav Shmulevitz was the *Rosh Yeshiva* of the Mir Yeshiva in Yerushalyim, and recognized as one of the foremost *Roshei Yeshiva* of Israel. It was in one of his year-end talks that he formulated the fright and despair that catches up with us as *Rosh Hashana* looms so large over all. The *Rosh Yeshiva* explained that even when a Jew feels that change and improvement are well beyond his grasp, there are strategies that *Chazal* have taught, with which we can prepare for the upcoming *yom hadin*.

Foremost is to remember the *Gemara* (*Rosh Hashana* 17a) that records Rav Papa's visit to the ailing Rav Huna (son of Rav Yehoshua), only to find him suffering the pain of imminent death. In fact, Rav Papa takes leave

Originally published on TorahWeb.org in 2004

of Rav Huna and commissions the necessary preparations. You can well imagine the surprise and embarrassment that overtook Rav Papa when Rav Huna appeared once again at his place in the *beis hamidrash*. Rav Huna, realizing Rav Papa's position, explained that he had been privy to the deliberations conducted on High as they prepared to greet his saintly soul. It was revealed then to him that although he had deserved to leave this world, his easygoing nature and willingness to cut everyone slack earned the same grace from *Hashem*, who granted him many more years in this world.

The *Gemara* sees in this story an illustration of *Hashem*'s approach to all those who, out of genuine humility, tolerate the barbs and lapses of others. It is referred to in the thirteen attributes of *Hashem*'s mercy: He is "נושא עוון ועובר על פשע - bears sin and forgives iniquities," which translates into נושא עוון לעובר על פשע, tolerates the sins of those who close their eyes to the insensitivities of acquaintances and friends.

Thus, Rav Chaim would encourage his students that when we find ourselves incapable of further improvement and perhaps even discouraged from introspection, we have by no means exhausted our preparations for the *Yemei Hadin*. If we could successfully muster up the inner strength to forgive others who may have wronged us, we would, in that merit alone, be eligible for *Hashem*'s compassion.

It is quite possible that we are asked to do more than simply tolerate the lapses of friends, swallow them and dismiss the hurt of the moment. Surely, one who does rise above the offenses of others shows greatness that the *Gemara* prizes. The peace that he and his family and friends will come to know will no doubt be a source of great blessing. Nevertheless the *mishna* that states "and judge everyone favorably" means just that, that we need to creatively and proactively judge our friends with a good and accepting eye.

The *Gemara* cites several examples of individuals who exercised mental gymnastics in order to explain the surprising and hurtful behavior of others. They were not satisfied with attributing it to circumstances that they could not question or understand. Rather, they thought through scenarios that would actually reinterpret the hurtful behavior into acts of concern and interest.

It is the deep-seated sense of goodness and trust in our fellows which allows us to be giving and accepting. In these days we pray for the same from *Hashem*, hoping that His trust in our goodness and dedication to Him will earn for us His patience and tolerance, so that we can grow and serve Him with greater vigor and happiness.

A Blueprint for Teshuva
RABBI MICHAEL ROSENSWEIG

In *Parashas Nitzavim*, which is generally designated to be read in advance of *Rosh Hashana*, the Torah records several crucial sections that depict the highs and lows of the national destiny of the Jewish people: the devastating impact of sin, exile, loss and destruction (*Devarim* 29:19-27), and the equally impressive phenomenon of rebirth and return to prosperity and Divine providence (30:1-11). After this wide range culminates with a direct reference to *teshuva* ("כי תשוב אל ה' א-לוקך בכל לבבך ובכל נפשך - when you return to the Lord your God with all your heart and with all your soul"), the Torah (30:11-14) dramatically introduces an ambiguous *mitzva* – "*ki hamitzva hazos*" – strikingly indicating that it is neither wondrous (*nifleis*) nor distant (*rechoka*), nor in the heavens (*bashamayim*), nor accross the sea (*meieiver layam*). Rather, this unspecified imperative is within our grasp – "בפיך ובלבבך לעשותו" - in your mouth and in your heart, so that you can fulfill it." The effect of the continuation, in which the Torah presents the choice of life and good or death and evil (30:15) is to convey urgency of implementation. Clearly a major principle of Judaism is being projected here, notwithstanding the ambiguity of the phrase "*ki hamitzva hazos*."

While the *Gemara* in *Eruvin* (55a), Rashi (op. cit.), and Rambam

---

Originally published on TorahWeb.org in 2003

(*Hilchos Talmud Torah* 3:8) interpret this imperative as a reference to study of Torah, deemed "*keneged kulam*" (*Peah* 1:1), the source for Jewish education and values, as crucial an institution as exists in Jewish life, the Ramban (30:11) suggests that the reference is to the obligation of *teshuva* – repentence. His reading is reinforced by an analysis of the context and language of the previous sections, as noted.

The Ramban's view is consistent with prominence of *teshuva* as a vehicle for personal, communal, and national transformation. The Rabbis perceived the very existence and possibility of *teshuva* – the ability to extricate oneself from past behavioral patterns, and to neutralize sin and past inadequacy, to literally reinvent oneself, a philosophically problematic notion, as it denies moral and behavioral causality – as a gift, even a miracle. This is particularly true of the more ambitious forms of *teshuva miyira* (fear of *Hashem*) and *teshuva mei'ahava* (love of *Hashem*) that have remarkable transformative impact on sin (*Yoma* 86a).

Yet, *teshuva* is a centerpiece in Jewish *halachic* outlook. That man can and must mold his spiritual destiny is axiomatic, and particularly urgent in the period beginning with *Rosh Hashana* and concluding with *Yom Kippur* (*Rosh Hashana* 18a).

An analysis of these *pesukim* according to the Ramban's reading constitutes a blueprint for the process of *teshuva*. It contributes significantly to our understanding of challenges and possibilities, and illuminates the process and methodology of this crucial institution-*mitzva*. Before the *Yamim Noraim*, such an assessment is indispensible to our own personal and collective preparation for what lies ahead.

The first element is accessibility ("לא רחוקה היא ... בפיך ובלבבך לע־שותו - it is not far away ... it is in your mouth and your heart, so that you can fulfill it"), which is conveyed repeatedly and emphatically in these verses. Meiri begins his work on *teshuva* (*Chibur Hateshuva*) by emphasizing the importance of not despairing in the quest for *teshuva*. Being cognizant of our capacity to succeed not only dispels counterproductive frustration, but also reflects the nature of *teshuva* and, by extension, of the *halachic* concept of religious growth more generally as a meaningful challenge.

Furthermore, the Torah's intriguing formulations preclude and reject a decisive role for extraneous factors, while at the same time, they hint at the obstacles that need to but most definitely can be overcome. They also underscore that misguided or overstated nostalgia, or overidealization of other eras or circumstances, are generally counterproductive unless they inspire and motivate, rather than frustrate by raising the bar to unattainable levels. In any case, a brief examination of what *teshuva* is not is also indispensible to the effort to achieve a proper *teshuva*.

The concept of "*lo bashamayim*" declares that Judaism, and by extension the process of *teshuva*, does not demand an angelic or otherworldly posture nor does it require perfection, either in deed or commitment. It is important to note that this verse is invoked by the Rabbis in a celebrated passage (*Bava Metzia* 59a: "*tanur shel Achnai*") to establish the principle of man's partnership with God in the development of the *halachic* system. The Talmud explains that precisely because of the perfection and self-sufficiency of the Torah given at Sinai, and due to its ambition for man's spiritual growth, there is no need for Divine intervention in *halachic* decisionmaking. The tools and methodology of interpretation and adjudication are all part of the Torah, and man is charged with implementing that system through its divinely ordained rules. The sincere *halachist* who is properly trained in these rules, and who is fully committed to Torah and *yiras Shamayim*, willing to surrender to its rule and sensibilities, becomes a significant partner in the endeavor of Torah, making Divine intervention – *lo bashamayim hi* – unnecessary. The fact that the *halachist's* sincere input is indispensable, even decisive, reflects *Hashem's* ambition for man, as well as the enormous responsibility that accompanies and is the basis for his prerogatives. Man's significant, if subordinate, role in the world of *halacha* also constitutes a leitmotif in the writings and thinking of the Rav zt"l. Rav Soloveitchik contrasts *halachic* man's creative contributions with the more generally passive posture of the admired heroic figures of other religions. This view reflects man's inherent value and potential for spirituality and sanctity.

This remarkable perspective attesting to man's vast potential qualifies man qua man (not as angel), as a candidate for the gift of *teshuva*. Man need not relinquish his humanity to restore his relationship with *Hashem*. Instead, he needs to elevate and sanctify his physical and human dimension and channel it to *Hashem*'s service. In Judaism, man is always superior to angels. Because of – not despite – his humanity, he is privileged to have and observe the Torah.

The motif of *"lo nifleis hi"* is equally important. In his magnificent depiction of the uniqueness of *halachic* Judaism, *"Ish HaHalacha,"* Rav Soloveitchik contrasts what he calls standard Religious Man and Halachic Man. He demonstrates that unlike other religions, Judaism first and foremost focuses on concrete this-worldly norms and the sanctification of the real world, not on mysticism and the flight to a more spiritual realm. The process of *teshuva*, by extension, is neither mysterious nor mystical. It is rooted in the accessible exoteric categories of the *halacha*. Man's ability to sanctify the mundane and the physical world that he inhabits is the basis for *berachos*, family laws like *taharas hamishpacha*, as well as *Choshen Mishpat*, the comprehensive code of civil law that governs every aspect of human interaction. *Halacha*'s vast scope contrasts with other religions that focus almost exclusively on the more obvious "spiritual, ritual" sphere. The *halachic* approach reflects not compromise of spirituality, but to the contrary, a greater ambition.

In *teshuva*, this consideration of *"lo nifleis,"* is particularly acute.

It is a crucial irony since sin reflects man's failure to attain his lofty goal, having succumbed to the pressures or temptations of the concrete world. Yet, in the process of *teshuva*, man is not asked to reject the physical world, but to rededicate to the struggle and ambition to sanctify his existence and the world around him. *Teshuva* is a rigorous, lengthy process, exoteric and human in every way.

At the same time, *teshuva* is also not "*mei'eiver layam.*" Halacha rejects a decisive normative role for the social-cultural environment in human behavior. This is most certainly not due to a denial of its profound impact. Indeed, the concept of "*shachen ra*" (bad neighbor influence) and the admonition to avoid "*moshav leitzim*" (clique of scoffers) etc. are pervasive and powerful themes in *Chazal,* who were keenly sensitive to the power of environment and prevailing sensibilities and norms. Rather, it is a testament to the ability and obligation to overcome such negative influences, and to the dominant concept of personal responsibility, the foundation for all reward and punishment. Personal choice (*bechira chofshis*) stands at the center of *teshuva*. (In the Rambam's work it appears in the fifth and sixth of ten chapters dedicated to *teshuva!*) According to the *halachic* view, man has the capacity, and therefore the obligation, to insulate himself from unacceptable attitudes and conduct, to extricate himself from or overcome his environment when necessary by strenthening his inner world that dictates his own responses, and when possible to help shape the world around him. (See Rambam, *Sefer Hamitzvos*, no. 3.) Yaakov indicated as much to his brother Esav when he declared that he was able to fulfill the 613 commandments in Lavan's home (Rashi, *Vayishlach*). He ultimately left that home when he felt Lavan's influence had became too intoxicating or confusing. Rav Soloveitchik often emphasized his belief that Judaism can thrive in any society with the proper *yiras Shamayim* and level of commitment. This conviction is predicated on the theme that Torah and its values are capable of fortifying a person, providing a powerful foundation enabling man to meet his challenges.

The concept of *"lo rechoka"* encourages man to reject the sense of frustration and hopelessness due to the apparently overwhelming distance that separates him and *Hashem*, particularly as a consequence of sin. This feeling can impede the effort toward *teshuva*. The Torah perceives the formidability of the task as a catalyst for greater effort, as the experience of loss and distance underscores the inimical effects of sin. Since man's purpose in the world is only to develop a relationship with *Hashem*, the sense of purposelessness and insignificance that results when he loses his spiritual bearings and anchor must trigger his motivation to return.

Finally, we turn from the challenge and misconceptions to the methodology. The words בפיך ובלבבך לעשותו ("in your mouth and your heart, so that you can fulfill it") constitute a remarkable guarantee that, notwithstanding all of the misconceptions, which are really reflections of enormous challenges, *teshuva* is within man's grasp and can be attained with nothing more than the basic core tools of his inner life. The first is the power of prayer through articulation. By virtue of a mechanism to reach *Hashem* and simultaneously achieve self-knowledge (from the reflexive *"lehispallel"*), man is able to place his needs and relationship to his Creator in better perspective. According to the Ramban, *"beficha"* also refers specifically to the *viduy* – the confession stage that is indispensible to *teshuva*, as it formulates and concretizes man's failings, stripping away rationalization and denial, paving the path for honest introspection and ultimately, for change. The second component, *"bilvavcha"* projects the emotional-intellectual resources of heart and mind that can reshape and regulate man's inner world and dictate his hierarchy of values and priorities. Finally, *"la'asoso"* establishes the role of actions that concretely implement the values of Torah through *halachic* norms. The this-worldly nature of *halachic* religious commitment alluded to earlier, which is not a concession to the physical world but a reflection of higher spiritual ambition, demands that profound inner change be concretized into physical and measured actions that also impact upon others.

The promise of accessibility of *teshuva* and the delineation of a well-defined program to achieve it does not dismiss or ignore the challenges and obstacles, as noted. Moreover, the *pesukim* indicate that success is contingent upon the intensity of one's commitment. As the *Gemara* in *Eruvin* and Rashi note, one need not storm the heavens, simulate conditions of *"eiver layam,"* immerse oneself in esoteric study and mystical actions to attain the goal and gift of *teshuva*, but one's devotion and dedication and conviction to religious self-improvement must match the intensity that would have been required had these radical, formidable standards been established as the sine qua non of *teshuva*! The gift of accessibility and attainability should not be misconstrued or exploited as a license for a tepid or mediocre effort to achieve so crucial a goal.

At the culmination of the *teshuva* period, on *Yom Kippur*, we withdraw temporarily from physical world, imitate the angels on high by standing and reciting the "ברוך שם כבוד מלכותו -Blessed is the name of His glorious kingdom for all eternity," etc. precisely to project the intensity of our commitment, our willingness to go to any lengths if they are demanded, and to project that our more balanced spiritual program springs from the same devotion that would have characterized a more ascetic and esoteric approach, and is just as passionate and tenacious. In this sense, the simplicity of *"beficha, bilvavcha, la'asoso"* does not belie the absolute comprehensiveness and ambitiousness of the task. The willingness to scale the heavens in our efforts to refashion our relationship with *Hashem*, combined with the accessibility guaranteed by the Torah, challenge and inspire each and every one of us to aspire for a complete *teshuva* (*sheleimah*), as individuals and as a community, in the *Yamim Noraim* period ahead. The multidimensional program outlined in the Torah is the blueprint for personal and collective introspection and transformation. May we achieve this goal כי המצוה הזאת בפיך ובלבבך – לעשתו, because this mitzva is in your mouth and in your heart, so that you can fulfill it.

Yom Terua and Zichron Terua: The Centrality of Mitzvas Shofar Even on Shabbos Rosh Hashana

RABBI MICHAEL ROSENSWEIG

The *Mishna* (*Rosh Hashana* 29b) rules that the *mitzva* of *tekias shofar* is suspended whenever *Rosh Hashana* coincides with *Shabbos*. The *Gemara* explains that this suspension is due to the concern that preoccupation with the performance of the *mitzva* might precipitate a violation of *Shabbos* (שמא יעבירנו ארבע אמות ברשות הרבים), lest he carry it four cubits in a public domain). The *Gemara* reports that same consideration was applied in suspending the practice of the *mitzvos* of *lulav* and *Megillas Esther* when they coincide with *Shabbos*. However, notwithstanding this policy, the *Mishna* records an exception: the *mitzva* of *shofar* was observed in the *Mikdash* (Temple) even on *Shabbos*. Moreover, in the aftermath of the destruction of the *Mikdash*, it was determined that *tekias shofar* would continue to have a *Shabbos* outlet in venues that housed a permanent *sanhedrin*.

Tosafos (*Rosh Hashana* 29b, s.v. *aval*; *Sukkah* 43a, s.v. *inhu*) notes

---

Originally published on TorahWeb.org in 2009

that we do not encounter a parallel manifestation with respect to the *mitzva* of *lulav*. During the Temple era, the *mitzva* of *lulav* was practiced universally if the first day of *Sukkos* was a *Shabbos* (*Mishna, Sukkah* 42b). After the Temple's destruction, the performance of *lulav* on *Shabbos* was uniformly terminated. What accounts for the discrepancy between these two biblically ordained commandments? Why was it deemed important to attempt to find some outlet for *tekias shofar* even on *Shabbos*, while the same risk of *Shabbos* desecration categorically precluded the performance of *lulav*?

Tosafos's response succinctly but profoundly highlights the indispensability of *tekias shofar* as a vehicle transmitting *Klal Yisrael*'s merits to *Hashem*: "דשופר הוא להעלות זכרונותיהם של ישראל לאביהם שבשמים, לא רצו לבטל לגמרי - because the *shofar* is to lift up the *zichronos* of Israel to their Father in Heaven, they did not want to nullify it completely." *Tosafos*'s formulation of the *shofar*'s function in communicating the nation's "*zichronos*" invokes Rabba's celebrated characterization of the interrelationship between the three themes of *Rosh Hashana* – *malchuyos*, *zichronos*, and *shofaros*. The *Gemara* (34b) reports that the integration of *shofar* blowing and its accompanying themes is unique, requiring that the various *berachos* be expressed in conjunction with the *tekios* ("תקיעות וברכות של ראש השנה ויום הכפורים מעקבות -[omission of] the *shofar* blasts and the blessings of *Rosh Hashana* and *Yom Kippur* do invalidate [one another]"(.

"*Tekios uvrachos shel Rosh Hashana veYom HaKippurim me'akvos.*" Rabba elaborates this interconnection by accentuating the different but mutually enhancing contributions: "אמר הקדוש ברוך הוא: אימרו לפני בראש השנה מלכויות, זכרונות, ושופרות. מלכויות כדי שתמליכוני עליכם, זכרונות כדי שיבואו לפני זכרונותיכם לטובה. ובמה? בשופר - Recite before Me *malchuyos*, *zichronos*, and *shofaros*: *Malchuyos* – so that you shall coronate me as your King. *Zichronos* – so that your remembrance comes before me for the good. And with what? With the *shofar*."

While the words of Rabba resonate in *Tosafos*'s pointed articulation of the need for a *Shabbos* outlet for *tekias shofar*, they also assume additional significance in its light. One might have conceived of *shofar*'s contribution to the triad of *malchuyos-zichronos-shofaros* in purely functional terms as an effective, optimal, even ideal, but hardly indispensable, vehicle through which to convey the substantive content of *zichronos* to the *Melech*. *Tosafos*'s insight imparts that *shofar* is a medium that shapes and redefines the message. The fact that *shofar* redefines, even transforms the message, and that it transcends its role as merely a medium can be demonstrated by the Torah's designation (in *Parashas Pinchas*) of *Rosh Hashana* as "*yom terua*." This depiction, alongside "*yom hazikaron*," dominates our *tefillos*.

Indeed, aside from the *Shabbos* outlet (the Temple, or *sanhedrin*), and in eras like our own in which there is no venue that will allow for *shofar* on *Shabbos*, it is noteworthy that we continue to project the message of *zichronos* in conjunction with the absent *shofar*, its ideal method of communication! When the *Gemara* considered the possibility that *shofar*'s suspension on *Shabbos* was rooted in biblical law, it cited as its source the phrase "*zichron terua*," the description of *Rosh Hashana* in *Emor*, the primary *parasha* of the *moadim*. Although that perspective was subsequently rejected by the Talmud, it is still our practice, based on *Massechet Soferim*, to formulate the *kedushas hayom* of *Shabbos Rosh Hashana*, in *Tefilla* and *Birkas Hamazon*, as "*zichron terua*"!

There are various (and probably interrelated) factors that underpin *shofar*'s special status as a medium that recasts its message. There is much evidence that *tekias shofar* is a form of prayer. Rav Soloveitchik conceived this perspective to be a major theme of *Rosh Hashana*. The fact that ideally we integrate the blowing of the *shofar* into the *Musaf* prayers on *Rosh Hashana* underscores this theme. Yet, *shofar* is far from conventional prayer, which focuses on the verbal articulation of needs and aspirations. *Shofar* constitutes inarticulate prayer, a piercing note conveying torrents of different, even contradictory impulses, as well as the ineffable. It constitutes the more subtle but also more powerful *kol demama daka* that can transcend rational expression. The Talmud explains that *terua* means "*yevava*," a cry that it is identified either with a more measured sighing-groaning (*shevarim – genuchei ganich*) or with uncontrollable staccato sobbing (*terua –yelulei yalil*) or the seemingly incompatible combination of both. When *zichronos* are transmitted by means of the *shofar*, not only is the experience different, the content-substance is affected as well.

Furthermore, the act of *tekias shofar* integrates seamlessly the entire gamut of human and halachic emotions and experiences. R. Saadia Gaon enumerates ten different themes of the *shofar*. They range from ecstatic heights to trembling fear, from inspired awe to joyous celebration. The fact that this range is compressed into a single note and that all of these dimensions are relevant, even trenchant on this special day, accurately captures the special *kedushas hayom* of Rosh Hashana. In this sense, it is truly a "*yom terua*."

Moreover, *tekias shofar* is perceived as an act of *ritzui* and *avoda*, akin to the sacrificial rite. Perhaps this is so precisely because it is a singular form of communication with *Hashem* and because it embodies the integrative expression of many crucial dimensions of religious life. The *Gemara* (*Rosh Hashana* 26a; see also Ramban's *derashah* on *Rosh Hashana*) explains that one cannot utilize a cow's horn as a *shofar* because of the principle of אין קטיגור נעשה סניגור – a prosecutor cannot become a defender (referring to the sin of the golden calf). The *Gemara* explains that while this principle may apply only to service in the inner precincts of the Temple (the *bigdei kehuna* of the *Kohen Gadol* on *Yom Kippur* cannot contain gold), *shofar* is judged by these standards since it transmits the message of *zichronos* ("כיון דלזכרון הוא, כלפנים דמי - since it is for a remembrance, it is as if it were in the inner precincts of the Temple"). Once again, the Talmud accentuates that the *shofar*'s unique method of bearing the *zichronos* qualifies it as having an elevated halachic status. Some *Rishonim* (Ritva, *Sukkah* 10a, 30a) argue that *shofar* may qualify for the disqualification of *mitzva haba'a be'aveira* because it constitutes an act of *ritzui* (worship). Possibly, the original special allowance of *shofar* on *Shabbos*, specifically in the Temple, is connected to this association of *shofar* and *avoda*. (See also Ra'avad, on the Rif *Sukkah* 43b, who argues that the *pesukim* in *Emor* imply that ideally *shofar* should be practiced within the Temple framework! The *Mikdash* also serves as the ultimate prayer venue: "כי ביתי בית תפילה יקרא לכל העמים - My House will be called a house of prayer for all the peoples.")

Finally, the piercing sound of the *shofar* is a catalyst for introspection and renewed halachic commitment. The Rambam eloquently captures this theme in *Hilchos Teshuva* (3:4) with his stirring depiction of the *shofar*'s message of עורו ישנים משנתכם (awaken from your spiritual slumber), galvanizing man to combat and overcome insidious spiritual complacency. When *Klal Yisrael's zichronos* are imparted by the *shofar*, they provide an ambitious framework for halachic renewal and maximalism.

Given the transformational impact of the *shofar* in conveying *zichronos*, it is unsurprising that the *halacha* expended every effort to manifest at least some expression of " יום תרועה יהיה לכם -it shall be a day of *shofar*-blasts for you" even on *Shabbos Rosh Hashana*. In this respect, the *mitzva* of *shofar* inspired greater urgency than *lulav*. When it was not possible to sufficiently protect against the risk of *Shabbos* desecration, it was still vital to accentuate *tekias shofar's* contribution to and expansion of *zichronos*. The *Emor* phrase *"zichron terua"* on *Shabbos Rosh Hashana* encapsulates the substantive impact of the medium on the message. It emerged as the focal point of *Shabbos Rosh Hashana*, challenging us not only to remember the *shofar*, but to ensure that our *zichronos* continue to reflect the *shofar's* high spiritual and halachic ambitions, even in its absence.

Zichron Terua: Perspectives on Tekias Shofar

RABBI YONASON SACKS

In describing the festival of *Rosh Hashana*, the Torah employs two very different epithets. In *Parashas Pinchas* (*Bemidbar* 29:1), the day is dubbed a *"yom terua"* (a day of blowing), while in *Parashas Emor* (*Vayikra* 23:24), it is referred to as a *"zichron terua"* (a remembrance of blowing). While the *Gemara* (*Rosh Hashana* 29b) initially assumes that *"yom terua"* refers to *Rosh Hashana* that falls on a weekday (hence the active "day" of blowing) and *"zichron terua"* refers to *Rosh Hashana* that coincides with *Shabbos* (on which *shofar* is not blown; hence the mere "remembrance" of blowing), the *Gemara* ultimately concludes that the disparity of language does not actually teach the abstention from *shofar* blowing on the *Shabbos*. Rather, the cancellation of *shofar* blowing on *Shabbos* is a function of a rabbinic, not biblical, injunction, enacted out of fear that one might come to carry a *shofar* in a *reshus harabim*.[15] In coming to this conclusion, however, the *Gemara* makes no mention of what the disparity of language – *"yom*

---

[15] Interestingly, the Talmud *Yerushalmi* concludes that the abstention from *shofar* on *Shabbos* is indeed a biblical commandment, derived from the aforementioned verses.

Originally published on TorahWeb.org in 2007

terua" versus *"zichron terua"* – comes to teach us.

To account for this discrepancy, Rav Soloveitchik *zt"l* suggested that perhaps the Torah is highlighting two components of the *mitzva* of *tekias shofar*. While the action of the *mitzva* (*"ma'aseh mitzva"*) is accomplished through merely blowing the *shofar* (signified through *"yom terua"*), the mere action of blowing, by itself, is insufficient. The ultimate fulfillment and completion of the *mitzva* (*"kiyum mitzva"*) occurs internally, through an emotional recognition of the *shofar*'s message (signified through the internally focused *"zichron terua"*). In most *mitzvos*, the *"ma'aseh mitzva"* and the *"kiyum mitzva"* occur simultaneously. The very moment one performs the action of eating *matza*, for example, one instantly completes the *"kiyum mitzva"* as well. However, with *shofar*, the action does not represent an end in and of itself, but rather a means of triggering an emotional response. It is this emotional response, the *"kiyum shebalev"* epitomized by the notion of *"zichron terua,"* which constitutes the essence of the *mitzva*.[16]

This distinction, between the action of blowing the *shofar* and the true fulfillment of the subsequent emotional recognition, may help explain an apparent contradiction in the Rambam. In *Hilchos Shofar* 2:4, the Rambam rules that if one does not have appropriate intent (*"kavana"*), he does not fulfill the *mitzva* of *shofar*. In *Hilchos Chametz uMatza* 6:3, however, the Rambam appears to give the exact opposite ruling: if one eats *matza* under duress, without intent to fulfill his obligation, he nonetheless fulfills his obligation. The Rambam's understanding of whether or not *mitzvos* require intent is thus obfuscated by apparently contradictory rulings in *Hilchos Shofar* and *Hilchos Chametz uMatza*. Rav Soloveitchik *zt"l* suggested that perhaps there is no contradiction whatsoever. A *mitzva*'s subjection

---

[16] It should be noted that *shofar* is not the only *mitzva* in which the action of the *mitzva* is separated from the fulfillment of the *mitzva*. *Tefilla* (see Rambam, *Hilchos Tefilla* 1:1), *simchas Yom Tov* (see *Pesachim* 109a), *aveilus/aninus* (see top of *Sanhedrin* 46b) are all examples of *mitzvos* which prescribe specific actions which are means towards a desired emotional state.

to the general requirement for "*kavana*" is a function of the nature of the particular *mitzva*. *Mitzvos* such as *matza*, in which the "*ma'aseh mitzva*" and "*kiyum mitzva*" are inseparable, do not require *kavana*. Their actions speak for themselves. *Mitzvos* such as *shofar*, however, in which the action is not an end in and of itself, but rather a means towards an internal *kiyum shebalev*, do require *kavana*.[17] Hence, if one lacks *kavana* during *tekias shofar*, he has not fulfilled his obligation.

Shofar's emphasis on a *kiyum shebalev* may also manifest itself in several relevant *halachos* which underscore an inextricable link between the *mitzva* of *shofar* and the *mitzva* of *tefilla*, the prototypical *avoda shebalev* (service of the heart).[18] For example, the *Ba'al HaMaor* (*Rosh Hashana* 10b *bedapei haRif*) assumes that the *berachos* which we recite before the blowing of *shofar* are a relatively recent innovation. In the times of the *Gemara*, he argues, *shofar* was not blown before beginning *Musaf*, as is common practice nowadays. The *Ba'al HaMaor* wonders: If the *shofar* was only blown during and after the *Tefillas Musaf*, when was the *birkas hamitzva* (blessing generally recited prior to performing a *mitzva*) for *shofar* blowing recited? He suggests that perhaps the very text of *Tefillas Musaf* itself, into which *shofar* blasts were inserted, served as a *birkas hamitzva*.[19] Apparently, even though *Tefillas Musaf* does not structurally resemble a classic *birkas hamitzva*, the conceptual relationship between the *kiyum shebalev* of *shofar* to the *avoda shebalev* of *tefilla* allows *Musaf* to serve as a *birkas hamitzva*.

This relationship is further highlighted by the *Gemara* later in *Rosh Hashana* (26b), which instructs that a *shofar* should be bent. Rashi, based on the *Gemara*, explains that a bent *shofar* resembles a person bent in humility and submission during *tefilla*. Apparently, the *shofar* fulfills a

---

[17] See *Kesef Mishneh* and *Maggid Mishneh* on the Rambam, ibid. This explanation may also be consistent with the Rambam's general understanding of *shofar*, underscoring the passive listening as opposed to active blowing.

[18] See *Ta'anis* 2a.

[19] See Rosh, beginning of *Masseches Berachos*, who cites Rav Amram Gaon as saying a similar idea regarding *Kerias Shema* and its *berachos*.

role strikingly similar to that of *tefilla*. Moreover, the *Gemara* on 26a develops this relationship in its discussion of אין קטיגור נעשה סניגור – a prosecutor cannot become a defender. A *shofar* may not come from a cow, because that resembles the *eigel hazahav*, a memory which we do not wish to evoke. The *Gemara* challenges this ruling, noting that the evocative problem of "*ein kateigor*" is seemingly only applicable to "*avodos shebifnim*" – services of the highest level of sanctity which take place in the *Kodesh Hakodashim* (such as selected parts of the *Kohen Gadol*'s *Yom Kippur* service). However, *shofar*, which is not blown specifically in the *Kodesh Hakodashim*, should not be included in this restriction. The *Gemara* answers that since *shofar* serves as a "*zikaron*" (commemoration), it is כלפנים דמי – as though it takes place in the *Kodesh Hakodashim*, and thus equally subject to restrictions of "*ein kateigor* ... " Apparently, *shofar*'s *kiyum shebalev* makes it similar to the service of the *Kohen Gadol* on *Yom Kippur*, and by extension to *tefilla*, which is directed toward the *Kodesh Hakodashim* as well.[20]

Shofar's subjection to the possibility of מצוה הבאה בעבירה (a *mitzva* fulfilled through a transgression) may also underscore *shofar*'s special *kiyum shebalev*. Based on the *Yerushalmi*, the Rambam (*Hilchos Shofar* 1:3) rules that *shofar* is not subject to the problem of *mitzva haba'a be'aveira*, because an intangible *shofar* blast cannot be stolen.[21] This technical reasoning implies that theoretically, *shofar* should be subject to *mitzva haba'a be'aveira*, and that its exemption is simply the result of a technical loophole. This implication is telling, however, since several *Rishonim*[22] opine that not all *mitzvos* are subject to *mitzva haba'a be'aveira*. *Mitzva haba'a be'aveira* only applies to supplicatory *mitzvos*, *mitzvos* which come "*leratzos*." If this is the case, apparently one must assume that *shofar*, too, is a *mitzva* whose aim is to supplicate and to beg, much like prayer, and would thus be subject to *mitzva haba'a be'aveira* if not for a technical solution.

---

[20] See *Berachos* 30a.
[21] See Ra'avad, who quotes a different possibility.
[22] See Ritva *Sukkah* 9a, who quotes the *Ba'alei HaTosafos*.

Finally, the Rav *zt"l* also pointed to the *Gemara* in *Rosh Hashana* 34b as a support to *shofar*'s essential relationship to *tefilla*. If an individual has the option to spend *Rosh Hashana* in a city where *shofar* will be blown but *tefilla* will not be recited, or in a city which will recite *tefilla* but not blow *shofar*, which is preferable? The *Gemara* answers that obviously, the biblical *mitzva* of *shofar* would take precedence over the rabbinic *mitzva* of *tefilla* (the *Gemara* concludes that even the mere possibility of *shofar* blowing would take precedence over a definite *tefilla*). The Rav, however, questioned the *Gemara*'s assumption that *tefilla* is simply a rabbinic *mitzva*. After all, numerous sources seem to suggest that reciting *malchuyos*, *shofaros*, and *zichronos* on *Rosh Hashana* might actually be a biblical commandment as well.[23] If so, would this *Gemara* not prove the contrary? The Rav suggested that perhaps, *Rosh Hashana*'s *Musaf tefilla* may indeed be biblical, but only when *shofar* is blown during services. If the *tefilla* is not accompanied by *shofar* blowing (as was the case in this *Gemara*), however, then everyone would agree that the *tefilla* is simply a fulfillment on a rabbinic level.

---

[23] See, for example, Rashi *Vayikra* 23.

Creating the Mood for Rosh Hashana
RABBI ZVI SOBOLOFSKY

Chazal instituted the reading of *Parashas Ki Savo* before *Rosh Hashana*. Much of the *parasha* deals with the terrible consequences for not observing the Torah. We read this prior to *Rosh Hashana* symbolizing that the year and all its curses should come to an end. In reality, however, we do not read *Parashas Ki Savo* immediately before *Rosh Hashana*. Rather, there is always a *Shabbos* after *Ki Savo* before the year ends. If we want to indicate that the year and its curses are ending, wouldn't it be more appropriate to read this *parasha* on the last *Shabbos* of the year? Why did *Chazal* leave a week between *Parashas Ki Savo* and *Rosh Hashana*?

We are taught (*Berachos* 5a) various methods to overcome one's *yetzer hara*. If one senses a temptation to sin, one should first focus on words of Torah. If this doesn't help, one should recite the *Shema*. If even this fails to assist in overcoming one's *yetzer hara*, as a last resort one should focus on death. If thinking about death is the most effective way to prevent one from sinning, why didn't *Chazal* suggest this as the first response to temptation? Why do we first attempt the less effective deterrents such as Torah study and *kerias Shema*?

Originally published on TorahWeb.org in 2010

When a person is ill there are often different potential treatments. Sometimes a more effective one will not be used at first because of its negative side effects. If the less effective cure is not sufficient and the condition necessitates, the illness must be cured notwithstanding the damaging side effects. Thinking of death is the most effective way of averting sin. However, using this as a constant deterrent can have negative repercussions. A person constantly focused on death will not be able to serve *Hashem* with joy. His morose mood will prevent him from interacting with others in a cheerful and pleasant way. Thinking of death as a first response to every temptation may be effective in preventing a particular sin, yet it may carry negative consequences that outweigh its benefits. Only if the gentler methods of Torah study and *kerias Shema* fail should one resort to the more drastic approach of focusing on death.

As we approach *Rosh Hashana* and try to perfect our *avodas Hashem*, we have many methods that we use. We increase our Torah study and focus on *kabbalas Malchus Shamayim* – accepting *Hashem*'s kingship over us through our *tefillos*. There is a last method that we use, and that is reflecting upon death. Perhaps the most powerful application of this is the *tefilla* of *Unesaneh Tokef*. Yet the majority of our *tefillos* on *Rosh Hashana* focus on *Hashem* being our King, rather than on our own mortality. The mood on *Rosh Hashana* is both serious and joyful. Constant focus on death would perhaps prevent sin but would also prevent us from celebrating *Rosh Hashana* appropriately.

During the weeks before *Rosh Hashana*, we prepare our different strategies for overcoming sin. We deliberately do not enter *Rosh Hashana* on a depressing note, having just read the curses of *Parashas Ki Savo*. Death and suffering are not the methods we want to invoke as we attempt to improve our *avodas Hashem*. We have these methods available to us in case of need. We read about them two weeks before *Rosh Hashana* to familiarize ourselves with them, but then have a break of a week so that they do not preoccupy our minds. We approach *Rosh Hashana* using the methods of Torah study and *kerias Shema* – accepting *Hashem* as King – as ways of combating sin. If and when we must resort to contemplating death as a way to assist us, we are equipped to do so. *Parashas Ki Savo* can be invoked if necessary, but we hope that Torah study and *kerias Shema* can assist us as we strive to perfect our *avodas Hashem*.

A Cry from the Soul
RABBI ZVI SOBOLOFSKY

The essence of *Rosh Hashana* is encapsulated in the phrase יום תרועה יהיה לכם - a day of blowing of the *shofar* it will be for you. *Chazal* had a tradition that the word *terua* refers to a broken sound similar to a cry. It is this tradition that is the source for the three different sounds of the *shofar*, the *shevarim*, the *terua*, and the *shevarim-terua*, which correspond to different types of crying. What is it about a cry that becomes the central feature of *Rosh Hashana*?

Tears are a reflection of a person's innermost feelings. Similarly, a proper fulfillment of the *mitzva* of *tekias shofar* emanates from the inside of one's soul. *Mitzvos* that are performed with different parts of the body express our desire to serve *Hashem* with those external parts. We dedicate our hands to *Hashem* by wearing *tefillin* and our mouths by reciting *berachos*, and yet the *mitzva* of *tekias shofar* is different. We blow the *shofar* with our breath, symbolically drawing upon our innermost soul to perform this *mitzva*. The word for breath, "*neshima*," is related to the word for soul, "*neshama*." When we blow the *shofar*, we are dedicating the very essence of our souls to the service of *Hashem*.

It is this dimension of *tekias shofar*, which represents our *penimius* – our

---
Originally published on TorahWeb.org in 2013

internal self, rather than our *chitzonius* – our external appearance, that explains a certain phenomenon we find about the *shofar*. There are three major historical events associated with the *shofar*. First, *Akeidas* Yitzchak culminated with a ram being brought as a *korban* instead of Yitzchak, and thus we prefer to use specifically a ram's horn for our *mitzva* of *tekias shofar*, harkening back to that ram. Additionally, the *beracha* of *zichronos* concludes with a plea to *Hashem* to remember *Akeidas* Yitzchak. The second time a *shofar* plays a prominent role is during *Matan Torah*, and we refer to the *shofar* of *Har Sinai* throughout the *beracha* of *shofaros*. Finally, the *shofar* associated with the future redemption is the culmination of the special *berachos* inserted into the *Musaf* of *Rosh Hashana*.

Besides a *shofar*, there is another unifying theme between these three events, and that is the prominent role of a donkey. Avraham and Yitzchak ride on a donkey on the way to the *Akeida*; *Yetzias Mitzrayim*, which began the process that culminates with *Matan Torah*, begins with Moshe returning to Mitzrayim on a donkey to lead the Jewish people to freedom; and the era of redemption will begin with *Mashiach* riding on a donkey. Why do the donkey and the *shofar* go hand in hand throughout our history?

A donkey is unique in that although it is a non-kosher animal, a firstborn donkey has sanctity and must be redeemed. Externally, a donkey seems very far removed from holiness, yet a donkey has an internal sanctity. A donkey and a *shofar* both symbolize our deepest innermost desires for holiness even if our external appearances and actions are not living up to that yearning.

As we approach *Rosh Hashana*, let us turn inward and draw inspiration from the *shofar* of the *Akeida*, *Har Sinai*, and Moshe. As we cry out our innermost feelings to *Hashem* on *Rosh Hashana*, let us focus on those feelings being desires for a life of *kedusha*. May we reconnect to the *shofar* of the *Akeida* and the sounds of *Har Sinai*, and thereby merit to hear the sound of the *shofar* of *Mashiach* in our days.

A Good and Sweet Year
RABBI ZVI SOBOLOFSKY

There is an age-old practice mentioned by *Chazal* to eat certain foods on the night of *Rosh Hashana*. These are known as *simanim* – signs that we pray will symbolize a good year. Short *tefillos* accompany the *simanim*, and the *poskim* comment that the intent and thoughts of *teshuva* that occur at this time can help make the *simanim* a reality. Perhaps the most popular of the *simanim* is the custom to partake of an apple dipped in honey. At this time, we fervently beseech *Hashem* for a *shana tova umesuka*, a good and sweet year. By analyzing what this dual request of "good and sweet" represents, we can gain a greater appreciation of where to concentrate our thoughts at this opportune moment.

Chazal teach us that when events occur that are especially good, we are required to recite the *beracha* of *Hatov Vehameitiv* – *Hashem* is good, and does good. There is another *beracha* that is recited when something bad happens, the *beracha* of *Dayan Ha'emes* – *Hashem* is the true judge. These different *berachos* are only recited in this world; in the world to come, only the *beracha* on good will be recited. The future is described as a day that is only good. Creation was originally supposed to be this way. When *Hashem* began the creation of the world with the creation of light, the Torah tells us that the light was good. Unfortunately for us,

---

Originally published on TorahWeb.org in 2017

this light could not be retained in this world, and *Hashem* hid it away for the righteous for days to come. When we ask *Hashem* for a *shana tova*, we are not just asking for good things in this world. We are elevating our thoughts by beseeching *Hashem* for a world that is all good. We are dreaming about a world in which the original light of Creation, of *Hashem*'s presence, is discernible.

In addition to a good year, we also ask for a sweet one. The words of Torah are compared to gold and honey. "More precious than gold and sweeter than honey" is Dovid *Hamelech*'s description of *Hashem*'s words (*Tehillim* 19:11). What is the significance of comparing the Torah to honey if it is already comparable to gold? Gold is obviously more valuable than honey.

Gold and honey are fundamentally different from one another. Although gold is more valuable, it is only significant because of what it can purchase. It does not provide actual pleasure, but rather it enables one to purchase worldly pleasures. Honey, although not particularly expensive, is intrinsically enjoyable. The words of Torah are compared to both gold and honey. Torah is like spiritual gold in that the acquisition of Torah knowledge enables one to better perform *mitzvos*, and Torah study helps perfect a person's character traits. Like gold, it is valuable for what it can accomplish. However, Torah is also much more than spiritual gold, because the words of Torah are sweeter than honey. Even without any other advantages gained by Torah study, learning Torah is the sweetest gift *Hashem* has given us. It is both more precious than gold and simultaneously sweeter than honey.

The *Or HaChaim* has a remarkable comment (*Devarim* 26:11) wherein he describes how we would react to the goodness and sweetness of Torah if we truly appreciated it to the fullest. We would be so overwhelmed by the sweet taste of Torah that we would not be able to pursue anything else. As we dip our apple in our honey on *Rosh Hashana*, we should be focusing on the lofty dreams of having a good and sweet year. We beseech *Hashem* to see His light and taste His Torah. May this year be a year of only goodness and sweetness for all of *Klal Yisrael*.

Wrong Way!
RABBI DANIEL STEIN

"Perhaps there is amongst you a man, woman, family, or tribe, whose heart strays this day from *Hashem*, our God, to go and worship the deities of those nations. Perhaps there is among you a root that produces hemlock and wormwood" (*Devarim* 29:17). The Torah juxtaposes in the very same *pasuk* two individuals who ostensibly seem vastly different from one another. The first has strayed entirely from the ways of the Torah and embraced idol worship wholeheartedly. The second merely has an eroded and infected "root." The Ramban explains that this second individual is presently committed to the *mitzvos* and *avodas Hashem*, but in the deep recesses of his heart there lies a kernel of doubt and insubordination. However, currently the two individuals are at opposite ends of the spectrum. The first individual in the *pasuk* has already abandoned *Yiddishkeit* completely, while the second is a practicing, loyal and faithful Jew. Why are these two people grouped together? What do they share in common?

Rav Henoch Leibowitz (*Majesty of Man*), explains that even though presently there might be a great distance between these two individuals, they are both on the same path, bearing an identical trajectory. One might be further down the road than the other, but ultimately they will be united. The Torah is teaching us that a critical component of our *teshuva* process is

---

Originally published on TorahWeb.org in 2016

not only evaluating our previous actions and assessing our current status, but also taking time to consider the path we are on and the direction in which we are heading, because inevitably that will determine our destination. Rav Elya Meir Bloch was once standing with his *talmidim* on a Chicago train station platform, waiting for the Pacemaker to New York. A few feet away, on the other side of the platform, stood the Sunshine Express to San Francisco. He asked his *talmidim*, "How far apart are these two trains?" They hastily conjectured that they were separated by about eight to ten feet. Rav Bloch disagreed, "The two trains are 3,000 miles apart, because one is headed to California, and the other to New York."

This is arguably the unique message of *Parashas Nitzavim*. *Parashas Nitzavim* seems to embody a very similar theme to that of *Parashas Ki Savo*. Both *parshiyos* convey and underscore the centrality of our covenant – *bris* – with *Hashem*. They both describe how if we will perform the *mitzvos* we will be rewarded, and if not we will be punished. However, the Netziv (*Ha'amek Davar*) notices a fundamental difference between the two presentations. *Parashas Ki Savo* focuses primarily on actions, on two possible modes of conduct; either "if you will listen to the voice of *Hashem* your God, to keep and perform all of His commandments" (28:1), or "if you will not listen to the voice of *Hashem* your God to keep and perform all of His commandments" (28:15). The lesson of *Parashas Ki Savo* corresponds to the aspect of *teshuva* which demands that we examine our previous actions and identify areas where we can improve.

However, *Parashas Nitzavim* adds an additional element, another dimension to the covenant, namely that of loving *Hashem*. As the *pesukim* state: "I have commanded you this day to **love** *Hashem* your God to follow His ways and keep His commandments" (30:16), "To **love** *Hashem* your God, to listen to His voice and to cleave to Him" (30:20), and "*Hashem* will circumcise your **heart** and the **hearts** of your children to **love** *Hashem* your God" (30:6). The Netziv explains that the Torah is teaching us in *Parashas*

Nitzavim that adherence to the *mitzvos* is not enough, because if our core commitment to the mission is weak and waning, if our hearts are lacking in love of *Hashem*, we will be trending off-course and ultimately religious decay will ensue. As the *pasuk* states, "If your **heart** turns away and does not listen, you **will** be drawn away and bow down to other gods and serve them" (30:17). Genuine *teshuva* demands not only that we evaluate our deeds, but our direction, because if we are headed down the wrong path, the results can be catastrophic.

The Rambam (*Hilchos Teshuva* 3:3) writes, "The sins of every inhabitant of the world together with his merits are weighed on the festival of *Rosh Hashana*. If one is found righteous, he is sealed for life; if one is found wicked, he is sealed for death. A *beinoni*, one who is in between, his verdict remains tentative until *Yom Kippur*. If he repents, he is sealed for life, if not, he is sealed for death."

The *Lechem Mishneh* questions why the *beinoni* must specifically repent and perform the *mitzva* of *teshuva* in order to receive a positive judgment on *Yom Kippur*. After all, once he performs any *mitzva*, that should tilt the scales in the *beinoni*'s favor. The *Lechem Mishneh* explains (and this is elaborated upon by Rav Yitzchak Blazer in his *Kochvei Or*) that the greatest of all sins is squandering the opportunity for change and *teshuva*. Therefore, any positive act that is performed by the *beinoni* will be eclipsed and outweighed by his failure to repent and do *teshuva*. Alternatively, Rav Aryeh Pomeranchek (*Emek Beracha*), Rav Chaim Shmulevitz (*Sichos Musar*) and Rav Aharon Kotler (*Mishnas Rebbe Aharon*) suggest that the performance of any additional *mitzva* will accrue toward the following year, and therefore will be ineffective in altering the previous year's tally. Only the *mitzva* of *teshuva* has the power to change the past, to rewrite history, and thereby favorably skew the judgment of the previous year.

However, the Meiri (*Chibur Hateshuva*), and later Rav Yitzchak Hutner

(*Pachad Yitzchak*), suggest that the Rambam does not view the *beinoni* as one who is literally caught in the limbo of a formal numerical stalemate between *mitzvos* and *aveiros*. For if that were the case, it would presumably be an exceedingly rare occurrence, yet the Rambam (*Hilchos Teshuva* 3:4) exhorts us all to view ourselves as *beinonim* throughout the Ten Days of Repentance and beyond. Rather, the Rambam understands the judgment of *Rosh Hashana* to be a function not only of our past performance but also of our direction for the future. Therefore, the *beinoni* represents all those who are wavering or feel conflicted about their religious arc and trajectory. Are we progressing toward *Hashem* or drifting further away? Is our religious commitment intensifying or subsiding? The only *mitzva* which can effectively address and impact this aspect of our lives is the introspective soul-baring process of *teshuva*, and that is why *teshuva* is the only avenue available to the *beinoni*.

As we stand at the doorstep of *Rosh Hashana* and the *Aseres Yemei Teshuva*, we must undertake, individually and collectively, not only to assess the validity of our actions, but also to inspect what lies within our hearts, and honestly ask ourselves, "Where are we headed?" Concerns regarding trajectory and direction should be welcomed and embraced as the indispensable hallmark of authentic *avodas Hashem*. We are enjoined to respond to the message of *Parashas Ki Savo* as well as the call of *Parashas Nitzavim*. We are obliged not only to recommit ourselves to a scrupulous observance of all of the *mitzvos*, but to reinvest in an honest and unadulterated love of *Hashem*, and to chart a course for the future based solely on that agenda. May we all be *zocheh* to be successful in this endeavor, and merit as individuals and as a community to have a *kesiva vechasima tova* and a *gut gebentched yohr*!

Malchus: The Theme of Rosh Hashana[24]

RABBI DR. ABRAHAM J. TWERSKI

Democracy may have diminished our *yiras Shamayim* (awe of Hashem). In the Talmud and Torah literature we often find parables that attempt to enhance our *yiras Shamayim* by saying, "If one were in the presence of a mortal king, how cautious one would be with one's words and deeds. How much greater should one's caution be in the presence of the Almighty King." This may not have much impact on us, since we do not relate to a mortal king today. We elect a president for a period of time, who does not have unlimited powers. To the contrary, his powers are limited by Congress and the courts. After his term is over, he is an ordinary citizen. Even in countries that do have a king, it is usually a ceremonial position, with power resting in the hands of an elected government.

Compare that with the talmudic account of R. Yochanan ben Zakai, whose disciples visited him when he was ill and found him crying. They said, "Light of Israel, the pillar of the right, why are you crying?" R. Yochanan replied, "If I were being led to trial before an earthly king, who is here today but

---

[24] Editor's Note: This is an excerpt from Rav Dr. Twerski's book, *Twerski on Machzor: Rosh Hashanah*.

Originally published on TorahWeb.org in 2011

in his grave tomorrow, who, if he is angry with me, his anger is not eternal, who, if he imprisons me, the imprisonment is not eternal, who, if he puts me to death, my death is not eternal, and I am able to appease him with words or bribe him with money, yet I would be fearful and cry, and now that I will be led before the King of Kings, the Holy One, Blessed is He, Whose life and existence is eternal, and if He is angry with me, His anger is eternal, and if He imprisons me, the imprisonment is eternal, and if He puts me to death, my death is eternal, and I cannot appease Him with words nor bribe Him with money, shall I not cry?"

The disciples then asked him, "Our teacher, bless us." R. Yochanan replied, "May your fear of *Hashem* be as great as your fear of mortals." The disciples said, "Is that all you can say to us?" R. Yochanan replied, "I wish that it were so. You must know, when a person commits a sin, he says, 'I just don't want a person to see me (but is not concerned that *Hashem* sees him).'"

Shortly before his death, R. Yochanan said, "Remove all the utensils so that they shall not become *tamei* (contaminated) when I die, and prepare a chair for Chizkiyahu, king of Judah, who is coming to escort me" (*Berachos* 28b).

This interchange between R. Yochanan and his disciples is most enlightening. We believe *Hashem* exists and is all-powerful, but this belief is an abstraction, and may not be enough to deter a person from sin. If we have the emotional experience of the awe we have standing before a powerful earthly monarch, we may perhaps be able to extrapolate and develop the awe of standing before *Hashem*, the King of Kings. But in a democratic country, where one may freely criticize the president or the ceremonial king, this reference point is lacking. R. Yochanan tells us that without this reference point, we may be remiss in awe of *Hashem*. We do not know what it means to tremble before a king.

Hashem said, "Recite verses of kingship before me, to enthrone

Me over you ... and with what? With the *shofar*" (*Rosh Hashana* 34b). The prophet says, "If the *shofar* is sounded in a town, will the people not tremble? ... When a lion roars, who does not fear?" (*Amos* 3:6-8).

R. Yeruchem of Mir said, "When I saw a lion, I understood its enormous might, and that as king of the beasts, all animals are in awe of him. Primitive peoples, seeing the might of the sun, worshipped it as a god, not realizing that the sun is but one of His many servants" (*Da'as Chochma Umusar* vol. 4, p. 248). In our *tefillos* we pray, "Let everything with a life's breath in its nostrils proclaim '*Hashem*, the God of Israel, is King, and His Kingship rules over everything.'" In our poverty of having an emotional experience of the awe of *Hashem*, we must extrapolate from objects that inspire us with awe, as a reference point for awe of *Hashem*.

"If the *shofar* is sounded in a town, will the people not tremble?" Beginning with the first day of *Elul*, we sound the *shofar* daily to inspire us with the awe of *Hashem*, that His Sovereignty is absolute. We must know that He controls everything in the universe, from the greatest galaxies to the most minute insects. The only thing that *Hashem* does not control is a person's moral decisions, because He has given a person freedom to choose between right and wrong.

It is of interest that when *Rosh Hashana* occurs on *Shabbos*, we do not blow the *shofar*. This is not only to avoid a person's carrying the *shofar* in a public thoroughfare, but also because the *kedusha* of *Shabbos*, and the awareness that *Hashem* created the world and is its only Master, can provide the appreciation of *Hashem*'s sovereignty. On *Rosh Hashana* we say, "Today is the birthday of the world." *Shabbos*, like *Rosh Hashana*, is a testimony to *Hashem*'s creation of the world.

Belief in the existence of *Hashem* is not yet *malchus*. Primitive peoples believed in the existence of God, but felt that God was too supreme to bother with this tiny speck of the earth and with mere mortals. That is why, in our *tefillos* of *malchus* we pray, "Reign over the entire universe in Your glory ... Let everything that has been made know that You are its Maker." The Israelites, upon their liberation from Egypt, did believe in *Hashem* (*Shemos* 4:31), but it was not until they witnessed the miraculous dividing of the Reed Sea that they exclaimed, "*Hashem* shall reign for all eternity!" (*Shemos* 15:18). Only then were they convinced that *Hashem* controls the world and His Providence is over all things, animate and inanimate. This is why on *Rosh Hashana* we begin saying *Hamelech Hakadosh*. *Kedusha* means that *Hashem* is separated and far above everything in the universe, but He is also the *Melech*, the King that operates and controls the universe.

Every day, we recite many *berachos* and say, "Blessed are You, *Hashem*, our God, King of the world ...." But precisely because we say these words so often, we do not concentrate on their meaning. *Rosh Hashana* should give us a much greater appreciation of *malchus*, so that when we say the words, "*Hashem*, our God, King of the world," we will think of *Hashem*'s absolute sovereignty.

When we think of the infinite greatness of *Hashem*, and that by comparison we are less than infinitesimally small, we may lose our sense of significance. We must be aware that as creations of *Hashem*, we are endowed with a Divine soul, which makes us potentially great. This is why R. Yochanan, having expressed his utter effacement before *Hashem*, nevertheless told his disciples before his death: "Prepare a chair for Chizkiyahu, king of Judah, who is coming to escort me." He knew that no less a personage than Chizkiyahu, king of Judah, would greet him.

Rosh Hashana marks the sixth day of creation, the day on which *Hashem* created man and endowed him with a Divine *neshama*. We appreciate the *malchus* of *Hashem*, and are proud that we are privileged to be His subjects.

Fear and Love, Truth and Peace

RABBI MORDECHAI WILLIG

I

The upcoming *Yamim Noraim*, Days of Awe, evoke fear of *Hashem* and His judgment. *Rosh Hashana* is the day that every person passes before *Hashem* individually (*Rosh Hashana* 18a). The dramatic *Unesaneh Tokef*, recited with great intensity and devotion, speaks of fear and trembling in the face of the Divine verdict of life and death. This universal theme is the central motif of the "sanctity of the day" on *Rosh Hashana*: *Hashem* is the King of the entire world, and all will recognize His sovereignty when He will appear with the splendor of His strength. The *shofar* awakens us to *teshuva*, primarily out of fear of *Hashem* and His judgment (Rambam, *Hilchos Teshuva* 3:4).

Yom Kippur emphasizes the need for complete atonement. Just as a *mikveh* purifies the impure, so *Hashem* purifies *Am Yisrael* (*Yoma* 85b). Just as a *mikveh* requires total immersion, *Yom Kippur* requires total *teshuva*. *Teshuva* out of fear is incomplete, a step towards *Hashem*, and only mitigates one's sins. *Yom Kippur* is a day of total *teshuva*, out of love, that converts sins into merits and reaches all the way to *Hashem*

Originally published on TorahWeb.org in 2011

(*Yoma* 86a-b).[25] Heartfelt confession, conspicuously absent on *Rosh Hashana*, is the central theme of *Yom Kippur*. It reflects a sincere recognition of one's mistakes, and is recited out of love of *Hashem* and resolve to improve, which is a meritorious result of the sins.

While *Rosh Hashana* is the universal day of judgment, *Yom Kippur* is a special gift to *Am Yisrael*. "You gave us with love this Day of Atonement so that we can return to You wholeheartedly" (*Neila*). "In Your abundant mercy, You have given us this fast day of atonement" (*Musaf*). *Hashem's* love of *Am Yisrael* in granting us *Yom Kippur* is reflected by our complete *teshuva* out of love.

II

Fear is praiseworthy only with respect to *Hashem*. Fear of *Hashem* should remove fear of man (*Berachos* 60a; *Rabbeinu* Bechaye, Introduction to *Ki Sisa*; *Al Hateshuva*, pp. 140-141). Love, on the other hand, is praiseworthy with respect to man, as well. A sincere Torah scholar is praised as one who loves *Hashem* and who loves His creatures, His *beriyos* (*Avos* 6:1).

On *Rosh Hashana*, the day of fear, we, as individuals, beseech *Hashem* for a good year and declare His kingship. On *Yom Kippur*, the day of love, we add the dimension of interpersonal forgiveness and closeness. It is a day of no jealousy, hatred or competition (*Musaf*), when even sinners pray with us (*Kol Nidrei*) and fast with us (*Kerisos* 6b).

Rosh Hashana is a day of truth, as we end its central *beracha*, "purify our hearts to serve You in truth, for You are the Lord of truth and Your word is true." *Yom Kippur* is a day of peace, as we make amends for our misdeeds and seek and grant forgiveness to foster peace with others.

---

[25] See "*Teshuva* and *Tefilla*: Two Paths to *Hashem*," http://www.torahweb.org/audio/rwil_090703.html; see also footnote 29 to "Reuven's *Teshuva*: A Model for Life-Long Growth," in this volume; see also "One Step At a Time" in *Mitokh Ha-Ohel* (Yeshiva University Press, *Tishrei* 5772).

On every holiday, we implore "bring us to Yerushalayim in eternal joy." On the *Yamim Noraim*, we add a prayer for "joy in Your city" and for *Hashem*'s rule in "Yerushalayim Your holy city." On *Rosh Hashana*, we cite the prophecy that all will return from exile and "will bow to *Hashem* on the holy mountain in Yerushalayim," and on *Yom Kippur* we recall and anticipate the service of the *Kohen Gadol* in the *Beis Hamikdash* in Yerushalayim.

How and when will Yerushalayim be rebuilt? *Hashem* promises to convert fasts into feasts of joy and gladness when the *Beis Hamikdash* will be rebuilt, if only we love truth and peace (*Zechariah* 8:19; *Rosh Hashana* 18b; see *Rabbeinu* Chananel). The very themes of *Rosh Hashana* and *Yom Kippur* hold the key to our ultimate redemption.

III

Indeed, the very name Yerushalayim reflects this duality. The *Midrash* (*Bereishis Rabba* 56:16) teaches that Shem called the city "*Shalem*" (*Bereishis* 14:18, see Rashi) and Avraham called it "*Yireh*." *Hashem* combined both names and called the city Yerushalayim.

The *Meshech Chochma* (*Bereishis* 22:14) explains that Shem saw that theft filled the world (*Bereishis* 6:11) and led to its destruction (*Bereishis* 6:13). Therefore, he devoted himself to improving interpersonal behavior. As such, he called his capital *Shalem* to emphasize character perfection and the idea that all of mankind comprises one organic whole, each person influencing and being influenced by one another.

Avraham, on the other hand, fought to teach mankind that *Hashem* is the Master of the world, a basic fact that had been forgotten (Rambam, *Hilchos Avoda Zara* 1:1-3). To emphasize this message, he called his capital, the site of the *Akeida* which demonstrated his fear of *Hashem* (*Bereishis* 22:12), "*Hashem* will see (*Hashem Yireh*) … on the mountain *Hashem* will be seen" (*Bereishis* 22:14).

Rosh Hashana, on which we read of the *Akeida*, and *Yom Kippur*, when we must appease others and improve our interpersonal behavior to achieve atonement (*Yoma* 85b), immediately follow the seven weeks of consolation. In the seven *haftaros* of consolation, Yeshaya describes our glorious future: "All your children will be students of *Hashem* and abundant will be your children's peace" (54:13). The two aspects of Yerushalayim, recognizing *Hashem* and achieving peace, will lead to its redemption.

In the previous *pasuk* (*Yeshaya* 54:12), *Hashem* promises to rebuild Yerushalayim with a stone called "*kadchod*." The *Gemara* (*Bava Basra* 75a) interprets that the angels (see *Netzach Yisrael* 51) or the scholars (see *Sheva Denechemta*) debated whether the stones should be *shoham* or *yashfeh*. *Hashem* said to them, "Let it be both" (*kedein uchedein*). Hence the word "*kadchod*," representing both stones.

The *Meshech Chochma* (*Shemos* 28:9) notes that *shoham* stones adorned the *efod*. This garment of the *Kohen Gadol* atones for idolatry (*Zevachim* 88b). The *shoham* represents its opposite, knowledge and fear of *Hashem*.

Yashfeh was the final stone of the *choshen* (*Shemos* 28:20). The *choshen mishpat* (*Shemos* 28:15), as its name implies, represents justice, interpersonal propriety. Yerushalayim will be rebuilt when both the themes of its name will be fulfilled. The two stones, *shoham* of the *efod* and *yashfeh* of the *choshen*, parallel *Yireh* and *Shalem*, truth and peace, respectively. When we love and pursue both, *Hashem* will rebuild Yerushalayim with both stones. All of *Am Yisrael* will be students of *Hashem*, *bein adam laMakom*, and will be blessed with abundant peace, *bein adam lechaveiro*.

The *Yefeh Toar* asks, why does *Yireh* precede *Shalem*? Chronologically, Shem preceded Avraham, so *Shalem* should precede *Yireh*. He answers that Avraham was a greater *tzaddik*, so his name, *Yireh*, takes precedence.

Alternatively, *Yireh* precedes *Shalem* conceptually. First we must establish our faith in *Hashem* and our adherence to the Torah's religious principles and observances. Only then can we develop appropriate interpersonal relationships, guided, and limited, by *yiras Shamayim*. Fear must precede love, truth must precede peace. *Yireh* must precede *Shalem*, even as *Rosh Hashana* must precede *Yom Kippur*.

May our *teshuva*, out of fear and love, lead to a year of truth and peace, and to the rebuilding of Yerushalayim.

The Months, Divine Attributes and Purpose of Creation
RABBI MORDECHAI WILLIG

I

"According to whom do we say [on *Rosh Hashana*] 'This is the anniversary day of the start of Your handiwork, a remembrance of the first day'? According to R. Eliezer who said that the world was created in *Tishrei*" (*Rosh Hashana* 27a). Elsewhere, we seem to follow R. Yehoshua, who said that the world was created in *Nisan*. *Tosafos* resolves the apparent contradiction as follows: in *Tishrei* the world rose in (*Hashem*'s) thought to be created, but it was not created until *Nisan*.

This enigmatic statement may be based on Rashi (*Bereishis* 1:1) who says: at first (*batechila*) "it rose in (*Hashem*'s) thought" to create the world with the attribute of strict judgment, but *Hashem* saw that the world could not last under such circumstances, so He gave precedence to the attribute of mercy and joined it to the attribute of strict judgment, as it says, "on the day of *Hashem Elokim*'s making of earth and heaven" (*Bereishis* 2:4).

Originally published on TorahWeb.org in 2017

Tishrei is the month of judgment, its symbol being scales of judgment. In *Tishrei* "it rose in (*Hashem*'s) thought" to create the world with strict judgment. Since the world could not last, actual creation was postponed until *Nisan*, the month of *Pesach*, which connotes mercy (Rashi, *Shemos* 12:23).

Rosh Hashana is the beginning of creation, in accordance with R. Eliezer. But actual creation occurred in *Nisan*, in accordance with R. Yehoshua. Thus we say on *Rosh Hashana*, "Today is the conception of [*haras*] the world," not its actual birthday.

Rashi's expression *"batechila"* (at first) implies that *Hashem* changed His mind. This is incorrect, as "He is not a human who changes his mind" (*Shmuel* I 15:29; see also *Bemidbar* 23:19), and heretical (Rashi, *Bereishis* 6:6). What then, does it mean?

II

"Moshe saw that people were weighing the flesh [from R. Akiva's body] in the meat market. He said 'Master of the world, this is Torah and this is its reward?' *Hashem* said to him 'Be quiet. So it rose in thought before Me'" (*Menachos* 29b).

The Shelah (*Bereishis, Torah Or* 9) explains that *Hashem* did not change His mind. Rather, the original plan to create the world with strict judgment remains for the exalted few, such as R. Akiva. *Batechila* is not chronological, indicating a change of mind, but rather conceptual, explaining the word *"Bereishis."* Ideally, the world should be created with strict judgment. Practically, the world could not stand, and mercy was added except for the likes of R. Akiva.

If so, we can understand *"batechila"* as *"lechatechila."* Ideally it rose in *Hashem*'s thought to create the world with strict judgment. Practically, as *Hashem* knew from the outset, this is impossible. *Hashem* answered

Rosh Hashana

Moshe that R. Akiva was judged strictly, as was the ideal system which rose in thought before Him. One question remains, however. Why is this the ideal system?

III

The answer lies in the purpose of creation, as explained by Ramchal (*Derech Hashem*, sec. 1, ch. 2): *Hashem*'s purpose in creation was to bestow of His good to another. His wisdom declared that for such good to be complete, the one enjoying it must have earned it himself. Therefore, He created man, the purpose of all creation, with the ability to choose good or bad. By choosing good, man earns closeness to *Hashem* (primarily in the world to come; see Ramchal's *Mesillas Yesharim*, ch. 1), and derives the greatest possible pleasure from His goodness, thereby achieving the purpose of creation.

Ideally, man should be judged strictly, earning his ultimate reward by right. However, practically, man is unable to do so and mercy must be added. Still, the choice to do good is rewarded in the world to come.

R. Akiva was judged strictly, thus enabling him to enjoy even greater reward in the world to come. The *Gemara* (*Berachos* 61b) describes the torturous death of R. Akiva. The ministering angels asked *Hashem*, "This is Torah and this is its reward? Is it not better to be among 'the dead who die at Your hand, *Hashem*, of old age' (*Tehillim* 17:14)? *Hashem* said to them, 'Their portion is in life [of the world to come]' (ibid.) A heavenly voice proclaimed, 'Fortunate are you, R. Akiva, that you will immediately enter the world to come [without judgment or pain. See *Tosafos, Kesuvos* 103b, s.v. *mezuman*].'"

IV

On *Yom Kippur*, the question of the angels is recounted (*Eileh Ezkera, Musaf*) with a different answer from a heavenly voice: "If I hear another sound, I will transform the world into water; I will turn the earth into *tohu vavohu* [desolation and emptiness] (*Bereishis* 1:2)."

This enigmatic response can be explained based on the words of the Ramchal. The purpose of creation is to bestow *Hashem*'s good on man. In its highest form, this requires the ideal system of strict justice, reserved for the exalted few such as R. Akiva. They are punished in this world for minor errors, so that they receive incomparable reward in the world to come. If the angels insist that strict justice not take place, then the highest purpose of creation no longer exists. Therefore, *Hashem* said He will return the world to the pre-creation state of desolation and emptiness. In fact, strict justice took place, the world continues to exist, and R. Akiva was amply rewarded in the world to come.

On *Rosh Hashana* and *Yom Kippur* we are all judged by *Hashem*. By focusing on the months of creation and the Divine Attributes utilized in creation, we can better understand the purpose of creation. Sincere repentance and self-improvement can tilt the balance of *Hashem*'s judgment, granting us a good year in this world and greater reward in the world to come.

Praying for What?
RABBI BENJAMIN YUDIN

The Gra, in his introduction to the *tefillos* of *Rosh Hashana*, notes a powerful and fundamental idea. The *Mishna* in *Rosh Hashana* (16a) teaches: "At four times during the year the world is judged ... on *Rosh Hashana* all of mankind is judged individually, like young sheep who pass through a small opening in the corral."

The seriousness and scope of the judgment is underscored in the *Unesaneh Tokef* prayer, authored by Rav Amnon of Mayence, wherein we are reminded of the nature of this judgment: "How many will die, how many will be born, who will be at rest, who will wander about, who will become poor and who will become wealthy."

One would have imagined that in response to such a reference to judgment, one would pray on *Rosh Hashana* to be pardoned and forgiven, for life for our children and sustenance. Moreover, at first glance the *Amida* of nineteen *berachos* that we recite daily would have been most appropriate for *Rosh Hashana*. The listing of thirteen requests, personal and communal, would precisely articulate the needs of all on *Rosh Hashana*. Indeed, having offered the specific personal and communal needs on *Rosh Hashana*, the *Shemoneh Esrei* for the rest of the year could well have been, "Reign

Originally published on TorahWeb.org in 2000

over the whole universe in your glory," the theme of all of the prayers of *Rosh Hashana*.

The *Rosh Hashana machzor* therefore teaches us a very basic principle regarding prayer. As Rav Chaim Volozhiner in *Nefesh HaChaim* (2:11) teaches, the main thrust and component of all prayer is *Hashem*, His kingship, glory and honor in this world. The personal needs of man are inconsequential by contrast and hence are omitted on *Rosh Hashana*. Moreover, even during the rest of the year, when we do articulate our needs, one learns from the *Rosh Hashana* liturgy that the primary purpose of our asking for health, wealth and religious growth is to serve *Hashem*. We are to channel these bounties to His service. Only then can we be rewarded.

This concept is found in the *Tiferes Yisrael*'s commentary to the last *mishna* in the third chapter of *Rosh Hashana*. The Torah informs us: "And it came to pass when Moshe raised his hand that Israel prevailed" (*Shemos* 17:11). The *mishna* asks, "Was it Moshe's hands that won or lost the battle against Amalek? Rather, the Torah teaches you: As long as Israel looked heavenward and subjected their heart to their Father in Heaven, they would prevail, but when they did not, they would fail." Similarly, *Hashem* instructs Moshe: "Go make a fiery serpent, and set it upon a pole, and whoever is bitten may see it and live" (*Bemidbar* 21:8). The *mishna* rules again that it was not the serpent which killed or gave life. Rather, when Israel looked heavenward and subjugated their heart to their Father in Heaven, they were healed, but when they did not, they perished. The *Tiferes Yisrael* notes that we learn from the above that whether one is praying for success in a new venture such as the war against Amalek, or even a business venture, or whether one is praying to be spared from an impending tragedy such as in the case of the serpents, or from sickness, man's prayer is only effective if the primary objective is to serve *Hashem*. *Bnei Yisrael*'s subjugating their hearts to *Hashem* enabled them to prevail.

Tefillas Chana, which is the *haftara* for the first day of *Rosh Hashana*, teaches us a great deal about prayer, and in particular, highlights the above concept. The *Gemara* in *Berachos* teaches that the *Musaf Amida* on *Rosh Hashana* has nine *berachos* instead of ten because Chana used *Hashem*'s name nine times in her prayer. (Instead of the expected ten *berachos* – the regular seven *berachos* of the *Shabbos* or *Yom Tov Amida* plus the three *Rosh Hashana berachos* of *malchuyos, zichronos* and *shofaros* – we only have six plus the three for *Rosh Hashana*.) Chana prayed for a son and was finally granted one.

The first chapter in *Shmuel I* recounts how Chana used to accompany her husband, Elkana, annually when he went to Shilo to pray. One would have imagined that once the child was born she would have been the first to go to Shilo to thank *Hashem*. The previous Lubavitcher Rebbe zt"l notes that Chana does not go, saying: "Until the child is weaned, then I shall bring him [*Shmuel* I 1:22]; my responsibility is to raise him to best serve *Hashem*." She asked for a child *lema'ancha* – for your sake, *Hashem*.

May we be privileged to have our *tefillos* answered, and to word them correctly.

On the Edge
RABBI BENJAMIN YUDIN

Blowing the *shofar*, which is the primary *mitzva* of Rosh Hashana, is a form of prayer. It is interesting to note that often the setting of a particular *mitzva* contributes to its fulfillment. Thus, the ideal synagogue structure places the *chazan* in a low position, thereby actualizing "ממעמקים" - "From the depths I have called You," (*Tehillim* 130:1). Similarly, the Rosh in *Gemara Rosh Hashana* (3:4) cites the *Yerushalmi* that teaches that we are to blow the *shofar* from the narrower end, as we are taught in Psalms, "מן המצר - From the straits I called God" (118:5). The *shofar* itself is to reflect the urgent need and total dependence of man on *Hashem*. The Talmud in *Rosh Hashana* (26b) also concerns itself with the shape of the *shofar*. R. Yehuda is of the opinion that a bent *shofar* is to be used, since "on Rosh Hashana, the more a person bows his mind," reflecting an attitude of submission and humility, the better it is.

We dare not overlook the obvious. No one would entertain the idea of eating *matza* during *Shemoneh Esrei*. Nor would we consider it proper to hold our *lulav* during *Shemoneh Esrei*. Yet the natural home of the *shofar* is the *Shemoneh Esrei*. This is seen with great clarity from the *Ba'al HaMaor*'s statement (*Rosh Hashana*, ch. 4) that originally the *shofar* was blown **only** in conjunction with the *Shemoneh Esrei*, and the blessings of the *Shemoneh*

Originally published on TorahWeb.org in 2002

Esrei served as the blessings for the *mitzva* of the *shofar* as well. However, in time, responding to the needs of the elderly, the sick, and those who could not stay for the entire service, the Rabbis instituted a set of *shofar* sounds prior to the *Shemoneh Esrei*. *Shofar* is naturally at home in the *Shemoneh Esrei*, since *shofar* is a form of prayer.

That *shofar* is prayer may be seen from the concluding blessing of the *shofaros* section of the *Musaf Shemoneh Esrei*, "Blessed are you *Hashem*, who hears the *shofar*-sound of His people Israel with mercy." If *shofar* is a *mitzva* like *mezuza* or *lulav*, then the request that our blowing be received with mercy is most incomprehensible. However, as we are accustomed to ask thrice daily for *Hashem* to accept our **prayers** with mercy, it is understandable that we do likewise in regard to *shofar*.

The *Beis Halevi* (*Derush* 15) notes a startling understanding of *shofar* as prayer. A prayer is as effective as the source from which it emanates. Indeed, the spoken word is the distinctive mark of man. The Torah (*Bereishis* 2:7) states that when *Hashem* blew the soul of life into man's nostrils, man became a "*nefesh chaya*," which the *Targum* translates as "*ruach mimalela*" (a spirit of intelligent speech). However, over the course of time, man sullies and misuses his Divine gift of speech. *Lashon hara*, *rechilus*, and *nivul peh* are not only forbidden forms of speech, but they limit the effectiveness and proficiency of the mouth. And thus the quality of the spoken prayer is often significantly diminished. Therefore, *Hashem* in His kindness allows us to communicate with a region that is deeper than the spoken words, namely the *ruach* – the spirit of man. When *Hashem* blew of His existence into man, part of the Divine became present in man. It is from this holy and pure source that the sounds of the *shofar* emanate. As this part of man is more holy, the prayer that issues forth is holier, and thus the concluding blessing asking God to accept the *shofar*-sound of His people Israel with mercy is most understandable.

Blowing from the narrow edge of the *shofar* is not only for the practical convenience of the *ba'al tokea* (the one blowing the *shofar*), but is to communicate the profound urgency of the moment. I blow the *shofar* because I recognize that I am in dire, difficult straits, and have no other place to turn for help. In *Devarim* 31:17, the Torah teaches that a time will come when the Jewish people will abrogate their covenant with *Hashem* and turn to other deities. At that time many troubles and afflictions will befall them, and Israel will say on that day, "Is it not because my God is not in my midst that these ills have befallen me?" Surprisingly the next verse teaches that *Hashem* will respond, "I shall utterly hide My face on that day." The Seforno explains that when the troubles befell the people, instead of realizing that they were sent as a punishment from *Hashem*, they attempted to solve their crises by turning to other venues and addresses, not realizing that they were to turn to *Hashem* in prayer and repentance. The *shofar* itself, which is blown from the narrow end, reminds the Jew how precarious life is and how dependent he is on *Hashem*.

Finally, *Devarim Rabba* (*Zos Haberacha* 11:10) presents an incredible *midrash* about the necessity of *tefilla*. R. Yochanan taught that in no fewer than ten places does the Torah speak of Moshe's impending passing. Initially, this was "*kal be'einav shel Moshe*"; Moshe was not immediately overwhelmed. Moshe reasoned: if the Jewish people committed major sins, and upon my praying on their behalf *Hashem* forgave them, *Hashem* will certainly forgive me, who did not sin from my youth, when I pray on my own behalf. When *Hashem* saw Moshe's complacent attitude and his failure to burst forth in **immediate** prayer, *Hashem* swore that Moshe would not enter the Promised Land. Moshe failed to see the urgency and immediacy of the crisis.

This past year has been a most difficult one for *Am Yisael*. Too often, one trouble after another has the effect of desensitizing us to the urgency of the moment. May we learn from Moshe *Rabbeinu*, and truly seize the moment of *shofar*, to realize the narrow and difficult straits in which we find ourselves, both individually and collectively, and thus realize that אין לנו להשען אלא על אבינו שבשמים, we are dependent only on our Father in Heaven.

If at First You Don't Succeed ...
RABBI BENJAMIN YUDIN

It is interesting to note that Rav Saadia Gaon counts among the *taryag* (613) *mitzvos* the convocation ceremony that happened at *Har Gerizim* and *Har Eival* on the day that the Jewish nation crossed the Jordan. The Torah in *Parashas Ki Savo* (chapter 27) details the exact way that the new immigrants to the land were to gather: six tribes on *Har Gerizim* and six tribes on *Har Eival*. The *Kohanim* and *Leviyim* stood in between the two mountains and first pronounced blessings to the nation if they kept the Torah, and then the curses if they did not.

Most commentaries do not count this event as one of the 613 *mitzvos*, as it was an experience that occurred only once. By definition *mitzvos* are eternal; thus, the placing of the blood on the doorpost in Egypt is not counted as a *mitzva*. Rav Yeruchum Perlow explains that the *mitzva* of *Har Gerizim* and *Har Eival* is the *mitzva* of *arvus*, the collective responsibility that the Jewish nation entered into at this time. The *mitvza* is not to regroup at the mountain but to practice and live by "*kol Yisrael areivim zeh lazeh*" (all of Israel is responsible for one another).

This is the source and foundation for the important halachic

Originally published on TorahWeb.org in 2004

Rosh Hashana

principle of *"yatza motzi."* Under normal circumstances, once an individual has fulfilled a particular *mitzva* he is **not** given a second chance to fulfill that *mitzva*. Case in point: One who has recited *kiddush* Friday night cannot recite *kiddush* again, claiming for example that he or she lacked proper *kavana* (concentration) the first time. Yet, the same individual, should he go for a walk that night and encounter a Jew who has not yet recited or heard *kiddush*, is obligated to recite *kiddush* for him, as all Israel is responsible for one another.

The meaning of the word *"areiv"* in the above context is that of a cosigner. As in a loan, the cosigner assumes responsibility for payment if the borrower reneges on his obligation. Similarly, each Jew is responsible to see that his fellow Jew observes Torah and *mitzvos*. Our *mitzvos* of *shofar*, *lulav*, *sukkah* and *tefillin* are incomplete if our neighbor has not yet fulfilled the *mitzva*, and we can positively correct the situation.

The *Noam Elimelech* suggests another interpretation to the word *areiv* in light of the passage in *Shir Hashirim* (2:14), "כי קולך ערב", "for your voice is sweet." *Kol Yisrael areivim zeh lazeh* – all of Israel sweetens one another. It is not coincidental that we read *Ki Savo* and *Nitzavim* each year prior to *Rosh Hashana*. We are taught תכלה שנה וקללותיה – may the year with its curses and adverse circumstances come to a close. I'd like to suggest that the *mitzva* of *arvus* is a critical one, especially at this time of year.

Rosh Hashana is a two-day holiday even in *Eretz Yisrael*. The Talmud *Rosh Hashana* (30b) gives an interesting halachic explanation for the two-day observance. Rav Dessler (*Michtav MeEliyahu* vol. 2) cites a fascinating *Zohar* (*Parashas Pinchas*) which offers the following philosophical approach: The first day of *Rosh Hashana* is that of *dina kashya* – strict judgment, while the second day is that of *dina rafya* –

soft judgment. Rav Dessler then brings the Arizal's explanation of each day. On the first day of *Rosh Hashana*, each individual is judged as an individual, regarding how each of us fared with our unique individual potential. Each person has character traits and understandings that are exclusively his or hers. The Talmud (*Berachos* 58a) teaches that just as each person's facial features are unique, so too is one's perception and intelligence. How one either elevated or used and abused one's individual personal gifts and potential is judged on the first day. All too often, the result is that one is found to be lacking, hence *dina kashya* – strict judgment.

The second day, however, explains the Arizal, we is judged as part of the *klal*, as a member of *Klal Yisrael*. Here there is greater opportunity for *dina rafya* – softer, kinder judgment, as each individual contributes, sweetens ("*areivim*") and enhances the community. Praying with a *minyan* in synagogue as opposed to praying alone at home is not only a higher-quality personal *mitzva*, but each participant contributes to ברוב עם הדרת מלך – "the King's glory is in a multitude of people." The quality, not just quantity, of the *minyan* is enhanced by each individual. Moreover, note the text of the *berachos* of the *Shemoneh Esrei*. They are all couched in the plural. We do not only pray for our health, wealth and personal redemption, but include the rest of *Klal Yisrael* as well.

As each person is singular – unique – so too is his or her prayer on behalf of the Jewish nation. Thus, everyone is needed. Therefore, a most important way to prepare for *Rosh Hashana* is to focus your prayers properly on behalf of the community, enabling one to merit a positive judgment on *Rosh Hashana*.

Finally, before *Rosh Hashana* pause and reflect how you can sweeten the lives of those around you. The smile that you bring to the faces of the senior citizens you visit, either alone or with your children; your telephone call to the shut-in inquiring of his or her well-being; your greeting a newcomer to shul with a warm welcome as opposed to ignoring him or her. These are but a few practical methods of implementing the lesson of the *Noam Elimelech*. Make a conscious effort to sweeten another's day, as there is no telling how it will impact your life.

Going "Sho-Far" for Hashem

RABBI BENJAMIN YUDIN

When *Rosh Hashana* falls on a *Shabbos*, we do not blow the *shofar*. There are several reasons for this law. I'd like to present three. The Talmud (*Rosh Hashana* 29b) cites the teaching of Rava that we are concerned lest a Jew somewhere violate the *Shabbos* by carrying the *shofar* in a public domain (*reshus harabim*). The Rabbis issued a decree, in order to protect the integrity of *Shabbos*, that it is preferable to remain passive and abstain from the biblical *mitzva* of *shofar*. This *halacha* speaks volumes about the *halachos* of *Shabbos* in general and specifically the laws of carrying. This is especially significant for many of us who are blessed with an *eruv*. We must educate our children regarding the laws of carrying and their need to inquire about the existence of an *eruv* when they go away for *Shabbos*.

The *Meshech Chochma* (*Vayikra* 23:24) provides another reason. He begins by extolling the significance and importance of *shofar*. The Talmud (*Rosh Hashana* 26a) equates the blowing of the *shofar* to a service that is performed in the Holy of Holies in the Temple. Not many other *mitzvos* are awarded such a distinction. Moreover, our Rabbis understand the blowing of the *shofar* as an antidote to the harsh charges of the *Satan*. The

Originally published on TorahWeb.org in 2006

shofar, as spiritual medicine, has the ability to combat the many different strands of spiritual virus hurled against us. Thus, not blowing the *shofar* is akin to a sick patient not taking his medicine. Whatever good excuse the patient has does not compensate for the absence of the medicine.

It is precisely because the *shofar* is so crucial and important to the welfare of the Jewish people that we abstain from blowing the *shofar* on *Shabbos*. The Jewish community is saying to *Hashem*, "Your Torah and Your *Shabbos* are even more important and dear to us than our individual and collective needs." Similarly, the Talmud (*Berachos* 6a) teaches that *Hashem* dons *tefillin* as do the Jewish people; our *tefillin* contain the *Shema* in praise of *Hashem*, while His *tefillin* contain the verse "and who is like Israel, a unique nation in the land," in praise of Israel. It is our sacrifice of foregoing the benefits of the *shofar* for the sake of the benefit of *Shabbos* that serves as our advocate. Our abstaining from blowing the *shofar* on *Shabbos* is placing *Hashem* before ourselves.

The *Chasam Sofer* offers yet another, most fascinating, reason for not blowing the *shofar* on *Shabbos*. He explains that the nature of Avraham's command to do the *akieda* was very different than Yitzchak's. Avraham heard the command directly from *Hashem*, which is likened to a command in the *Torah Shebichsav*, the Written Torah, which emanated directly from *Hashem*. Yitzchak heard the will of *Hashem* through his father, which the *Chasam Sofer* compares to the *Torah Shebe'al Peh*, the Oral Law. Avraham was ready to offer his son based upon God's direct instruction, while Yitzchak demonstrated his willingness to offer his life for the sake of the *Torah Shebe'al Peh*.

It is for this reason that Yitzchak's sacrifice was even greater than that of his father's. Therefore, the *Chasam Sofer* explains, in our *Musaf* service we refer to this event as the binding of Yitzchak: "*ve'Akeidas Yitzchak lezaro tizkor*" "and remember the binding of Yitzchak for the sake of his progeny." We do not say "the binding of Yitzchak by Avraham," as Yitzchak proved himself ready to sacrifice his life based on the *Torah Shebe'al Peh*. Avraham was convinced that he heard God speaking to him, but Yitzchak, who did not hear it from *Hashem*, demonstrated his absolute trust and faith in the *masora*, the Oral Tradition.

Incidentally, the Torah (*Bereishis* 22:6) describes the journey of father and son as "*vayeilchu shneihem yachdav*," "and they both went together." This refers to the integration and synthesis of the Written and Oral Law.

The Talmud (*Rosh Hashana* 16a) provides a reason for the blowing of the *shofar*. "*Hashem* said 'blow the ram's horn before Me so that I shall recall *Akeidas* Yitzchak for your sake.'" That is, to recall the sacrifice of Ytitzchak for the sake of *Torah Shebe'al Peh*. Therefore when *Rosh Hashana* falls on a *Shabbos*, our abstaining from blowing the *shofar* based upon *Torah Shebe'al Peh* is a living implementation of a teaching of the *Akeida*. As Yitzchak demonstrated his absolute allegiance and commitment to the *masora*, our refraining from blowing the *shofar* on *Shabbos* is our affirmation of the *masora* as well.

Group Coverage
RABBI BENJAMIN YUDIN

I

The opening verse of *Parashas Nitzavim* is understood on many levels. Rashi understands it as a source of consolation. The Torah in *Parashas Ki Savo* enumerated ninety-eight curses, and simply listening to them conveys the fear of extinction and annihilation. Therefore, the Torah says, despite the punishments and catastrophes, "*atem nitzavim hayom kulchem,*" you are all standing today. The Jewish nation endures and will endure forever.

The *Zohar* understands the word "*hayom*" – today – to refer to the day of *Rosh Hashana*. The Talmud *Megilla* (31b) teaches that Ezra instituted that *Parashas Nitzavim* be read as a buffer between the curses of *Ki Savo* and the holiday of *Rosh Hashana*. The Alter of Kelm, citing the *Tur* at the beginning of the laws of *Rosh Hashana* in the name of R. Chanina and R. Yehoshua, sees a great lesson in the word "*kulchem*" – the entire nation – as a modifier of "*nitzavim.*" Ordinarily, an individual on trial for his life will not be concerned regarding his personal appearance before the court. He will not necessarily shave or get a haircut, nor dress in any other garments but black. In sharp contrast, *Am Yisrael* get haircuts, don white clothing, and eat and drink *Yom Tov* meals. They know *Hashem* will per-

---

Originally published on TorahWeb.org in 2010

form a miracle on their behalf.

Where does this state of optimism come from? The Alter of Kelm explains that each individual indeed should worry and enter *Rosh Hashana* in a state of personal fear and trepidation. Regarding his personal fate this forthcoming year in the areas of health, family tranquility and prosperity, he has no assurance and guarantee that what was will necessarily continue to be. But one thing he can be absolutely assured of and guaranteed: the Jewish nation as a people will survive, and play a significant role in the unfolding of world history.

The way for the individual, therefore, to overcome, or at least assuage, his or her personal fears is to connect his or herself to the *Klal*, to the community, to the Jewish nation. *Kulchem* is the answer! The more an individual is needed by the community – not only studying Torah, but being part of a Torah study group – the more he encourages others to participate, the more essential he is to the group, the more the merits of the *Klal* will encompass and embrace him. This is true in regard to *gemilus chasadim*. Involvement in various *gemachs*, societies that assist neighbors in all different ways, raises our stature from that of an individual to a member of the *klal*. In the area of *tefilla*, if one is an integral part of the *minyan* – if one contributes not only financially but experientially, by one's *kavana* (concentration and seriousness of purpose) – one's personal station and position becomes upgraded, and hence he is "*nitzavim*" on *Rosh Hashana*, thanks to the coattail effect of the guaranteed survival of the Jewish nation.

II

In the Ashkenazic community, we begin the recitation of *Selichos* this Saturday night. This too fits very comfortably with *Parashas Nitzavim*. Our *parasha* speaks of the phenomenon of *teshuva* in *perek* 30, and *Selichos* is based on the foundation of *teshuva*. To the Rambam, our Torah reading is a Divine prediction that the Jewish nation will repent.

The essence of *Selichos* is not to plead before *Hashem* for mercy by claiming that after all, "I'm sorry, we are frail and mortal; let bygones be bygones." We believe that He only asks of us what we can definitely do and fulfill. The essence of *Selichos* is found in *Rosh Hashana* (17b), where R. Yochanan taught that following the sin of the golden calf, *Hashem* enveloped Himself in a *tallis*, like a *shaliach tzibbur* (*chazan*), and recited the Thirteen Attributes of Mercy. He taught that when the Jewish people are in need of forgiveness, they should "*ya'asu*" (perform) before Him this order of attributes. The commentaries highlight the fact that it does not say "recite" before Him these attributes, but "perform," implying a substantive act; man is to resolve to change. This is the essence of *Selichos*, articulating the resolve but also pledging oneself to perform the 611th *mitzva* of "*vehalachta bidrachav*," to emulate His attributes. As He is kind, compassionate, and slow to anger, so will I endeavor to be.

The *Midrash* in *Parashas Noach* illustrates *Hashem*'s attribute of patience. On the verse that *Hashem* smelled the sweet aroma, "*reiach nichoach*," of Noach's offering, the *Midrash* teaches that He smelled Avraham being thrown into the furnace, and Chananel, Mishael and Azaryah being cast by Nebuchadnezar into the great furnace. The commentary *Ma'asei Hashem* explains this challenging *midrash*. Given that *Hashem* is incorporeal, what does it mean that He "smelled" and savored the *korban*? He explains that the sense of smell is different from the other senses. Without seeing or touching the object, one can often identify the source of the fragrance from a distance. One can stand outside a home on *Erev Shabbos* or *Erev Yom Tov* and smell and anticipate the delicacies. Similarly, *Hashem* saw in the future the sacrifice and *Kiddush Hashem* of Avraham and the other *tzaddikim*, and thereby decided never to destroy the world again.

Be Basket-like
RABBI BENJAMIN YUDIN

Rabbi Yitzchak Zilberstein, *shlita* (*Veha'arev Na*, vol. 3, p. 450) addresses an interesting and sensitive question regarding a group of men who study Talmud together. When they begin a new tractate, they rotate who purchases the volumes of Talmud for the group. With the great variety of *Gemara* volumes available, including those with more features, the more affluent members purchased more costly texts, and the more economically strapped purchased more basic texts. The question was: should the *maggid shiur*, instructor of the group, make a policy that only one type of *Gemara* should be bought, to protect the dignity of the poorer members?

The *Mishna* (*Bikkurim* 3:8) teaches that poor farmers gave the *kohen* both their *bikkurim* fruits and the simple myrtle baskets in which they brought the *bikkurim*, while the affluent farmers took back their baskets of gold and silver. Rabbi Zilberstein, discussing the above issue of *Gemara* purchases, cites the following question of the *Tosfos Yom Tov* on this *mishna*: just as the *Mishna* (*Ta'anis* 26b) teaches that girls borrowed dresses on *Tu Ba'av* and *Yom Kippur* in order to not embarrass the poor girls, why not legislate here that everyone should bring *bikkurim* in simple baskets? *Tosfos Yom Tov* answers that the honor of the *Beis Hamikdash*, and allowing the wealthy farmers to enrich their *mitzva* and beautify it, thus fulfilling "*zeh Keili ve'anveihu*," "this is my God and I will beautify Him" (*Shemos*

Originally published on TorahWeb.org in 2013

15:2), override the concern of sensitivity to the poor.

Rabbi Zilberstein brings an exciting comment of the Malbim (*Devarim* 26:4), who teaches that there is a significant difference between the baskets of the rich and the poor, and that the poor man's basket is actually the more elevated. The poor man, postulates Malbim, wove the basket out of myrtle leaves specifically for this purpose. Since it is a labor of love, reflecting his personal *mesirus nefesh* for the *mitzva*, the basket thus becomes an integral part of the *mitzva*. It is not simply a means to an end, enabling the farmer to give the fruit to the *kohen*, but rather it assumes the status of the *mitzva* itself; the poor man who toiled and gave of himself in making the basket elevates the basket to become part and parcel of the *mitzva*. It is for this reason that we honor the poor, and the *kohen* keeps the basket in recognition of his noble efforts.

I believe this insight of the Malbim is extremely significant and poignant. The Torah is teaching that when one invests in something, it becomes an integral part of oneself. The Talmud (*Bava Metzia* 38a) teaches that a person prefers a *kav* of his own produce to nine *kavin* of his fellow's produce, which could be purchased with the proceeds from a timely sale of his produce. Rashi explains that this is the case because that which one toils to produce is most precious to him. What is true in the physical and materialistic realm is equally true in the spiritual realm. *Avos DeRabi Nasan* (3:6) teaches that one *mitzva* observed with *tza'ar* – difficulties and challenge – is more dear to *Hashem* than one hundred *mitzvos* performed with ease.

Dovid *Hamelech*, in his opening chapter of *Tehillim*, praises the one "whose desire is in the Torah of *Hashem*, and in his Torah he meditates day and night" (1:2). At first it is called the Torah of *Hashem*, but once an individual has studied it and mastered it, it is called "his Torah," namely that of the scholar (*Kiddushin* 32b).

Moreover, when the Torah, in the beginning of *Vayikra*, speaks of the *korban olah*, it begins with the bringing of an animal, then the bringing of a bird, and finally the bringing of a meal offering. Interestingly, it is only regarding this last offering that the Torah describes the donor as *nefesh* ("if a soul [*nefesh*] will bring a meal offering" [*Vayikra* 2:1]). Rashi cites from the Talmud (*Menachos* 104b) that since most often it is a poor man who brings a meal offering as his *korban olah*, Hashem looks upon this act as though he offered his soul.

The lesson of the Malbim is most appropriate as we prepare for *Rosh Hashana* and *Yom Kippur*. Make the *mitzvos* yours. One way, suggests the *Chazon Ish* (*Emuna uBitachon*, chap. 3, 5-10), is to study the *mitzvos*. The more one understands what appears to be the technical aspects of the *mitzvos* and the philosophical teachings of the *mitzvos*, the more they become part of you. Why do we blow thirty sounds, the *tekios demeyushav*, before the *Musaf* prayer on *Rosh Hashana*? Why do we blow thirty sounds during the *Shemoneh Esrei*? Why forty at the end of the *Musaf*? What is biblical and what is rabbinic? Studying the above enables one to make the *mitzva* of *shofar* theirs.

Finally, as the handmade basket is upgraded and reckoned as an integral part of the *mitzva*, may we who perform and are about to approach a season of many *mitzvos* become basket-like, namely, not just to do good, but to be good.

Aseres Yemei Teshuva

Bechira Chofshis
RABBI HERSHEL SCHACHTER

The *Gemara* (*Pesachim* 54a) tells us that the ability of man to do *teshuva* was one of the seven things that *Hashem* instituted before He created the world. The whole purpose of the entire creation was to create man to serve Him. Man's service only has meaning if man has *bechira chofshis*, so man had to be created with the ability to choose to sin.

This is assumed to be the meaning of the *pasuk* that says that man was created "*betzelem Elokim*," in the image of God. Man was created with total freedom of choice[26]. Just as there is nothing forcing God to choose one thing or another, so too man is completely free in his decisionmaking.

The Torah (*Bereishis* 2:7) tells us that *Hashem* took sand from "*ha'adama* – the earth" to form man. Rashi in his commentary quotes the understanding of the *Midrash* that the word "*adama*" is an allusion to the earth of the altar in the *Beis Hamikdash*. Man has built into his being the ability to do *teshuva*. Freedom to choose on which path to proceed is essential to the make-up of man. Even after having made his initial choice, man has the ability to totally undo a decision, in either direction (for the good or for the bad), and choose a totally different route.

---
[26] *Mesech Chochma* in the name of the Mabit, in his *sefer Beis Elokim*

Originally published on TorahWeb.org in 2015

In the weekday *Shemoneh Esrei*, the first request we make in the middle section (containing all of our *bakashos*) is for intelligence and wisdom, i.e., that we should be able to function as normal human beings. What distinguishes the humans from the animals is our *sechel*. The very next request in the *Shemoneh Esrei* is that we should be able to exercise our ability to do *teshuva*. This too is integral to the human condition. All people are prone to sin, but *Hashem* built into all of us the ability to do *teshuva*.

The *Midrash* (*Bereishis Rabba* 3:9) says that *Hashem* originally created other worlds and destroyed them, until He finally created this world with which we are familiar. Certainly if *Hashem* had willed a beautiful and wonderful world in the first place, that would have come about, so why did He initially will several imperfect worlds into existence just to destroy them and then start all over again? Apparently *Hashem* wanted to teach man the lesson of "starting all over" (see *Nefesh HaRav*, p. 68).

Some have the attitude that by sinning and going against the wishes of *Hashem*, they are exercising their *bechira chofshis* to the greatest degree! From a perverted perspective this is certainly correct. But also included in the concept of *tzelem Elokim* is using the power of *bechira* for a creative, positive and productive purpose. *Hashem* chose freely to create an entire universe, so we should emulate His ways by using our *bechira chofshis* for positive purposes. "ובחרת בחיים - choose life" (*Devarim* 30:19); choose to go *bederech Hashem*. Even after having already made an improper choice, we must use our *bechira chofshis* to scrap "our world" and "start all over again," just as He did.

Shabbos and Teshuva: Remaking the World, Remaking the Self
RABBI YAKOV HABER

Shabbos Shuva, the name for the *Shabbos* between *Rosh Hashana* and *Yom Kippur*, most directly gets its name from the first verse of the dramatic and poignant *haftara* read on this *Shabbos*: "'שובה ישראל עד ה' א-לקיך כי כשלת בעונך-. Return O Israel to *Hashem*, your God, for you have stumbled with your sin."

Many contemporary writers have noted additional connections between the themes of *Shabbos* and repentance. Among these explanations is a fascinating exposition presented by the late Slonimer Rebbe *zt"l*, Rav Shalom Noach Berzovsky, in his *Nesivos Shalom*. The language of the Torah concerning the first Sabbath of Creation, "And *Hashem* finished His work on the seventh day" (*Bereishis* 2:2), implies that something was created on *Shabbos*. This seemingly contradicts other verses indicating that the work of Creation was completed in six days. Expanding on statements by *Chazal*, Rav Berzovsky explains that *Shabbos* was the first day of **re-creation**. Nothing in the world exists fundamentally. It is only through the continued will of God that all of the billions of molecules in the universe and all its myriad

---

Originally published on TorahWeb.org in 2007

laws continue. In the language of the prayers, "מחדש בטובו בכל יום תמיד מעשה בראשית - He renews with His kindness each day, constantly, the acts of creation."²⁷ This phenomenon of re-creation rooted in the very Creation itself, first occurring on the first *Shabbos*, serves as the cornerstone of the ability to change. Through the *teshuva* process, the individual breaks with his past and becomes a new being. R. Moshe Chaim Luzzato and others point to this aspect of repentance as that which allows for the erasure of the past evil acts. The acts are not attributed to the person who sinned, because he is now someone else.

Rav Aharon Kahn, *shlita*, suggested a similar approach in his analysis of a midrashic statement on a passage oft-recited on *Rosh Hashana*: "תקעו בחודש שופר בכסה ליום חגנו", "Blow the *shofar* at the time of the renewal of the month …" *Yalkut Shimoni*, expanding on the verb forms of the words "baChoDeSH" and "SHoFaR," comments: "CHaDSHu ma'aseichem; SHaPRu ma'aseichem" – "Renew your actions; better your actions." Sometimes one may merely "fine-tune" one's past actions to achieve perfection. Quite often, though, one needs an entirely different outlook, one which is God-centered and not self-centered, in order to properly repent. This is the mystery of the human being's ability to take advantage of the God-granted ability to perform true *teshuva*: to re-create one's life and devote it to the service of *Hakadosh Baruch Hu*, just as the Creator Himself constantly re-creates His world.

---

²⁷ There is an interesting physical, natural phenomenon highlighting this very concept – that of constant cell division, the emergence of new cells and the death of the old, while the organism remains the same.

Becoming Bound to Each Other and to Hashem

RABBI YAAKOV NEUBURGER

At the outset of every *Shemoneh Esrei* of the *Yamim Noraim*, at a moment when we would want to focus on our dreams and our worries, our minds are quickly directed to pray for a time when *Hashem*'s presence will dominate the plans and proceedings of all people. It is then that we ask that *Hashem* instill awe throughout His creation, establishing a time that will fully realize the phrase: "ויעשו כלם אגודה אחת לעשות רצונך בלבב שלם -that [all people] will become bound as one to do Your will with complete hearts."

I have often wondered why our Sages chose to conjoin two seemingly disparate prayers into one sentence. Why did they not continue the style of the forgoing sentences, and in one brief phrase ask for a peaceful time when we will all live comfortably together, and subsequently in a separate sentence beg for the purity and sincerity of "complete hearts"? Further, why did *Chazal* phrase this one request differently from the rest, putting it in the passive form, "that we become bound" rather than scripting for us a request for the strength and tolerance that it takes to proactively bind ourselves together?

Originally published on TorahWeb.org in 2008

Perhaps these two passions, to serve *Hashem* genuinely and to extend and enjoy loving and respectful relationships, stem from the same environment and culture. It may be that the roads to both begin at the same point and end at each other's doorsteps. No doubt both will demand ridding oneself of the pettiness that so often overtakes our minds and decisions.

The naturalness and thrill of competition certainly shape within us a predisposition which is unfriendly to respecting and appreciating the strengths of others. Yet investing in acquiring a positive and open frame of mind is truly an *"avoda"* – requiring dedicated and persistent applications to greater nobility. If we are really going to earn our membership in an *aguda achas* – a unified group of *Klal Yisrael* – it will no doubt require great introspection and soulful thinking; being on guard against harboring ill feelings toward other individuals and other groups, challenging ourselves to prioritize, and focusing on that which is genuinely precious.

In sum, aspiring to live in true harmony requires putting much ahead of private concerns, and as a result nurtures a purity of heart and deed in the direct service of *Hashem* as well. *Chazal* further intimate that once we have achieved comfort and closeness with our peers, we will feel as though we have "become bound" – as though it had happened naturally and was always meant to be.

Of course, it is important to keep in mind that our most powerful prayers may be our actions moving ourselves in the direction of our wishes.

May we all be blessed to come into the *Yamim Noraim* with the potent prayers of improved relations with family and friends, and may we all be blessed with peace, health, spiritual growth, prosperity and happiness.

Reaching Our Destination
RABBI ZVI SOBOLOFSKY

Closeness to *Hashem* is a primary theme of the upcoming *Aseres Yemei Teshuva*. The *navi* Yeshayahu describes a time when *Hashem* is especially close, and *Chazal* have the tradition that this is referring specifically to this time of the year. In *Parashas Nitzavim*, Moshe beseeches the Jewish people not to view "this *mitzva*" as being far away, but rather very near to us. According to the Ramban "this *mitzva*" is *teshuva*, and thus these *pesukim* are especially appropriate to read right before *Aseres Yemei Teshuva*.

How does one attain closeness to *Hashem*? When a person is distant from a geographic location he desires to reach, he must travel on the road that will take him there. Similarly, there is a road to travel to reach *Hashem*. In addition, just as there are impediments that prevent one from reaching a physical destination, so too there are factors that prevent one from achieving spiritual goals.

In *Sefer Melachim* we learn that Yeravam, the king of the northern kingdom, was concerned that his position would be weakened if the Jews under his rule would travel to Yerushalayim, which was located in the southern kingdom. He therefore implemented a two-pronged system

---

Originally published on TorahWeb.org in 2015

to prevent the people from being influenced by Yerushalayim: he set up physical roadblocks to turn back those who wished to travel to Yerushalayim, and he also set up idolatrous temples that would serve as alternatives for those seeking the religious experience of visiting the *Beis Hamikdash*.

When traveling on a physical journey, there are two things that can prevent us from reaching our destination: there are "roadblocks," such as traffic or construction, which we often encounter on today's roads, and there is also the possibility of getting lost. A wrong turn can take us miles in the wrong direction.

As we travel on a spiritual journey, we are faced with similar challenges. First, there are "roadblocks" of different types on the way. When we feel we are not accomplishing our goals, we often want to turn around and go back. Frustrated by the "traffic and construction," we question whether we will ever reach our desired destination. Second, there are also wrong turns – thinking we are heading to "Yerushalayim," we may end up in a very different place. One small detour can lead us in the opposite direction from the destination we want to reach.

When traveling today, many of us avail ourselves of technology that addresses these two potential obstacles on our course. We are no longer as concerned about traffic, since Waze weaves us around the most difficult traffic jams. It also gives such precise directions that we no longer fear making a wrong turn and getting lost for miles. Even if we miss a turn, we are immediately rerouted to enable us to reach our correct destination.

As we travel down the road of spirituality, there is a time-tested system that will enable us to reach our final destination and avoid any roadblocks or wrong turns: closeness to *Hashem*. The *mitzva* we read about in *Parashas Nitzvaim*, which is described as being so close to us and which was understood by the Ramban to refer to *teshuva*, is understood by Rashi to refer to *talmud Torah*. These two views are not contradictory, but rather complimentary. *Teshuva* to attain the desired closeness to *Hashem* can only come through Torah. Studying Torah will prevent us from getting stuck in the obstacles along the way and from getting lost.

Especially at this time of the year, let us be certain that we are traveling in the right direction and not getting delayed by obstacles along the way. Let us listen carefully to the directions the Torah gives us as we are guided to our destination. Only the Torah will enable us to reach our desired goal of closeness to *Hashem*. May we all merit attaining that closeness during the days ahead, and may we be inspired to maintain that closeness throughout our lives.

Remember Your Creator
RABBI MAYER TWERSKY

Rambam[28] writes that while it is never too late to do *teshuva*, optimally one should repent while at the same age and stage of life. Optimally, the only difference between past *cheit* and present compliance with *mitzvos Hashem* should be the penitent's *teshuva*. Rambam adds that Shlomo Hamelech was speaking of this timing when he said, "And remember your Creator in the days of your youth" (*Koheles* 12:1).

Rambam hitherto had been discoursing about *teshuva*; he quotes proof text from *Megillas Koheles* where Shlomo *Hamelech* speaks about remembering *Hashem*. A fundamental, all-important equation emerges. *Teshuva* means remembering *Hashem*.

The background to this equation lies in an understanding of *cheit*. Consider the following *mashal*. Even someone whose temptation to cheat on an examination is so strong as to potentially overpower his scruples will not cheat when the proctor is watching. Cheaters engage in their dishonesty when they feel that their actions are not being observed.

---

[28] *Hilchos Teshuva* 2:1.

Originally published on TorahWeb.org in 2010

Aseres Yimei Teshuva

The analogue is clear. The *yetzer hara* manifests itself in different ways, pushing us in different directions. The temptation to speak or listen to *lashon hara* differs from the *yetzer hara* for inappropriate physical pleasure. There is a common denominator, however. Every *yetzer hara*, every manifestation of the *yetzer hara*, would be inhibited if only we were cognizant of being in the presence of *Hakadosh Baruch Hu*, who is always watching us. *Cheit* involves forgetting *Hakadosh Baruch Hu*,[29] *rachmana litzlan*; thus *teshuva* means remembering *Hashem*.[30]

As we seek, *besiyata dishmaya*, to take advantage of the *Aseres Yemei Teshuva*, we must, through persistent and consistent reflection, work to increase our awareness of *Hakadosh Baruch Hu*. We must constantly remind ourselves of the ultimate truth of *Hashem*'s omnipresence, ultimately internalizing this fundamental awareness. We must not only confess our particular sins, but also more generally our forgetting *Hashem*, which allowed for those sins. As we recite the *al cheit*s we must be careful to stress the *lefanecha*, in Your presence. May we all be *zocheh* to *teshuva shleima mei'ahava*, a *kesiva vachasima tova*, and a *shenas chaim veshalom*.

---

[29] See *Rabbeinu* Yona, *Sha'arei Teshuva*, *sha'ar* I, *ikar* 6
[30] Besides *Hilchos Teshuva* 2:1, see also 3:4.

Teshuva:
A Mandate for Change
RABBI MAYER TWERSKY

The impending *din* of *Rosh Hashana* and *Yom Kippur* focuses our attention upon [the need for] *teshuva*. This is obviously entirely appropriate and commendable. The problem is that we inappropriately associate *teshuva* exclusively with the *din* of *Yamim Noraim*. This distorts the *mitzva* of *teshuva* in two crucial, interrelated ways. Firstly, the *mitzva* of *teshuva* is perennial, not seasonal. *Rabbeinu* Yona opens *Sha'arei Teshuva* by underscoring the vital obligation to repent immediately, as soon as one becomes aware of *cheit*. Likewise, *Maharsha* comments that when *Chazal* detail the *mitzva* of studying the appropriate seasonal *halachos* on the respective *Yamin Tovim* (*halachos* of *Pesach* on *Pesach*, *Shavuos* on *Shavuos*, *Sukkos* on *Sukkos*) they conspicuously omit mention of *Rosh Hashana* and *Yom Kippur*, lest one erroneously think that *mitzvas teshuva* is seasonal and limited to the *Yamim Noraim*.

Secondly, the exclusive association of *teshuva* with *din* yields a truncated, distorted view and vision of *teshuva*. The goal of *teshuva* becomes settling accounts, attaining forgiveness and winning a favorable ver-

---

Originally published on TorahWeb.org in 2010

Aseres Yimei Teshuva

dict. Completely absent from that vision is change. The *mitzva* of *teshuva* actually entails affecting formidable, even dramatic personal change – transforming our character and very persona.

צריך לחפש בדעות רעות שיש לו ולשוב מהן
One has to identify his bad character traits and repent from them
מן הכעס ומן האיבה ומן הקנאה וכו'
from anger and enmity and jealousy etc. ...
ומן רדיפת הממון והכבוד ומרדיפת המאכלות וכו'
from pursuit of money, honor and food ...
(*Hilchos Teshuva* 7:3)

משנה שמו, כלומר אני אחר ואיני אותו האיש שעשה אותן המעשים
He changes his name, so as to say that I am different; I am not the same person who committed those [sins]
(*Hilchos Teshuva* 2:4)

Haughtiness, Humility and Din

RABBI MORDECHAI WILLIG

Last week's terrorist attacks[31] are being reported, analyzed, and reacted to in many ways throughout the world. In Yerushalayim, Rav Moshe Shapiro described the proper Torah perspective with the words of the prophet Yona (1:12) "*Besheli*," on my account. A tragedy of biblical proportions is a message from *Hashem*. We must find the lesson in *Nevi'im*, which include only prophecies for all generations (*Megilla* 14a), and learn it well.

In *Sefer Yeshaya*, Yeshaya *Hanavi* chastises *Am Yisrael* for abandoning the good deeds which made them a special people (2:6, Rashi); they content themselves with foreign ideas and not following the Torah's way of thought (2:6, *Metzudos*). The land of the nations became full of silver and gold, with no end to its treasures; it became full of horses, with no end to its chariots (2:7). *Am Yisrael* absorbed the foreign ideas of limitless wealth and military power, which led to haughtiness.

Hashem has a day against every proud and arrogant person, who will be lowered (2:12, Radak); against all the lofty mountains, symbolizing

---

[31] The September 11, 2001 attacks.

Originally published on TorahWeb.org in 2001

pride and perceived invulnerability associated with great heights (2:14, Radak); against every tall tower, and the conceit of great wealth accumulated by overseas trade (2:15, Radak). Humankind's haughtiness will be humbled and men's arrogance will be brought down, and *Hashem* alone will be exalted on that day (2:17).

The destruction of the Twin Towers, the World Trade Center, is a fulfillment of this prophecy. In this pre-messianic era (2:5, Rashi), a wealthy and powerful nation will be humiliated. On that day, people come to understand that only *Hashem* is exalted. As long as man is high and mighty, *Hashem* is not "allowed" to rise above all others, and "that day" cannot occur.

The lesson for the Torah Jew is crystal clear. We must recognize our vulnerability. We dare not allow affluence to lead to arrogance. This unprecedented attack is a message from *Hashem* that He alone is exalted. We dare not ignore it.

The *navi* is confident that *Hashem* will not forgive the arrogant (2:9, Rashi). *Selichos* are introduced by the prerequisite of shamefacedness (*Daniel* 9:7). We knock on *Hashem*'s door as paupers (*rashim*), who have nothing (*Shmuel* II 12:3). The only thing that we have is the understanding that we have nothing.

Based on a passage in *Devarim* (11:12), indicating that in Egypt agricultural success is guaranteed by the abundance of river water whereas Israel is dependent upon rain and on *Hashem* who provides it, the *Gemara* explains that every year that is poor at its beginning becomes prosperous at its end (*Rosh Hashana* 16b). That means that when *Yisrael* make themselves paupers (*rashim*) at the beginning of the year by praying to *Hashem* brokenheartedly, divine mercy and forgiveness are forthcoming (Rashi, *Tosafos*).

Egypt was the center of wealth and power in ancient times. When *Hashem* took us out, and destroyed Mitzrayim, He was "*mashpil gei'im*," He lowered the arrogant. The lesson to us, in *Eretz Yisrael* or elsewhere, is that we avoid arrogance and realize our dependence on *Hashem* for life and sustenance.

When cataclysmic events take place just before *Rosh Hashana*, the message is even more powerful. The books of life and death are open before *Hashem*. Our very existence hangs in the balance.

On the very first *Yom Kippur*, we were threatened with extinction ("*va'achalem*") because of the sin of the golden calf (*Shemos* 32:10). Atonement was achieved only by the lengthy prayers of the humblest of men, Moshe, to whom *Hashem*'s Attributes of Mercy were first revealed ("*le'anav mikedem*"). Only through humility are forgiveness, and survival, possible.

When Bilam wished to destroy us by saying "*Kalem*" ("destroy them"), *Hashem* transformed the curse (*Devarim* 23:6), a literal reversal of the letters, so that it became a blessing by saying "תרועת מלך בו", "and the King's acclaim is in their midst" (*Bemidbar* 23:21) (*Tosafos, Avoda Zara* 4b). The reversal from "*kalem*" to "*melech*" is not merely in the order of the letters. Extinction is avoided only by proclaiming *Hashem*'s kingship.

Hashem created us only for His glory (*Avos* 6:12). When a year ends, so does our lease on life. Only by proclaiming *Hashem*'s kingship, as we do on *Rosh Hashana*, is our lease on life renewed, because we declare our readiness to fulfill the singular purpose of creation, namely the service of *Hashem*. The phrase "*teruas Melech bo*" is found in *malchuyos* and must be said sincerely to reverse the threat of extinction ("*kalem*").

The headlines of last week were written in heaven last *Rosh*

Hashana, as were the terrorist attacks in *Eretz Yisrael*. Apparently, the year 5761 was not poor enough in its beginning. In these biblical times, we can achieve atonement and hasten the redemption only by realizing our poverty, our nothingness, before *Hashem*. In these *Aseres Yemai Teshuva*, we dare not ignore *Hashem*'s thundering message, which teaches precisely this lesson.

Reuven's Teshuva: A Model for Life-Long Growth
RABBI MORDECHAI WILLIG

I

"Reuven returned to the pit" (*Bereishis* 37:29). The *Midrash* (*Bereishis Rabba* 84:19) understands "returned" to mean repented (see Rashi). *Hashem* tells Reuven, "No one has ever repented. You are the first to repent. By your life, your descendant will be the first to call for general repentance, as it is written, 'Return, Yisrael, unto *Hashem*' (*Hoshea* 14:2)." Reuven was the first to repent without being confronted and chastised by *Hashem*, as Adam and Cain were before they repented. His *teshuva* did not stem from fear, but rather was the first repentance stemming from love. This *teshuva mei'ahava* reaches *Hashem*'s throne of glory, as indicated in Hoshea's words, "unto (**ad**) *Hashem*" (*Yoma* 86a; *Midrash Hamevoar*).

Hoshea continues, "Return to (*shuvu el*) *Hashem*" (14:3). Perhaps "return to" means "return toward *Hashem*." Even if one cannot return all the way unto *Hashem* and His throne of glory, he must, nonetheless, move closer to Him.[32] The plural "*shuvu*" may indicate that most *teshuva*

---

[32] The Malbim interprets *el* (14:3) as closer than *ad* (14:2). He believes that "*ad*" is *teshuva*

Originally published on TorahWeb.org in 2004

Aseres Yimei Teshuva

is incomplete. The singular *"shuva"* may refer to the rare person who does reach all the way unto *Hashem*. Anticipated failure to reach the end of the road should not deter one from beginning the journey.

On *Yom Kippur*, even turning to face (*lifnei*) *Hashem* enables purification (*Vayikra* 16:30). In contrast to those whose backs are to *Hashem*, our eyes look to *Hashem* (*Sukkah* 51b). On *Sukkos* we rejoice that *Hashem* grants purity for minimal *teshuva* on *Yom Kippur*. However, we must continue to strive to return toward *Hashem* and even unto Him.

II

In a place where *ba'alei teshuva* stand, the originally righteous, *tzaddikim gemurim*, cannot (*Berachos* 34b). Maharsha rejects the simple meaning, and interprets a *ba'al teshuva* as one who was tempted by sin and overcame the temptation. Thus a *mosheil berucho* is greater than a *chasid hameuleh* (Rambam, *Shemoneh Perakim* chap. 6).

The proof text, " שלום שלום לרחוק ולקרוב- peace, peace to the far and to the near" (*Yeshaya* 57:19), may provide a different interpretation. A *karov* is one who is near to *Hashem*, in contrast to a complete *ba'al teshuva* who has reached all the way to *Hashem* and is considered greater.

Frequently, today's *ba'alei teshuva* observe laws too often neglected by others, who suffer by comparison. This is analogous to righteous converts, whose zeal in performing *mitzvos* is "difficult" for born Jews who are not so meticulous (*Tosafos, Kiddushin* 71a).

"When does a *ba'al teshuva* become an indistinguishable part of the *tzibbur*? When he begins to talk in shul!" This recently printed comment

---

from fear, as the end of the *pasuk* – "for you have stumbled through your iniquity" – is understood (*Yoma* 86b). It is possible, however, to partially reconcile the *midrash* with the Malbim. If *Midrash Hamevoar* is correct, the opening phrase of 14:2 calls for preemptive *teshuva* from love, by which one can reach *Hashem* and His throne. The subsequent phrase, which chastises iniquitous stumblers, refers to *teshuva miyira*. If *el* is indeed less far-reaching than *ad*, then the next *pasuk* (14:3) refers to this lesser form of *teshuva*.

illustrates the extraordinary single-mindedness associated with *ba'alei teshuva*. This includes a refusal to succumb to the failings of most originally-observant Jews.

In the *Shema*, we are commanded to love *Hashem* with all our hearts, souls, and powers (*Devarim* 6:5). Such love is able to overcome all other loves – of others, of life and of money (Rashi). Only by repenting from non-observance or imperfect observance with love, *mei'ahava*, can one reach this level.

The second paragraph of the *Shema* is in plural form and omits "*meodechem*" ("your powers"). The community at large, even if serving *Hashem*, cannot reach the level of loving *Hashem* totally (*Tanchuma Noach*, 2). A *ba'al teshuva*, unburdened by the accepted foibles of the *tzibbur*, is sometimes able to rise above "*tzaddikim gemurim*."

Perhaps "*gemurim*" connotes completed, one who has finished his spiritual development. Although a *tzaddik gamur* may be close to *Hashem*, a *ba'al teshuva*, who is constantly striving for perfection, can surpass him.

Since no one is perfect, all of us should aim to be *ba'alei teshuva*. After all, Reuven repented for only one indiscretion. Yet, since he did so out of love, his example, and the articulation of his descendant Hoshea, continue to inspire *teshuva* forever.

The colloquial usage of *ba'al teshuva*, limited to one who repents from non-observance, is unfortunate. It reflects insufficient desire by observant Jews to transcend their "completed" state of righteousness, formed, and limited, by communal norms. A great *rav* once mistakenly assumed that a questioner was from a non-observant background. The individual protested, "Rebbe, I am not a *ba'al teshuva*." The *rav* responded, "Why not?" Indeed.

Yom Kippur

Yom Kippur, the Yom Tov of Torah Shebe'al Peh

RABBI HERSHEL SCHACHTER

The Talmud tells us (*Ta'anis* 30b) that every year on *Yom Kippur* we commemorate the fact that on that very day, so many years ago, Moshe *Rabbeinu* came down from Mt. Sinai with the second set of *luchos*. But we also know that every year on *Shavuos*, both in the *davening* and in the *kiddush*, we identify *Shavuos* as " Why do we need two holidays for the sake of commemorating the same thing, our receiving the Torah?

R. Betzalel *Hakohen* (the *dayan* of Vilna) suggested that perhaps on *Shavuos* we commemorate our receiving the *Torah Shebichsav*, while on *Yom Kippur* we commemorate our receiving the *Torah Shebe'al Peh* (see *Nefesh HaRav*, p. 293.)

Rav Soloveitchik explained that this suggestion is not merely an arbitrary "*teretz*," that there are two holidays because there are two parts of the Torah, but that it is really a "*milsa debeta'ama*," a matter with a rationale. In the essays of the *Beis Halevi* (#18), a thesis is developed based on many passages in the Talmud, the *Midrash* and the *Zohar*, that on *Shavuos*, when *Hashem* proclaimed the *Aseres Hadibros*, the plan was to give Moshe *Rabbeinu* the *luchos* which would contain all of the Torah.

Originally published on TorahWeb.org in 2004

According to this original plan, there would have been no need for any *Torah Shebe'al Peh*. Everything would have appeared on the *luchos*. After the Jewish people sinned with the *eigel*, they were weakened to the point that it became possible for other nations to dominate them. Those other nations might also possibly dominate the Torah as well, and claim that they are "the chosen nation," since they have the Torah. For this reason, God instituted the *Torah Shebe'al Peh*, which would only remain transmitted among the Jews. In this way, the Jewish people would maintain their uniqueness and their chosenness, by virtue of the fact that they alone would have the oral transmission of the *Torah Shebe'al Peh*. And this is what the prophet *Hoshea* (8:12) was referring to: "I write for them the great things of My Law; like a strange thing they are considered." *Hashem* says: "If I were to have the entire Torah committed to writing, then the enemies of the Jewish people would be able to claim that the Jews were 'strangers,' that they had lost their status as '*am hanivchar*,' and that they (the enemies) were now the chosen people!" (see *Gittin* 60b).

Therefore, the Rav explained, on *Shavuos*, when we commemorate *Ma'amad Har Sinai*, and our receiving the Torah the first time, this really relates only to our receiving the Written Torah; because according to the first plan, there was not going to be any Oral Torah at all. Had *Bnei Yisrael* not sinned, there would not have been a need for it. However, by the time Moshe *Rabbeinu* came down on *Yom Kippur* with the second set of *luchos*, the entire plan had changed, and the first *Yom Kippur* was the beginning of the *Torah Shebe'al Peh* (see *Yemei Zikaron*, p. 245).

In that same prophecy of Hoshea (8:10), the *navi* encourages the Jewish people that "if they emphasize the study of *Mishna* (i.e., *Torah Shebe'al Peh*), God will redeem them" (see *Midrash Vayikra Rabba* 7:3). The Rabbis had a tradition that God, who instilled within all of us a *yetzer hara*, also gave us the Torah to serve as an antidote to that *yetzer hara* (*Kiddushin* 30b). Until the period of the *Anshei Keneses HaGedola*, the dominant *yetzer hara* was for *avoda zara* (see *Sanhedrin* 102b), and apparently the main antidote for that *yetzer hara* was the study of *Torah Shebichsav*. After the *Anshei Keneses HaGedola* succeeded in abolishing the *yetzer hara* for *avoda zara* through their *tefillos* (*Yoma* 69b), a new *yetzer hara* was instilled within us for *minus* (heresy) and *apikorsus*. The main antidote for that *yetzer* is to emphasize the study of *Torah Shebe'al Peh* (see *Be'ikvei Hatzon*, p. 139). The *Seder Olam* records that the death of Chaggai, Zecharia and Malachi was the end of the period of the prophets, i.e., the end of the period of the *Torah Shebichsav*. From that point we were instructed to bend our ears and pay good attention to what the Rabbis have to tell us (i.e., the *Torah Shebe'al Peh*.) The *navi* Hoshea was alluding to our period of history when he spoke of emphasizing the study of *Mishna* and *Torah Shebe'al Peh*.

Regarding *Torah Shebe'al Peh*, the key word is "*mesora*." The attitudes and the style of thinking must be transmitted from *rebbi* to *talmid*. The opening *mishna* in *Avos* tells us that Moshe received the Torah from God at Mt. Sinai, and transmitted it (*mesarah*) to Joshua; and each succeeding generation transmitted the *Torah Shebe'al Peh* to the next generation. There cannot be *Torah Shebe'al Peh* without *mesora*. One lacking such a *mesora* cannot sit down with a *sefer* of *Mishnayos* or *Gemara* and come up with new ideas and claim that they are in the spirit of the *Torah Shebe'al Peh*. Strictly speaking, there is no text to *Torah Shebe'al Peh*. It is a system of ideas and attitudes, giving an approach which was intended to be transmitted orally, along with the full depth and flavor of meaning and understanding of those attitudes and ideas. At one point in history, the Rabbis were afraid that due to the many persecutions and exiles, much of the Oral Torah would be forgotten, so they felt compelled to preserve it by writing it down. But that text cannot really stand alone. It requires a strong *mesora* to understand what the text of the Talmud is driving at. The *mesora* did not end when R. Yehuda *Hanasi* edited the *Mishna*; nor did it end when Ravina and Rav Ashi edited the *Gemara*. The *mesora* has extended to our generation and will continue to be transmitted.

From the very beginning and throughout the entire period of the Second Temple, there were groups who challenged the *mesora* of the Oral Torah. In later years there were Karaites, and yet later, the *Haskala* movement. As we say in the *Haggada*, "בכל דור ודור עומדים עלינו לכלותנו -in every generation they rise against us to destroy us." The *navi* Hoshea has warned us that in our period in history, in order to maintain our identity and not get washed away by assimilation, we must emphasize *mesora* of the Oral Torah.

Often there are traditions which we find difficult to understand, or difficult to accept. Parts of the *Torah Shebe'al Peh* seem not to be politically correct. Rav Soloveitchik offered a homiletic interpretation of the passage in the *Gemara* (*Menachos* 29b), that Rabbi Akiva, rather than be apologetic, would be more meticulous and place extra emphasis on all of the *halachos* at which the enemies of Torah had thrown thorns. Rather than discard anything that at first glance we are uncomfortable with, we must preserve our *mesora*, and try to develop a deeper insight into what it represents. The superficial mind will often misunderstand Torah, and cast away very precious traditions.

This added theme of *Yom Kippur* as being the day to commemorate the start of the *Torah Shebe'al Peh* was especially obvious during the period of the Second Temple. Every *Yom Kippur*, the Rabbis would make the *Kohen Gadol* swear that he would not deviate from the Oral Tradition in doing the *avoda*.

Many years later, the Orthodox Jewish community of Alexandria would have an annual march – on *Yom Kippur* – to declare that they subscribed to the *Torah Shebe'al Peh*. Rav Soloveitchik felt that our practice to recite the lengthy *seder ha'avoda* in *chazaras hashatz* of *Musaf* is also for the same purpose: to reaffirm our commitment to the *mesora* and the *Torah Shebe'al Peh* (see Rabbi Joseph B. Soloveitchik, *Before Hashem You Shall Be Purified*, p. 144).

The Torah of Chesed and the Day of Chesed

RABBI HERSHEL SCHACHTER

The *Mishna* at the end of *Masseches Ta'anis* records that one of the two happiest days of the year is *Yom Kippur*. The *Gemara* there gives two reasons for this special joyous atmosphere. One of the reasons is that on *Yom Kippur* we celebrate the anniversary of our receiving the second set of *luchos*. Every *Shavuos*, however, we celebrate the anniversary of *Ma'amad Har Sinai* and refer to that day as *zeman Matan Toraseinu*. Why do we need two *Yamim Tovim* celebrating our receiving of the Torah?

The *Beis Halevi* (*drush* #18) explains that according to the original plan there was not going to be any *Torah Shebe'al Peh*. Rather, everything would have been included in *Torah Shebechsav*. Only after the *cheit ha'eigel*, when *Hakadosh Baruch Hu* decided to punish *Bnei Yisrael* and allow other nations to rule over them, was it necessary to give us the *Torah Shebe'al Peh*. The *umos ha'olam* dominating the Jewish people would be able to claim that we lost our status as *am hanivchar* and that they took over that special role. The *Midrash* comments on a *pasuk* (*Hoshea* 8:12) that if the entire Torah were to have been written down, the Jewish people would have become like "outsiders" and "strangers." Therefore *Hashem* gave us the *Torah Shebe'al Peh* which was not supposed to be shared at all with other nations.

Originally published on TorahWeb.org in 2014

Through the transmission of the *Torah Shebe'al Peh* from generation to generation, we preserved (even in the eyes of the world) our unique status as *am hanivchar*. We alone had this vast section of Torah that was never shared with anyone else. On *Shavuos* we celebrate the receiving the *Torah Shebichsav*, while on *Yom Kippur* we celebrate the receiving of the *Torah Shebe'al Peh*.

In *sifrei chasidus* an idea is developed, based on a passage in the *Zohar*, that the *Torah Shebichsav* was generally given *bemiddas hadin* while the *Torah Shebe'al Peh* represents *middas hachesed*. An obvious example of this would be the way the *Chumash* describes the punishment for one who maims another person. The simple reading of the text of the *Torah Shebichsav* would lead one to believe that we actually maim the assailant, as the *pasuk* reads, "עין תחת עין - an eye for an eye" (*Shemos* 21:24). The *Torah Shebe'al Peh*, however, teaches us that we should not take that literally. Perhaps "*ayin tachas ayin*" is the punishment that the person deserves *bemiddas hadin*, but the *middas hachesed* dictates that instead of maiming him we have him make a cash payment.

The other reason the *Gemara* in *Ta'anis* gives as to why *Yom Kippur* is a day of such unusually joyous celebration is that *Yom Kippur* is the day on which *Hashem* forgives all of our sins. The forgiving of sins is certainly *bemiddas hachesed*. When we refer to *Yom Kippur* in the *piyutim* as a *yom hadin* ("לא-ל עורך דין, ביום דין") we don't mean *din* in the sense of strict judgment, but rather describe the day as a *yom hadin* in the sense of a day of calculations (like "*din vecheshbon*"). *Yom Kippur* is a *yom hachesed* and not a *yom hadin*. It certainly fits in that the *Torah Shebe'al Peh* was given on *Yom Kippur* since it is the day of *chesed* and the *Torah Shebe'al Peh* represents *middas hachesed*.

Rav Soloveitchik pointed out that according the simple reading of the *pessukim* in *parshas Acharei Mos*, the *korbonos* on *Yom Kippur* were brought in three units: first there was *avodah* done by the *kohain gadol* wearing his golden uniform, then *avodah* done by *kohain gadol* wearing his special white uniform, and finally, the third unit of *avodas hakorbonos* was performed by the *kohain gadol* wearing the golden uniform. The *Torah Sheb'al Peh* teaches us that we should not follow the simple reading of the *pessukim*, and the *avodah* must be divided into five units and not three. *Yom Kippur* is the day on which we celebrate our receiving the *Torah Sheb'al Peh* so perhaps this is the reason why the text of the *chumash* is so vague on this point and we are required to follow the tradition of the *Torah Sheb'al Peh* to know the correct way of doing the *avodah*.

And Rejoice in Trembling: The Mitzva of Seudas Erev Yom Kippur

RABBI YAKOV HABER

The *mitzva* of eating on *Erev Yom Kippur* at first glance presents an enigma. The festive nature of the meal seems to contradict the serious mood of the next day, which is filled with beseeching, pleading and multiple confessions repeated ten times in five separate *tefillot*.

Rabbeinu Yona (*Sha'arei Teshuva* 4:8) offers three explanations for this meal. First, a person expresses joy anticipating the day when his sins will be forgiven. This joy indicates a person's concern about his sins and their effects and his yearning for them to be removed. Second, just as a festive meal is served on *Yom Tov*, so too we have a festive meal on *Erev Yom Kippur* reflecting the joy of *Yom Kippur*. This meal cannot take place on *Yom Kippur* because of the obligation to fast, so it takes place a day earlier. Third, we prepare for the service of the day to pray and confess our sins by strengthening ourselves beforehand by partaking of a meal. Much discussion as to the halachic ramifications of these three reasons appears in

---

Originally published on TorahWeb.org in 2009

poskim. (See *Moadim beHalacha* for an overview.)

This meal further demonstrates a dual theme begun on *Rosh Hashana*. On the one hand, the *shofar* blasts instill a sense of dread and awe; in the language of Rambam, the *shofar* calls out: "Awaken O you slumberers, and examine your deeds!" On the other hand, we partake of festive meals in accordance with the passage in *Nechemia*: "Go and eat savory foods... for the joy of God is your stronghold!" (*Nechemia* 8:10). So too on *Yom Kippur*, the climax of the Ten Days of Repentance, we are filled with dread at the final day of the "sealing of the judgment" of *Rosh Hashana*, the day when the *beinonim* will be judged whether their repentance merits their being inscribed in the Book of Life. But on the other hand, in the language of Rabbi Akiva (*Yoma* 8:9), "Praiseworthy are you, Israel, before Whom are you purified, and Who purifies you? Your Father in heaven! ... *Hashem* is the *mikveh* of Israel. Just as a *mikveh* purifies the impure, so too the Holy One Blessed is He, purifies Israel." *Rabbeinu* Yona's first reason especially highlights these seemingly contradictory themes. We are happy, says *Rabbeinu* Yona, for the opportunity to have our sins forgiven. But this very happiness "serves as testimony about his worry over his sin, and his sorrow over his iniquities."

"וגילו ברעדה - And be joyful with trembling" (*Tehillim* 2:11) is an oft-quoted verse expressing this common duality of fear and love, trembling and joy (see *Berachos* 30b). It is especially relevant for *Yom HaKippurim*, a day suffused with *Hashem*'s Divine Presence, which, many commentaries explain, is the *mikveh* referenced by R. Akiva which causes the purification from sin. Being in the presence of the Divine is frightening but uplifting, paralyzing but gladdening. The same dual sense of awe overcoming the *Kohen Gadol* entering the *Kodesh Hakodashim* with the incense – clearly accompanied by his joy in serving as the agent of achieving atonement for the sins of Israel – guides us in our synagogues, our *mikdeshei me'at* (minor sanctuaries), on this unique day.

Yom Kippur

Rav Yosef Dov Soloveitchik *zt"l* suggests that the *viduy* (confession) on *Yom Kippur* serves not in the classic role of the *viduy* of *teshuva* but as a *viduy* on a *korban*. The one bringing the *korban* must lean his hands on it and mention the sin for which it was brought. This is in addition to the *viduy* and *teshuva* process already begun before bringing the offering. So too on *Yom Kippur*, the *teshuva* process was already to have begun before *Yom Kippur*. We recite *viduy* on the vehicle of atonement, which is the Day of Atonement itself. Chasidic masters would only refer to this day as *Yom HaKadosh*. The Talmud calls it *Yoma*, "the Day." Its holiness and mystery not surprisingly fill us each year with the sense of *"gilu birada!"* May we merit with our *teshuva* and our confession the dual promise of *kappara* and *tahara*, atonement and purification, "כי ביום הזה, יכפר עליכם לטהר אתכם מכל חטאתיכם לפני ה' תטהרו!‎ - For on this day He shall atone for you to purify you; from all your sins before God, you shall be purified!"

The Two Goats and the True Self

RABBI YAKOV HABER

One of the most prominent aspects of the *Avodas Yom HaKippurim* in the *Mikdash* is the service of the *shnei haseirim*, the two goats. The *halacha* requires them to be identical in height and appearance (*Yoma* 6:1). A lottery was performed on them with one being designated as a *korban laShem*, its blood being sprinkled in the Holy of Holies, something done with no other *korban* other than the bull of the *Kohen Gadol* also offered on Yom Kippur. The second was designated as the *sa'ir la'azazel* to be thrown off a steep cliff and which, in the language of the *Mishna*, "did not reach halfway [down] before it was turned into a pile of limbs" (ibid. 6:6).

This out-of-the-ordinary service is clearly one of the *chukim* of the Torah, with no explicit reason given for it. However, many approaches have been taken attempting to uncover a glimpse into the Divine messages inherent within this service.[33] I have heard an approach whose source I do not recall which seems to match the details of the *mitzva* well.[34] This ap-

---

[33] See Ramban, Rav Hirsch, and Rav Soloveitchik in *Al HaTeshuva* for various approaches.
[34] I would be indebted to a reader who can provide the source.

Originally published on TorahWeb.org in 2013

proach can serve as a central focus of what we attempt to accomplish on the "*Shabbos Shabbason.*"

God created man originally pure, without a tendency toward evil (see *Koheles* 7:29). The *yetzer hara* was external, as represented by the primeval snake. When man sinned, the evil inclination became internalized. This led to a state of "*tov vara,*" in which good and evil were seemingly intermingled in the human mind. Confusion, lack of clarity, and indecision became the new reality for mankind. Only by studying and fulfilling the Torah would mankind be able to rise beyond the confusion of this new reality. However, the ultimate plan of the Creator is to restore the original state of perfection, which will occur in the Messianic era with the circumcision of the heart (see Ramban to *Nitzavim* 30:6), meaning the elimination of the evil within each and every one of us.

However, even before that era, *Yom Kippur* gives us a glimpse of our real selves. The two goats similar in appearance both represent the same individual. Each of us has a "split personality": the fundamental, true personality and the superimposed, fake persona infused into us with the entrance of the *yetzer hara*. On this day, we separate the real from the fake, the fundamental from the artificial. The real personality, represented by the *sa'ir laShem*, created in the image of God, is brought into the Holy of Holies, symbolizing man's calling to cleave to God throughout his existence. The fake persona is dispatched and meets a violent end on a rocky mountain. This represents the end of evil, the end of confusion, the end of indecision.

Yom Kippur is the day when we "take a break from the world", when we rest not only from labor, but we "rest" from most aspects of *olam hazeh* (see Rambam *Hilchos Shevisas Asor* 1:5-6). The numerous drives and desires inherent in the world, when channeled properly, elevate us, and even make us higher than the angels who do not have the ability to elevate the physical. This occurs when we listen to our real personality. But the drives of the world also have the potential to, and often do, drive us away from God when we view these drives and desires as reality itself. This is a result of the fake persona within us. On *Yom Kippur* we rediscover who we really are.

This concept is further highlighted by a beautiful insight of the Maharal (*Nesivos Olam, Nesiv Ha'avoda*). We recite the phrase "ברוך שם כבוד מלכותו לעולם ועד - Blessed is the name of His glorious kingdom for all eternity," silently during the whole year but aloud on *Yom HaKippurim*. The *Midrash* explains that Moshe *Rabbeinu* heard the angels reciting this verse and taught it to the Jews. But since it is an angelic declaration of Divine sovereignty, we recite it silently. Why then do we recite it at all if we are not angels? Maharal explains that we do so because there is part of us that **is** angelic; the soul, the core of who we really are, is constantly on the level of the angels capable of declaring this angelic form of acceptance of *Malchus Shamayim*. But this part of us is seemingly inaccessible to us, hidden as it were in the inner recesses of our existence. We recite "*baruch sheim*" silently during the rest of the year because only the silent, hidden part of us is on that level. On *Yom Kippur*, though, when the "soul emerges," we are capable of reciting this verse aloud. *Yom Kippur* shows us who we really are.

With this renewed awareness of the intense sanctity of the human personality and especially of the covenantal Jewish people, coupled with our repentance, may we achieve, with Divine mercy, forgiveness for our sins and the reawakening of the central attitude necessary to face the "regular world" as we march one step closer to the era when evil will be eradicated forever.

The Torah's Song; the Song of Torah

RABBI YAKOV HABER

I

"ועתה כתבו לכם את השירה הזאת ולמדה את בני ישראל, שימה בפיהם למען תהיה לי השירה הזאת לעד בבני ישראל", "And now, write for you **this song**, and teach it to the Children of Israel, place it in their mouth, in order that this song shall be a witness for the Children of Israel" (*Devarim* 31:19).

This verse is inherently vague. On the one hand, the context in which it is written, before *Shiras Ha'azinu* and immediately preceding verses predicting the Jewish people's entry into the Land of Israel, their turning to idol worship and subsequent punishment, followed by: "and this song will testify as a witness" (v. 21), indicates that the song being referenced is *Shiras Ha'azinu*, the song of Jewish history. On the other hand, the nearby verse, "And when Moshe finished writing down the words of this Torah in a scroll until completion" (v. 24), and the subsequent command to the Levites, "Take this *sefer Torah* and place it on the side of the *Aron Habris*, and it should remain there as a testimony" (v. 26) imply that the reference is to the entire Torah.

Indeed, the commentaries explain that two meanings inhere

Originally published on TorahWeb.org in 2016

within the commandment of writing "*hashira hazos*," one referring to the specific portion of *Shiras Ha'azinu* and one to the entire Torah (see *Rashi, Ralbag, Sha'arei Aharon*). The Talmud (*Sanhedrin* 21b) teaches that even if one inherits a *sefer* Torah from his ancestors, he still has an obligation to write one himself, and quotes *Devarim* 31:19 as the source for this ruling. This implies that the entire Torah is being referenced. But the Talmud (*Nedarim* 38a) also indicates that both *Shiras Ha'azinu* and the entire Torah are being referenced.

Many approaches have been suggested as to how the commandment "to write this song" can imply the *mitzva* to write the entire Torah. After all, the entire Torah is presumably not a song! Rambam (*Hilchos Sefer Torah* 7:1) famously explains that the commandment is primarily to write the song of *Ha'azinu*. But since the Torah cannot be written in separate mini-scrolls (*parshiyos, parshiyos*), the entire Torah must be written. Rav Naftali Tzvi Yehuda Berlin *zt"l* (Netziv) in his *Ha'amek Davar* (see also *Torah Temima*) challenges this understanding since the Torah's intent might be to write *Ha'azinu* separately, just as there is a commandment to write the *parshiyos* of *tefillin* separately.

Netziv alternatively suggests that the phrase "this song" has both meanings. Firstly, it refers to the song of *Ha'azinu*; secondly it refers to the entire Torah. Because of this second meaning, the plural "*kisvu*" is used, since every Jew has an obligation to write a *sefer* Torah. By contrast, only Moshe was commanded to write *Ha'azinu*. As to why the Torah is called a song, *Netziv* elsewhere (introduction to *Ha'amek She'eila, Kidmas Ha'emek* 2:3) explains that there are two types of writing: prose and poetry, the latter also being referred to as verse or song. *Hashem* formulated the Torah in a purposefully ambiguous manner to allow for multiple meanings to be derived from the text.[35] As any student of the Talmud knows, *Chazal* are at-

---

[35] In *Ha'amek Davar*, Netziv references *Kidmas Ha'emek* to explain why the Torah is called a song. There, the nature of Torah being written in a manner to allow for many layers of interpretation is discussed at length. Admittedly, I did not find a direct reference there to

tuned to every extra letter, every textual anomaly and every textual similarity, from which many *halachos* are derived. (See also Malbim's *Ayeles Hashachar*.) R. Akiva is famously described as deriving "mounds and mounds of *halachos*" from even the crowns on top of the letters (*Menachos* 29b.) In the *aggados*, *midrashim*, and in *sifrei chasidus*, verses are interpreted *bederech haremez*, by way of allusion, often taking them totally out of context. All of these meanings lie within the "song" of Torah, purposefully implanted by its Author to enable those who study it to extract those multiple layers of meaning from the text.[36] As an additional example, Malbim, in his commentary to *Tanach*, often collects many different interpretations of the commentaries preceding him and shows how each interpretation is alluded to in the text. The Gaon of Vilna, toward the end of his life, worked on demonstrating how all the *halachos* of the Torah are alluded to in the text of the Torah.[37]

This important idea developed by Netziv gives us great insight as to the nature and complexity of how a finite text of the Torah can ultimately have infinite interpretations. The Torah is a manifestation of the *chochmas Hashem*. In the language of the *Zohar*, "קודשא בריך הוא ואוריתא חד הוא"- *Hashem* and the Torah are one." Learning Torah is, on a deeper plane, studying *Hashem* Himself. In one of the daily blessings recited over Torah study we refer to those who know Torah as "*yodei shemecha*," "those who know Your name." Ramban writes in his introduction to Torah that if we were to remove all the spaces between the words of the Torah and create different words by spacing them differently, we would be reading different names of *Hashem*. Rav Schneur Zalman of Liadi, the first Rebbe of

---

the concept of the Torah being called a song. Above, I wrote what I thought the Netziv's intent was.

[36] In his introduction to *Chumash Devarim*, Netziv explains that the title *Mishneh Torah* should not be translated as "repetition of Torah" but as "double-meaning Torah." Specifically in this *Chumash*, even on a *peshat* level, multiple layers of meaning often apply. *Ha'amek Davar* throughout *Devarim*, including here, applies this principle repeatedly.

[37] Famously, he posited that all the 613 *mitzvos* are alluded to in the very first word, "*bereishis*."

Lubavitch, explains, based on kabbalistic sources, that each commandment represents a different aspect of Divinity. This gives us insight into how the Talmud could describe *Hashem* as "wearing *tefillin*" (*Berachos* 6a) or "wrapping Himself in a *tallis*" (*Rosh Hashana* 17b). The *mitzvos* which we do are an allegorical representation of Divine ideas. The real "*tallis*" and "*tefillin*" are esoteric Divine concepts; the physical *tallis* and *tefillin* allow finite human beings to connect to these infinite concepts. The "song" of Torah, with its multi-dimensional and even infinite layers of meaning, provides for us a window into the Eternity and all-encompassing nature of its Author.[38]

II

Yom HaKippurim was established originally as the Day of Atonement for the sins of *Klal Yisrael*, since it was on that day that Moshe *Rabbeinu* came down for the final time from *Har Sinai* with the second *luchos*. This central event was the climax of the *kappara* for the sin of the golden calf. In essence then, the Torah was given a second time on *Yom Kippur*. Since the second *luchos*, not the first, were the ones that lasted, the Jewish people are perhaps more connected to this day of *Matan Torah* than even to *Shavuos*. The last *mishna* in *Masseches Ta'anis* teaches that there was no happier holiday in Israel than *Yom HaKippurim*, since it was the day of the giving of the Torah. Perhaps the reason that *Shavuos* is not listed as day of the giving of the Torah is that since the first *luchos* were broken, we relate to *Yom HaKippurim* more intensely.

But of course, *Yom Kippur* is not just the day of the second *Matan Torah*; it also the "*keitz selicha umechila*," "culmination of pardon and forgiveness"; it is a day of national and individual repentance and return to God. It is a day whose very essence is infused with Divine

---

[38] For further elaboration on these themes, see "Talmud Torah at the Center of Family Life" http://torahweb.org/audio/rsch_091805.html, by *Mori veRabi* Rav Hershel Schachter *shlita*.

Presence and mercy; it is a day we **enter into** as we would a *mikveh*, not just a day that we experience. "*Mikveh Yisrael Hashem.*" Just as a *mikveh* purifies the impure, so *Hakadosh Baruch Hu* purifies Israel (*Mishna Yoma* 8:9). Apparently, there is a strong link between *Yom Kippur*'s role as a day of *teshuva* and *kappara*, and its role as a day of *Matan Torah*.

Rav Betzalel Zolty *zt"l*, the former chief rabbi of Jerusalem (*Mishnas Ya'avetz* 54:3-4), elaborates at length about how *teshuva* is not just the commitment to not violate *aveiros* and not just the determination to perform the *mitzvos* properly, but to return to the totality of Torah and specifically to its study – "and in it we will speak day and night" (*Tehillim* 1:2). This is a manifestation of the highest form of *teshuva*, *teshuva mei'ahava*, out of love. Among his other sources for this concept, Rav Zolty quotes the *haftara* for *Shabbos Shuva*, wherein Hoshea the prophet adjures us: "שובה ישראל עד ה' א-לקיך כי כשלת בע‑וניך: קחו עמכם דברים ושובו אל ה' - Return O Israel unto God for you have stumbled in your sin; **take words with you** and return to God." On this, the *Sifrei* (*Ha'azinu* 306:2) comments that the phrase, "Take words with you" refers to words of Torah. Similarly, we implore *Hashem* daily in the blessing of *teshuva*, "השיבנו אבינו לתורתך - return us, our Father, to Your Torah," and only afterward do we pray, "והחזירנו בתשובה שלמה לפניך - and bring us back in complete repentance before You."[39]

The song of Torah has to permeate our thoughts, our words as well as our actions. Perhaps demonstrating the idea of the Torah being called a song, the Torah is read with *trop*, musical notes, and the Jewish people have traditionally sung the Talmud to a characteristic *niggun*. Just as a symphony has many different instruments, each with its own purpose, all joining together to create a majestic musical masterpiece, so too does each *mitzva* elevate another limb, physical and spiritual, and each Torah idea develop another aspect of our inner personality in

---

[39] Refer also to the *shiur* referenced in the previous footnote.

our quest for *sheleimus*.

May *Hashem* grant us the assistance to realign our lives individually and collectively to play our unique role in the Divine symphony that is the Torah, the greatest gift that *Hashem* has bestowed upon His creation.

Teshuva on Yom Kippur
RABBI MICHAEL ROSENSWEIG

The obligation to repent (*teshuva*) is a central theme in Judaism that applies throughout the year and throughout one's lifetime. *Chazal* register the effectiveness of *teshuva* even at the end of a lifetime of sin: "אפילו רשע כל ימיו ועשה תשובה באחרונה אין מזכירים לו עוונותיו - even one who is an evildoer all his life, but repents at the last, his sins are not mentioned to him."

However, *teshuva* attains special prominence in the period defined as *Aseres Yemei Teshuva*, inaugurated by *Rosh Hashana* and culminating with *Yom Kippur* (*Rosh Hashana* 18b). The special requirement of *teshuva* during these days cannot be attributed only to the urgent need to achieve a positive judgment for the upcoming year. Nor does the fact that this period, punctuated by the spiritually inspiring experiences of *Rosh Hashana* and *Yom Kippur*, is particularly conducive to accomplishing *teshuva*, sufficiently explain the phenomenon.

The singular status and character of *teshuva* in this period is reflected in numerous sources. The *Sefer Hachinuch* (no. 364) concludes his general discussion of the *mitzva* of *teshuva* by asserting that one who neglects to engage in this ubiquitous obligation of repentance specifically on *Yom Kippur* is guilty of actively rejecting this imperative. The Rambam

Originally published on TorahWeb.org in 2005

(*Hilchos Teshuva* 2:7) formulates the broader *mitzva* of *teshuva* as the obligation to accompany one's repentance with *viduy* – confession. Only in connection with *Yom Kippur* does he actually record an obligation to repent! R. Yona, in his classic exposition on *teshuva*, *Sha'arei Teshuva* (2:4, 17), lists *teshuva* on *Yom Kippur* as an obligation independent of the universal *mitzva* of *teshuva*, based on the verse, "לפני ד' תטהרו", "before *Hashem* you shall be purified" (*Vayikra* 16:30), which he interprets not as a promise but as an imperative. What is the special character of repentance on *Yom Kippur* reflected by these unusual treatments?

The constant obligation to do *teshuva* is generated by the act of sin which distances the transgressor from *Hashem* and triggers punishment. In order to redress this specific violation and absolve oneself, one must engage in the process of repentance and confession. The Rambam begins *Hilchos Teshuva* with a description of these factors and this process. The focus of such repentance is the neutralization of each specific sin and the restoration of the relationship with *Hashem* that prevailed prior to the individual infraction.

However, precisely because the period of *Aseres Yemei Teshuva* is triggered by the calendar, by the need to face judgment and by the opportunity to begin a new year with an intensified religious commitment, the focus and orientation of the *teshuva* is different. The fact that one needs to address all previous transgressions at once contributes to the singular nature and ambition of *Yom Kippur*'s *teshuva* process. In the effort to contend with and confront all sins, one necessarily engages in a holistic reassessment that includes but transcends individual halachic violations. Moreover, the *teshuva* of this period is linked to the central motif of total devotion to *Hashem* (*kulo laShem*) that is accentuated on *Yom Kippur*, a day of pure spirituality in which human beings vie with the angels on high in expressing their absolute and single-minded religious commitment.

The long confession of *Yom Kippur* (*al cheit*) begins with accidental transgressions (*ones*) that do not actually engender punishment and that possibly do not even require repentance according to the rules that govern the rules of *teshuva* all year long. The fact that intentional and accidental infractions (*ones veratzon*) are grouped together at the outset of the process, despite evident crucial differences, reflects the wide range and transcendent ambition of a more holistic repentance. The list includes broader categories of sin, as well as the mere intention to sin, alongside specific violations. It is noteworthy that the entire confession litany is recited irrespective of specific guilt. Significantly, the *halacha* asserts that one continue on *Yom Kippur* to confess transgressions that were neutralized in years past. Moreover, we seek on this day not merely to restore our relationship with *Hashem* but to intensify and enhance it. The sense of alienation experienced due to sin becomes a catalyst for the refashioning of one's religious persona.

The confession list introduces *olah* (burnt offering sacrifices) violations before *chatas* (sin offerings) transgressions. This seems perplexing since the offering of *korban chatas* always precedes *korban olah* (*Zevachim* 7b; see the parallel discussion of *Magen Avraham Orach Chaim* 1:5.) However, it is the *olah* that uniquely captures the opportunity, ambition and focus of *Yom Kippur*. While the *chatas* focuses on neutralizing each individual sin, and that, too, is a priority on *Yom Kippur*, it is the *olah* that conveys the total commitment of "*kulo laShem*," snymbolized by the fact that it is totally consumed on the *mizbeach*. Moreover, the *olah* addresses the totality of the religious personality and experience, confronting also the neglect of spiritual opportunity (*mitzvos aseh*) and improper attitudes and intentions (*hirhurei aveira*). The *teshuva* of *Yom Kippur*, then, accentuates *olah* even as it includes *chatas*.

This ambitious, transcendent and holistic approach to *teshuva* is conveyed by the independent source for repentance on *Yom Kippur* that is cited by R. Yona, "לפני ד' תטהרו", "before *Hashem* you shall be purified."

Tahara (ritual purity) demands a holistic and comprehensive approach; it cannot be achieved piecemeal. Only one who immerses himself fully in the *mikveh*, addressing all of his impurities simultaneously, can attain the objective. *Sefer Hachinuch* projects the idea that while ignoring individual violations year-round is an act of neglect and the squandering of an opportunity, the failure to confront the challenge of *teshuva* on *Yom Kippur* in the context of the stakes and opportunities for a comprehensive realignment of one's relationship with *Hashem* constitutes an emphatic rejection of the very concept of *teshuva*. The Rambam formulates repentance as an obligation only on *Yom Kippur* precisely because the artificial timeframe underscores and facilitates *teshuva*'s transcendent orientation.

Despite their assertion of the unique character of the *teshuva* of *Yom Kippur*, it is noteworthy that, unlike R. Yona, the Rambam and *Sefer Hachinuch* integrated their treatment of *teshuva* on *Yom Kippur* with their discussion of year-round and life-long *teshuva*. In fact, the Rambam omits any reference to *teshuva* in *Hilchos Shevisas Asor*, the section dedicated to the laws of *Yom Kippur*. This reflects a profound truth that is echoed by the Maharsha (*Megilla* 32a). He notes that Moshe's enactment that one begin to review the *halachos* of a particular festival in the preceding month was never articulated with respect to *Rosh Hashana* and *Yom Kippur*. The Maharsha explains that the theme of *teshuva* that dominates this period belongs to the entire year, while Moshe's *takana* applies only to themes that are unique to a particular festival. The concept of *teshuva*, as manifest on *Yom Kippur*, is a paradigm that is meant to inspire us to achieve great spiritual heights and to develop a comprehensive halachic personality all year round. Because of its singular character, *Yom Kippur* is both the most unique and most relevant day of the year!

Yom Kippur: The Day of the Kohen Gadol

RABBI MICHAEL ROSENSWEIG

The centerpiece of Yom HaKippurim, the most singular and pivotal day in the Jewish calendar (referred to thrice in the Torah as "achas bashana"), is the elaborate avoda that enables the Kohen Gadol to enter into the innermost sanctum (lifnai velifnim) of the Beis Hamikdash. Even in the aftermath of the Temple's destruction, the elaborate description and ecstatic depiction of the avoda dominates tefillas Musaf, mesmerizing all those who contemplate and reflect upon it. Chazaras hashatz of Musaf on Yom Kippur is an inimitable experience, though it is barely "uneshalma parim sefaseinu" relative to the drama that unfolded in the actual avoda.

The *avoda* is exotic, unique and profound in its elaborate shifting between *Kohen Gadol* wardrobes (five *tevilos*, and ten *kiddushin*), in its range of interspersed *korbanos*, in the drama of the two parallel and opposing *seirim* (*lifnai velifnim* and *la'azazel*), as well as other singular features. However, it is particularly atypical in projecting a single actor, the *Kohen Gadol*, who not only presides but almost completely dominates this intricately complex halachic protocol that is vital to every member of *Klal Yisrael* and to the collective of *Am Yisrael* (Rambam, *Hilchos Teshuva* 2:7, "זמן תשובה לכל, ליחיד ולרבים, והוא קץ מחילה וסליחה לישראל", "the time set aside

Originally published on TorahWeb.org in 2017

is consistent with this theme. Extraordinary steps (that defy the routine rules of *safek* and *chazaka* – preparing a replacement, a replacement wife, undergoing extra purity measures, etc.) are taken to preclude any mishap that might sideline him or preclude him from his destiny to preside over the *avodas Yom HaKippurim*. It is possible that numerous norms that regulate the *Kohen Gadol*'s life and status year-round stem from the anticipation of his *Yom Kippur* mission that defines and qualifies his very persona! (See Rav Soloveitchik's explanation of Rambam, *Hilchos Issurei Biah* 17:13 and *Klei Hamikdash* 5:10 – the prohibition against multiple spouses.)

The most striking evidence of the intricate bond between the *Kohen Gadol* and *Yom Kippur* is found in the protocol of the *avoda* itself, as well as in its presentation in *Parashas Acharei Mos*. The Torah introduces *avodas Yom HaKippurim* by focusing on the circumstances and methodology in which Aharon and his *Kohen Gadol* successors would warrant entry into the *Kodesh Hakodashim*. We encounter "בזאת יבוא אהרון אל הקודש - with this shall Aharon enter the Holy," (*Vayikra* 16:3), many verses before the Torah finally elaborates the concept of *Yom Kippur*! Moreover, what enable the national *korbanos* – the *seirim*, etc. – that achieve the collective *kappara* for *Klal Yisrael* are the personal *korbanos* – the *par* and *ayil* – of the *Kohen Gadol* which precede them. The *Yom Kippur* protocol calls for three *viduyim* and ten *shemos Hashem*, two thirds of which stem from the personal *par* of the *Kohen Gadol*, the blood of which is ultimately actually merged with the communal *sa'ir hapenimi* when they are sprinkled on the *mizbeach haketores*! It is fascinating that the Talmud (and commentaries) debate the exact status of these offerings which had to be personally financed by the *Kohen Gadol*, but which play such a central and indispensable role in the *Yom Kippur* process. (See *Yoma* 6b-8a, 49b-51b. The issues that reflect the status of these *korbanos* [*korban yachid, tzibbur, shutafim*] – *temura, hutra betzibbur, chataos hameisos*, etc. are complex and subject to numerous interpretations. I hope to elaborate these in a different context.) Numerous other indications cement the impression that the *Kohen Gadol* is more than merely the appropriate, even the exclusive, functionary of the *avoda*.

Evidently, the *avodas Yom HaKippurim* requires the *Kohen Gadol* because *Yom Kippur* itself is a day that both enhances and is enhanced and elevated by the ideal persona of the *Kohen Gadol*. The *Kohen Gadol*'s role and the norms that govern his conduct and standards accentuate the interlocking themes of *kulo laShem*, total devotion and loyalty of *Hashem*'s service, as well as an absolute commitment to the collective of *Klal Yisrael*. The *Kohen Gadol* even sets aside personal grief and bereavement in order to uphold the principles of Divine and national service. He is *makriv onen*, and abstains from *tumas meis* even for close family members. Only a *meis mitzva*, perhaps because that is a *Klal Yisrael* obligation, justifies his ritual impurity. While the Rambam rules that regular *kohanim* may not wear their priestly garb when they are not in service, he excludes the *Kohen Gadol* from this injunction (Rambam *Hilchos Klei Hamikdash* 8:12, *Hilchos Kilayim* 10:32 – see Ra'avad and Radvaz ad loc.). Radvaz links this distinction to the fact that the *Kohen Gadol* is enjoined from disrupting his *mikdash* duties even for family bereavement: "*min hamikdash lo yeitzei*," "he should not leave the *Mikdash*." The *Kohen Gadol* is existentially always connected to the *avodas Hashem*, as his idealistic persona embodies *kulo laShem* and absolute devotion to *Klal Yisrael*. The Rambam rules (*Hilchos Klei Hamikdash* 5:7 – absent a known source!) that the *Kohen Gadol* should live in Yerushalayim! Perhaps this view is consistent with his celebrated position (Rambam *Peirush Hamishnayos Sukkah* and *Rosh Hashana*, and reflected also in *Hilchos Beis Habechirah* chapter 6) that Yerushalyim has the legal status of *mikdash*, as well. Moreover, Yerushalyim ("עיר שחוברה לה יחדיו' – שלא נתחלקה לשבטים - a city united with itself" [*Tehillim* 122:3] – it was not divided among the tribes" [*Yoma* 12a]) represents the locus of collective *Klal Yisrael*! Even when the *Kohen Gadol* leaves the "*mikdash*," he remains ensconced in the *mikdash* region!

During the *Musaf* services, we focus on the personal fate, success, and persona of the *Kohen Gadol*. Certainly this emphasis is related to his high-stakes *Yom Kippur* mission representing *Klal Yisrael*, but the jubilant "*Mareh Kohen*," which accentuates his radiance and other esthetic facets, seems to transcend the mission. Indeed, the *Yom Tov* that his success occasioned was also a celebration of his institutional persona, an appropriate expression not only on his most high-profile day, but on the day that magnificently manifests the values he personified.

Yom Kippur is most emphatically not a manifestation of vicarious atonement, a concept that is completely foreign to *Yahadus*. Rather, it constitutes a day of pure loyalty and commitment, the day of the *avoda lifnai velifnim*, the day of the persona of the *Kohen Gadol*. It is a profound appreciation-celebration of the converging themes of the exclusive institutional persona devoted *kulo laShem* on the day, *achas bashana*, in which through fasting, *kedushas hayom*, and the intricate, ambitious *avoda*, all of *Klal Yisrael* reaffirms that very capacity.

Angels or Sinners: Who Are We?
RABBI ZVI SOBOLOFSKY

Our actions, prayers and even external clothing on *Yom Kippur* appear to be replete with one fundamental contradiction – are we presenting ourselves as sinners humbly requesting forgiveness, or are we portraying ourselves as pure angels in the service of *Hashem*?

In *Tefilla Zakka* (the prayer many recite before *Kol Nidrei*), we describe the prohibitions of *Yom Kippur* as methods of atonement for our sins. We beseech *Hashem* to consider our refraining from eating as atonement for sins in the realm of food. Each aspect of physical abstention is seen as a method to correct some flaw in our behavior. Yet the imagery of refraining from food and drink and other physical pleasures also conjures up an entirely different picture. Moshe *Rabbeinu*, upon ascending to *Har Sinai*, came as close to being an angel as a human being can. He no longer needed food or drink. Similarly, on *Yom Kippur*, when we completely dissociate ourselves from our physical existence, we are transformed to an angelic state.

This dual existence, as sinners and angels, is reflected throughout our *tefillos* on *Yom Kippur*. Our constant reference to sin, highlighted by

---

Originally published on TorahWeb.org in 2007

the numerous times *viduy* is recited, portrays us as contrite sinners. Yet we also play a very different role throughout our *tefillos*. Unlike any other day, we recite "*baruch sheim kevod Malchuso le'olam va'ed*" in a loud voice. A phrase normally reserved for angels to cry out, we take advantage of our angelic status in this unique praise. More than any other day, we elaborately praise *Hashem* in many different ways. Many have the custom of reciting the entire *Shir Hayichud* – a prayer of intricate praise of *Hashem* – following *Ma'ariv* on *Yom Kippur*. When reciting *Kedusha*, the prayer most associated with angels, we introduce it with praises reserved for *Yom Kippur*. Even the text of the actual *Kedusha* is unique – we recite the longer form of it for all the *tefillos* of the day, unlike other days where it is reserved for *Musaf*. Each time a prayer which is usually in the domain of angels is recited, we take the opportunity to cast ourselves in the role of these angels.

Even in our external appearance, we are simultaneously sinners and angels. It is customary for married men to wear a *kittel* on *Yom Kippur*. The *kittel* is representative of death; we stand before *Hashem* in shrouds, acknowledging our mortality. Knowing that our very lives are now on the line, subject to our repentance from sin, the most appropriate garment to don is the one which conjures up the image that frightens us the most. Yet the *kittel* also has a very inspiring message as well. The angels are described as wearing white robes. The *Kohen Gadol* on *Yom Kippur* upon entering the *Kodesh Hakodashim* wears such a robe. We, too, emulating the *Kohen Gadol* and the angels, dress in white, which radiates the purity of the heavenly angels.[40]

How should we understand these apparent contradictions on *Yom*

---

[40] The *kittel* as the embodiment of two very different messages is true for the other time during the year that many wear a *kittel*, i.e., the *Pesach seder*. There are two reasons suggested by the *poskim* as to why many don a *kittel* then. The first explains that at a time when we celebrate our freedom, we are concerned lest we lose sight of our fragile existence. Therefore, even as we dine as kings, we are reminded of our mortality by the clothing we wear. Others suggest that the *kittel* worn during the *seder* is reminiscent of the special robes worn in the time of the *Beis Hamikdash* when *korbanos* were eaten. These robes of white, symbolizing purity, befit those who eat from the table of *Hashem*.

Kippur in the realms of action, prayer and dress? Who are we really on this special day – sinners focusing on the frailty of life, or angels in the service of *Hashem*?

This apparent contradiction teaches us a fundamental lesson that we must internalize on *Yom Kippur*. The *Yom Kippur* service in the *Beis Hamikdash* revolved around the two goats that were brought – one as a *korban laShem* and the other thrown off a cliff as the *sa'ir la'azazel*. These two goats had to be identical in size, appearance and cost. Although externally identical, their fates were completely different. One would be chosen for the noble task of being a *korban laShem*, whereas the other would be destined for destruction.

On *Yom Kippur* we are faced with the decision whether to become a *sa'ir laShem* or a *sa'ir la'azazel*. These two images play out before us throughout the day and are reinforced by our actions, prayers and dress. Who are we? Are we the sinners who seek atonement by abstaining from pleasure, or are we the angels who have no need for physical pleasure? Are we laden with sin that we must repeatedly confess, or are we angels singing the praise of *Hashem*? Are we mere mortals who fear death as a result of our sins, or are we heavenly beings dressed in white, symbolizing our purity?

The essence of *Yom Kippur* is to undergo a transformation. We begin the day with these two images before us. Are we going to become the *sa'ir la'azazel*, laden with sin, destined for destruction, or are we going to chose the path of the *sa'ir laShem*, whose very existence is to enter the *Kodesh Hakodashim* as a *korban laShem*? By the end of the day we realize that the only path to take is the path of the *sa'ir laShem*. We are no longer sinners, suffering from our abstaining from pleasure, confessing our sins dressed in shrouds. We have become angels, praising *Hashem*, dressed in white robes of purity. May we all merit making this transformation on this *Yom Kippur*, and in this merit may *Hashem* bless all of us with a *gemar chasima tova*.

Torah and Chesed: The Secrets of Kappara

RABBI ZVI SOBOLOFSKY

As *Yom Kippur* approaches, the concept of *kappara* – atonement – is foremost on our minds. There are many ways to achieve different degrees of *kappara*. When the *Beis Hamikdash* stood, *korbanos* were brought to atone for various *aveiros*. The elaborate service of *korbanos* offered in the *Beis Hamikdash* on *Yom Kippur* included several *mechaprim*. *Korbanos* offered on behalf of the *Kohen Gadol*, the regular *kohanim*, and all the Jewish people culminated with the *sa'ir hamishtaleach*, the goat sent out for atonement, completing the *kappara* process. After we reenact the *avodas Yom HaKippurim* through our *tefillas Musaf* on *Yom Kippur*, we lament in great detail our inability to achieve the level of *kappara* that was once available to us.

Chazal teach us that there is a method of *kappara* even greater than *korbanos*. The study of Torah and the performance of acts of kindness can achieve *kappara* even in a situation in which *korbanos* are not effective. *Chazal* comment concerning the house of Eli *Hakohen*, that although their sins cannot be atoned for through the mechanism of *korbanos*, *talmud Torah* combined with *gemilus chasadim* can bring them atonement. We, who do not have the opportunity to offer *korbanos*, can still avail ourselves of *talmud Torah* and *gemilus chasadim* as our *mechaprim*. While *talmud To-*

Originally published on TorahWeb.org in 2012

rah and *gemilus chasadim* are two fundamental aspects of *avodas Hashem*, why should they have the ability to be *mechaper* for *aveiros*?

In the *tefilla* of "*Hineni*," recited by the *shaliach tzibbur* before *Musaf* on *Rosh Hashana* and *Yom Kippur*, we beseech *Hashem*, "ופשעינו תכסה באהבה - cover all of our sins with love." This request expresses a basic concept concerning *kappara*. *Chazal* observe that the ultimate *mechaper*, *teshuva*, elicits different levels of *kappara* depending on the type of *teshuva* that is performed. *Teshuva mei'ahava*, a *teshuva* that results from an expression of one's love for *Hashem* and from a sincere desire to return to a close relationship based on that love, is the highest form of *teshuva*. *Teshuva* that merely emanates from *yiras Hashem* – fear of *Hashem* – is more limited in nature and cannot accomplish a complete *kappara*. As such, as we strive to obtain *kappara*, it behooves us to perfect our *ahavas Hashem*, which is the prerequisite for *teshuva mei'ahava*. As we reach greater heights in our *ahavas Hashem*, we can beseech *Hashem* to express His love for us by covering our sins with that love.

How do we practically demonstrate *ahavas Hashem* and thereby merit the highest level of *kappara*? It is precisely *talmud Torah* and *gemilus chasadim* that express and strengthen this love, and as such are our ultimate *mechaprim*. Regarding the obligation of "*ve'ahavta es Hashem*," the *Sifrei* comments "איך? אתה אוהב – How do we attain this love?" The next *pasuk* answers this dilemma: "והיו הדברים האלה -Let these matters [… be upon your heart …]"; the *mitzva* of *talmud Torah* is the key to *ahavas Hashem*. As the Rambam in *Hilchos Teshuva* develops the principle, "לפי הדעה תהיה האהבה - According to one's knowledge of *Hashem* will be one's love for *Hashem*." Knowledge of Torah is our way of attaining knowledge of *Hashem*, enabling us to experience *ahavas Hashem*.

There is another way we express our *ahavas Hashem*. Through acts of *gemilus chasadim*, we imitate *Hashem* and fulfill the *mitzva* of "*Vehal-*

achta bidrachav," "You shall walk in His ways" (*Devarim* 28:9). Modeling our behavior after *Hashem*'s is a testament to the love and admiration we have for Him, since we try to imitate that which we love.

These two manifestations of *ahavas Hashem, talmud Torah* and *gemilus chasadim*, are our most sincere expressions of *teshuva mei'ahava*, and as such are our most effective methods of *teshuva*. May *Hashem* grant us the privilege to be *chozer bitshuva sheleima* and fulfill for us, "*upeshaeinu techaseh be'ahava.*"

Atonement on Yom Kippur
RABBI MORDECHAI WILLIG

I

"*Yom Kippur* atones only for the repentant (*shavim*) who believe in its atonement. But one who scoffs at it and thinks, 'What does *Yom Kippur* do for me?' does not gain atonement on *Yom Kippur*" (Rama, *Orach Chaim* 607:6).

"*Yom Kippur* atones with *teshuva*; without *teshuva* it does not atone. Rebbe says it does atone without *teshuva*" (*Yoma* 85b).

"What is *teshuva*? The sinner must cease sinning, regret his sin, and resolve not to commit the sin again" (Rambam, *Hilchos Teshuva* 2:2).

At first glance, there is absolutely no atonement on *Yom Kippur* unless a person does *teshuva*; but, when accompanying *teshuva*, *Yom Kippur* completes atonement for the violation of *mitzvos lo ta'aseh* – negative commandments (*Yoma* 86a, Rambam, *Hilchos Teshuva* 1:4). The Rama, however, implies that as long as one **believes** in the effectiveness of *Yom Kippur* it atones, even in the absence of *teshuva*. The Rama's source is the Rambam (*Hilchos Shegagos* 3:10, based on *Kerisus* 7a), but the Rambam

---

Originally published on TorahWeb.org in 2005

himself states that the essence of *Yom Kippur* atones for the **repentant** (*shavim*) (*Hilchos Teshuva* 1:3)! The *Kesef Mishneh*, in his explanation of the Rambam, cites the aforementioned dispute between Rebbe and the Rabbanan on *Yoma* 85b. The citation from *Hilchos Teshuva* 1:3 implies a need for full *teshuva* according to the Rambam, following the Rabbanan, not merely a belief in the effectiveness of *Yom Kippur*, as the Rama says.

Perhaps the harmonization of the Rama and Rambam is that only a full atonement on *Yom Kippur* requires a full *teshuva*. However, there is a partial atonement on *Yom Kippur* for anyone who believes in it. Such a person is in the class of *shavim*, even though he does not regret and cease his sin, and does not resolve not to repeat it.

The concept of a partial atonement on *Yom Kippur* is found, according to Rebbe, for one who is unrepentant and eats on *Yom Kippur* (*Tosafos Yeshanim*, *Yoma* 85b). *Yom Kippur* serves to avoid *kares*, but *teshuva* is needed to achieve full atonement.

A similar concept exists according to the Rabbanan for one who is repentant. If he believes in the effectiveness of *Yom Kippur*, it provides partial atonement. Full atonement, however, requires *teshuva*.

II

Yom Kippur is the day on which *Am Yisrael* was forgiven for the sin of the golden calf. For this reason it was established as a day of atonement (Rashi, *Devarim* 9:18).

The origin of this sin was stiff-neckedness (*am keshei oref* [*Devarim* 9:6]). It was this attribute that triggered *Hashem*'s threat to destroy us (*Shemos* 32:9, 10). A stiff neck contains, metaphorically, a metal rod that makes a person unable to turn his neck. This prevents him from turning to face a *rav* whose compelling message deters sin. This trait eliminates any hope for *teshuva* (Seforno, *Devarim* 9:6-8).

The ideal *teshuva*, based on love of *Hashem*, returns a person all the way to (*ad*) *Hashem* and His throne (*Hoshea* 14:1, *Yoma* 86a). The next *pasuk* (*Hoshea* 14:2) exhorts *teshuva* to (*el*) *Hashem*, which may refer to one who does not reach all the way to *Hashem* but returns toward *Hashem*.

On *Yom Kippur* we need only turn around to face (*lifnei*) *Hashem* in order to gain a measure of atonement and purity. Belief in *Yom Kippur*'s effectiveness is, in itself, such a gesture, which makes a person repentant. Turning around is the opposite of stiff-neckedness. Since the origin of *Yom Kippur* is atonement for the stiff-neckedness of the *cheit ha'eigel*, even a mere turning around toward *Hashem* achieves partial atonement.

At *Ne'ila* we proclaim that we, and our eyes, look to *Hashem*. Our ancestors faced east and worshipped the sun. In the *Beis Hamikdash* the *kohanim* turned around to the west, to the *mikdash*, and said, "We and our eyes look to *Hashem*" (*Sukkah* 51b). Turning one's face to *Hashem* at *Ne'ila* confers upon one the status of repentant and grants a measure of atonement. The full atonement of *Yom Kippur*, however, requires *teshuva* – regret, sincere confession, and acceptance not to sin in the future.

III

"All of the nation [has sinned] unintentionally (*bishgaga*)" (*Bemidbar* 15:26). The literal context of this *pasuk* atones for those who sin based on an error of the *Beis Din*. The recital of the *pasuk* three times after *Kol Nidrei* clearly applies it to all the sins of *Am Yisrael*. The reality of intentional sin, however, makes this generalization quite problematic.

The expressions "*chatasi*" and "*avisi*" refer to unintentional and intentional sins, respectively (*Yoma* 36b). Yet the Rambam (*Hilchos Teshuva* 1:1) seems to require both expressions in the confession of even a single sin.

Rav Soloveitchik *zt"l* explained that on can never be completely sure whether a particular sin was unintentional. Perhaps he should have known better, and thus some intention was present. Conversely, an intentional sin may be extenuated by a deficient education, a pervasive zeitgeist, difficult personal conditions or the negative influence of friends (see *Al Hateshuva*, p. 64).

While these mitigating factors may not technically qualify as *shogeig*, one cannot be certain and should therefore say *chatasi* even if he sinned intentionally. On *Yom Kippur*, we invoke *Hashem*'s mercy and characterize the sins of all *Am Yisrael* as *shegaga*, worthy of at least partial atonement.

Indeed, *Hashem* forgave the sin of the golden calf on *Yom Kippur* based on Moshe's words, as *Hashem* said "סלחתי כדבריך", "I have forgiven according to your words," (Rashi, *Devarim* 9:18, although סלחתי כדבריך's original context is the sin of the spies [*Bemidbar* 14:20]). The recital of סלחתי כדבריך three times after *Kol Nidrei* indicates that the key to the atonement of *Yom Kippur* lies in Moshe's defense of *Am Yisrael*'s idolatry.

"Moshe said before *Hashem*, 'Because of the silver and gold that You lavished upon *Yisrael*, they made the golden calf … What should that son [who is placed in a vulnerable and tempting situation] do that he not sin? … *Hashem* concurred with Moshe, as it says [*Hoshea* 2:10] 'And I lavished silver upon her, and they made [a statue of] gold to the Baal'" (*Berachos* 32a). Although Moshe advanced mitigating factors only, and not complete exoneration (*Maharsha*), *Hashem* forgave *Am Yisrael* based on his defense.

IV

As we prepare for *Yom Kippur*, the following lessons emerge from our analysis of the sources.

Every person must aim for a complete *teshuva*, regretting and confessing his sins and resolving not to repeat them. This *teshuva*, which is

Yom Kippur

for repentance for all, for individuals and for the collective, the culmination of pardon and forgiveness for Israel"). It is striking and atypical that such a crucial and urgent dimension of halachic life is undertaken in a manner that renders *Klal Yisrael* observers-spectators. *Yahadus* fundamentally rejects anything that even approximates vicarious atonement, instead demanding participation and responsibility. Why, then, is the most crucial of all religious experiences the exclusive domain of a single figure, the *Kohen Gadol*? Even the modicum of wider communal participation, also emulated by the *tzibbur* in the *Musaf* prayers, "והעם ... בעזרה כשהיו ... שומעים את השם ... היו כורעים ומשתחוים ... ונופלים על פניהם" "And the people ... standing in the courtyard, when they would hear the Name ... they would kneel and prostrate themselves ... and fall upon their faces," is triggered by and is a response to the actions of the *Kohen Gadol*.

This phenomenon contrasts sharply even with other *avoda* protocols which tend to be inclusive at least of multiple *kohanim*. The institutions of *payasim*, *mishmaros*, *batei av*, etc. reflect an effort to widen priestly participation. On *Yom Kippur*, however, the *Kohen Gadol*'s exclusive role extends not only to the singular aspects of *avodas Yom Kippur*, but even to the daily or generic services – *temidim*, *musafim* – as well (see *Yoma* 32b, etc.). While there are fundamental debates among the *rishonim* (*Ba'al HaMaor* and *Milchamos* on *Yoma* 26a, Ritva 12b, Rambam, *Hilchos Avodas Yom HaKippurim* 1:2, etc.) regarding the precise scope of the *Kohen Gadol*'s expanded responsibility, the principle is endorsed by all and formulated as an important dimension of the *Kohen Gadol*'s prominence and indispensability.

Moreover, aside from his daily *korban minchas chavitin*, the *Kohen Gadol*'s primary *mikdash* obligation and role is the once-yearly *avoda*. The Talmud establishes that there can only be a single qualified *Kohen Gadol* for this unique function on this singular day (see also Rashi, *Megilla* 9b). The fact that he leaves his home to begin a weeklong preparation for this *avoda* effective all year long, combines with *Yom Kippur* to atone completely for negative commandments.

One who is unable to achieve this level of *teshuva* should not despond. *Hashem* looks at extenuating circumstances, especially on *Yom Kippur*. Turning toward *Hashem* and believing in the effectiveness of *Yom Kippur* achieve partial atonement.

Finally, in judging others, these factors must be emphasized. The importance of this idea is the very essence of the *pesukim* we recite after *Kol Nidrei*. Indeed, the opening line of the *machzor*, permitting us to pray together with sinners, is the preface to all of *tefilla* on *Yom Kippur*.

Our charitable attitude toward sinners reflects the indispensability of their participation in our fast (*Kerisus* 6b). Remarkably, even today many alienated Jews fast on *Yom Kippur*. We should encourage and appreciate this phenomenon, even as we hold ourselves to a higher standard. May we all be worthy of atonement on this *Yom Kippur*, and may all of Israel be blessed with a *gemar chasima tova*.

Communal Atonement
RABBI MORDECHAI WILLIG

I

The scapegoat atones for all sins if one repents ... Otherwise, it atones only for lesser sins ... Grave sins, punishable by *kares* or *misas beis din*, as well as false or vain oaths [are not atoned] (Rambam *Hilchos Teshuva* 1:2).

Two questions arise. First, atonement without repentance, achieved vicariously via a scapegoat, seems impossible. After all, an offering of a wicked person is abominable (*Mishlei* 21:27). Second, why the distinction between lesser and grave sins?

Rav Soloveitchik *zt"l* answered both questions based on the Rambam's introductory phrase: "The scapegoat ... is an atonement for all Israel." A wicked, unrepentant person has no individual atonement. However, he partakes of the communal atonement granted to *Am Yisrael* as such. Grave sins remove the person from the nation and preclude participation in the national atonement. *Kares* cuts the soul off from its people (*Bemidbar* 19:13).

The Rav *zt"l* cited the *beracha* recited on *Yom Kippur*: "The King who pardons and forgives our sins and the sins (*avonos*) of His people Israel."

Originally published on TorahWeb.org in 2010

Hashem forgives individuals, and the nation as a whole. He also removes our guilt (*ashma*), a term associated with desolation (*shemama*; Ramban, Vayikra 5:19). Since *Klal Yisrael* will never be destroyed, the term "guilt" (*ashma*) is limited to individuals (*On Repentance*, 1996 ed., p. 97-109).

Presumably, removal from the nation by capital punishment resembles *kares*. And one who swears falsely or in vain is distanced by everyone, because others are punishable when one close to them swears falsely, more so than for other sins (*Shevuos* 39a-b). As such, communal atonement is not possible for these sins.

Yom Kippur itself achieves atonement even in the absence of complete *teshuva* [see "Atonement on *Yom Kippur*," in this volume]. We can postulate that this, too, is a national atonement, as the *beracha* implies. According to Rebbe (*Yoma* 85b), *Yom Kippur* atones for (nearly) all sins without *teshuva*. Why, then, was the *Beis Hamikdash* destroyed? [See *Tosfos Yeshanim*, who ask this question and suggest that the atonement is only partial.]

A nation is judged based on the majority of its people (Rambam, *Hilchos Teshuva* 3:1). Therefore, as the sins of *Am Yisrael* increased, the scapegoat no longer achieved full national atonement, symbolized by the red thread turning white (*Yoma* 39a, 67a). Similarly, *Yom Kippur* lost its effectiveness, according to Rebbe. As a communal atonement, *Yom Kippur* requires a majority of individuals who repent and deserve atonement. Only then can the unworthy be included.

II

Yom Kippur does not atone for interpersonal sins until one appeases [yeratzeh] the wronged person (Yoma 85b).

Even if the appeasement is continually rebuffed, Yom Kippur atones. It does not state until the wronged person is appeased (yisratzeh) (Pri Chadash, Orach Chaim 606:1).

Conversely, if one grants forgiveness without being asked, it is not fully effective. For this reason, Rav appeared before the butcher who had wronged him, hoping that the butcher would appease him (*Yoma* 87a). Rav did not merely forgive him from afar.

Nonetheless, forgiving from afar is partially effective. This is evidenced by our forgiving all those who wronged us in *Tefilla Zakka* on *Yom Kippur* eve. We pray that no one should be punished on our account, a phrase many say nightly. Forgiving others nightly results in longevity (*Megilla* 28a, *Mishna Berura* 239:9). Apparently, forgiving sins is comparable to forgiving money. It removes punishment on account of the one who was wronged and forgives. But it does not entitle the sinner to the atonement of *Yom Kippur*.

This can be explained based on our earlier analysis. One cannot enjoy communal atonement when removed from the community. Interpersonal sins remove the sinner from the wronged person and, by extension, from the community. If he appeases his fellow and asks repeatedly for forgiveness, he has done all that he can to make amends. As such, he reenters the community and benefits from *Yom Kippur*'s communal atonement.

By contrast, the wronged person who does not grant forgiveness after three requests is the sinner. For this reason one should not ask forgiveness more than three times (Rambam, *Hilchos Teshuva* 2:9). It is now assumed (*chazaka*) that the wronged person will not grant forgiveness. Asking him again would only make him a bigger sinner and, as such, is not allowed.

III

It is customary to ask forgiveness on *Erev Yom*

Kippur, as the *Midrash* teaches: *Hashem* ordained ten days of *teshuva*, during which even if one person repents, his *teshuva* is accepted like the *teshuva* of the community. Therefore, all Israel should repent and make peace between a man and his fellow, and forgive one another on *Erev Yom Kippur* so that their repentance and prayer should be received by *Hashem* with peace and with love (Mordechai, *Yoma* 723).

This citation proves the aforementioned thesis. *Yom Kippur* is special because an individual's repentance is treated like that of a community. If one asks forgiveness of his fellow, he is included in the community, since he seeks closeness with everyone, even someone whom he has wronged and had been distanced from him.

The *midrash* adds two points. It includes all the ten days of *teshuva*, and mentions prayer as well. This is based on the *Gemara* (*Rosh Hashana* 18a), which explains varying levels of *Hashem*'s closeness based on the whether the community or individual is reaching out:

"*Hashem* is close to us whenever we call Him" (*Devarim* 4:7). Yet it states (*Yeshaya* 55:6): "Call *Hashem* when He is close," i.e., during *Aseres Yemei Teshuva*. The former refers to the community, the latter to an individual.

The *midrash* interprets that even in *Aseres Yemei Teshuva*, the time of individual closeness, we require the merit of the *tzibbur*, but the *teshuva* of an individual is treated like that of a community. This is achieved only by asking forgiveness of one's fellow, which reintegrates the petitioner into the community and its atonement.

"To whom does *Hashem* grant atonement? To one who forgives others who wrong him" (*Rosh Hashana* 17a). One who overcomes his natural inclination to respond in kind to a person who pained him, but rather forgives the wrongdoer, belongs more strongly to the community. As such, he is granted the all-important communal atonement.

> The angels asked, "Why does Yisrael not say *Hallel* on *Rosh Hashana* and *Yom Kippur*?" Hashem said, "The King judges, the books of life and death are open, and Israel should say *Hallel*?" (*Arachin* 10b)

The angels' very question is perplexing. It must be based on the statement, "There was no greater holiday for Yisrael that *Yom Kippur*" (*Ta'anis* 26b), "a day of atonement" (30b). *Am Yisrael* is guaranteed atonement. This warrants *Hallel*, as the angels asked. *Hashem* responds that no individual is guaranteed to be part of the communal atonement. The individual fears judgment and death and cannot recite *Hallel* (Rav Chaim Yaakov Goldvicht *z"l*).

As we approach *Yom Kippur*, we should do all that we can to become more strongly connected to the *tzibbur*. We should both seek and grant forgiveness. We should do more to help other individuals and the community at large.

On *Yom Kippur* itself, we must include even sinners in our fast (*Kerisus* 6b) and prayers (introduction to *Kol Nidrei*). It is a day to institute love and friendship and to forsake jealousy and competition (*Musaf*).

May each and every one of us merit both the individual and communal atonement of *Yom Kippur*. May *Am Yisrael* forsake the baseless hatred which caused the *Churban* and merit the rebuilding of the *Beis Hamikdash* and the restoration of the powerful communal atonement of the *Yom Kippur* service.

Sukkos

Shemini Atzeres and Simchas Torah: One Simcha

RABBI HERSHEL SCHACHTER

The prohibition against getting married on *Shabbos* is rabbinic in origin. It was part of the *gezeira* against *mekach umemkar* (buying and selling) *shema yichtav* (lest one write by mistake). However, the prohibition against marrying on *Yom Tov* or even on *Chol Hamoed* is biblical, based on the principle of *ein me'arvin simcha besimcha*. On *Yom Tov*, and even on *Chol Hamoed*, there is a *mitzva* to rejoice, and one who marries is engaged in a different form of *simcha*, which detracts from the *simcha* of *Yom Tov*. (On *Shabbos* there is no *mitzva* of *simcha*, hence no problem of contradiction.)

In talmudic times, there were several differences between the practices of the Jewish community in Babylonia and the practices of the communities in *Eretz Yisrael*. One of these differences was regarding *kerias haTorah*. In Babylonia they would complete the reading of the entire Torah every year on the last day of *Sukkos*, hence the name *Simchas Torah*. In *Eretz Yisrael* the *sidra* read each *Shabbos* was only about one third of the length of the *sidros* read in Babylonia; hence it would take about three years to complete the entire Torah. *Simchas Torah* would only be celebrated

Originally published on TorahWeb.org in 2002

once every three years, upon the completion of the entire Torah. Already in the times of the Rambam, the practice all over the world followed that of Babylonia, to celebrate *Simchas Torah* every year, on the last day of *Sukkos*.

The *Achronim* raise a problem regarding this practice: why is this celebration not in violation of the principle of *ein me'arvin simcha besimcha*? On *Sukkos* there is clearly a *mitzva* of *simcha*, and the celebration of the *siyum* of the Torah also certainly involves an element of *simcha*. Why should we not insist on observing *Simchas Torah* only on a *Shabbos* or a weekday, as opposed to having the celebration on a *Yom Tov*?

Perhaps the answer to that question lies in the nature of the *Yom Tov* of *Shemini Atzeres*. Each of the *Yomim Tovim* has its own theme. The theme of *Pesach* is the redemption from Egypt; on *Shavuos* it is *Matan Torah*; and the theme on *Sukkos* is the ability of the Jewish people to have survived miraculously throughout the years of the *galus*. For seven days we leave our permanent home and dwell in the shaky *sukkah*, with very little protection. We rely on the Divine protection, which has maintained the Jewish people throughout the years, despite all odds against survival. In the language of Rav Kook *zt"l*, the continued existence of the Jewish people is a "*halacha leMoshe miSinai*" (i.e., there is no rational way to explain it).

What is the theme of *Shemini Atzeres*? The *halacha* declares *Shemini Atzeres* as a separate *Yom Tov*, and is not merely the last two days of *Sukkos*. (This is the reason that the *beracha* "*Shehechiyanu*" is recited at the end of the *Kiddush* on the evening of *Shemini Atzeres*, but not on the evening of the last days of *Pesach*. *Shemini Atzeres* is a separate *Yom Tov*, and has not been celebrated since a year prior.) What is the special theme of the new *Yom Tov*?

Rashi, in his commentary on the Torah (*Vayikra* 23:36), quotes from the *Tanaim* that after the seven days of *Sukkos* are all over, and the millions of Jews have spent their *Yom Tov* in Jerusalem (fulfilling *aliya lar-*

egel), *Hakadosh Baruch Hu* exclaims, "I love you so much; I find it difficult to say goodbye; please stay on another day." *Shemini Atzeres* does not come to commemorate any particular historical event, but rather it emphasizes *bechiras Yisrael*, the uniqueness of *Am Yisrael*. From all the nations of the world, the Jews alone were chosen to be designated as "*banim laMakom*," as "*beni bechori Yisrael*."

The entire uniqueness of the Jewish people lies in the fact that the *malach* (angel) teaches every baby the entire Torah before he or she is born. The *simcha* of the completion of the entire Torah is not something separate from the *simcha* of the *Yom Tov*. The whole essence of the *Yom Tov* of *Shemini Atzeres* is interconnected with Torah study. Only through Torah study did we become the *Am Hanivchar*, and hence our *minhag* of celebrating the *simcha* of completing the learning of the entire Torah not only does not compete with the *simcha* of the *Yom Tov* of *Shemini Atzeres*, rather it complements and enhances it.

One Continuum of Jewish History

RABBI HERSHEL SCHACHTER

Some *chasidim* have the practice of leaving *shul* after *Shacharis* on each day of *Sukkos*, in order to shake their *lulav* in the *sukkah* before reciting *Hallel*. The origin of the *minhag* most probably was that one who had slept in the *sukkah* all night would wash his hands first thing in the morning and recite the *beracha* over the *lulav* right after sunrise. But based on kabbalistic sources, there has developed a *minhag* that even when one has not slept in the *sukkah*, and even if it's not first thing in the morning, one should combine the two *mitzvos* of *sukkah* and *lulav*.[41]

The *mitzva* of *sukkah* symbolizes the survival of the Jewish people during the forty-year period after leaving Egypt prior to entering *Eretz Yisrael* (under the leadership of Yehoshua bin Nun). By now this *mitzva* has also come to represent the miraculous survival of the Jewish people through all the exiles and all the pogroms they suffered. The mere existence of our people today is really "stranger than fiction"[42] and supernatural!

On the other hand, the *mitzva* of *lulav* represents those time pe-

---

[41] Based on *Shelah, Masseches Sukkah* (p. 75d), cited by the *Magen Avraham* (652:3).

[42] Which is the title of an English book on Jewish history by Lewis Browne.

Originally published on TorahWeb.org in 2006

riods when the Jews lived in *Eretz Yisrael*. The farmer would dance before *Hashem* thanking Him for the bounty with which He had blessed him.[43]

Perhaps the idea behind combining the two *mitzvos* of *lulav* and *sukkah* is to emphasize the idea that all of Jewish history was designed by *Hashem*. There are those who feel that the many years we spent in *galus* were an accident of fate, and that now that we have our own Jewish *medina* in *Eretz Yisrael*, we ought to discontinue the study of the Babylonian Talmud, along with all of the other *sefarim* which were composed during the years of *galus*. They feel that we should disassociate ourselves from everything that was developed during the *galus* period. This is not our approach. One of the reasons given by the Rabbis of the *Midrash* as to why the Torah refers to Avaraham *Avinu* as "Avraham *HaIvri*," and the entire Jewish nation after him are known as "*Ivrim*," is because he came *mei'ever hanahar* (from the other side of the river).[44] The Rabbis did not mean this simply as a geographic description. They meant to bring out that Avraham maintained all the principles of faith that he had discovered "on the other side of the river," even after *Hashem* gave him *Eretz Yisrael*.

The Talmud (*Avoda Zara* 5a) records a tradition that *Hashem* showed Adam *Harishon* a book that consisted of דור דור וחכמיו – "each generation and its Torah scholars." In that book there was mention of Rav, Shmuel, Ravina, and Rav Ashi as leading figures in the development of the Torah *Shebe'al Peh* in Bavel (*Bava Metzia* 85b-86a). Toward the end of the *tochacha* in *Parashas Bechukosai* (*Vayikra* 26:44) we read that even when the Jews are in *galus*, *Hashem* has totally despised them or totally rejected them, because of the *bris* (the covenant) that He had previously made with them. The Talmud (*Megilla* 11a) takes the *pasuk* in *Bechukosai* as an allusion to the prominent leaders that *Hashem* had sent to guide us.

---

[43] See Rambam in *Moreh Nevuchim* (III:43) and *Insights of Rabbi Joseph B. Soloveitchik*, by Rabbi Saul Weiss, p. 103.

[44] See Rav Soloveitchik's essay on Avraham *HaIvri*, section 4 in *Chamesh Derashos*.

The two *mitzvos* of *Sukkos* – the *sukkah* and the *lulav* – represent the two parts of Jewish history; the years of *galus* and the years of living in *Eretz Yisrael*. We believe that all is from *Hashem*, and that all that *Hashem* does is for the good.[45] Even during periods of *hester panim*,[46] it is not the case that *Hashem* was not watching over us! *Hashem* was hiding from us in such a way that we could not see His face (i.e., *hester panim*), but all the while He was, so to speak, "peeking through the cracks" (see *Shir Hashirim* 2:9) and looking after us.[47] *Hashem* has guided, from behind the scenes, the history of the Jewish people, as well as the development of the Torah *Shebe'al Peh*, in such a way that both continue to reach successful conclusions.

---

[45] See *Berachos* (60b) where the famous story about Rabbi Akiva being denied lodging and forced to sleep in a field, then losing his candle, his donkey and his rooster, is recorded. The Rabbis felt that even something that seems to us to be absolute evil actually contains something good which we can not perceive. Some have commented on the expression used in the Torah (*Devarim* 25:19) in connection with the *mitzva* to wipe out Amalek "from under the heavens," that the connotation is that from *Hashem*'s perspective (*mei'al haShamayim*), there is some good in Amalek also. And, indeed, the Rabbis of the Talmud had a tradition (*Gittin* 57b) that many years later, descendants of Haman the Amalekite converted and learned Torah in Bnei Brak. See also *Sanhedrin* 96b.

[46] See *Devarim* 30:17-18 and 32:20.

[47] See *Yad Haketana*, pp. 39, 242.

Lashon Hara in the Sukkah

RABBI HERSHEL SCHACHTER

The *halacha* requires that one dwell in the *sukkah* for the duration of the *Yom Tov* in the same way one would live in his own home: eating, sleeping, learning, etc. In the language of the Talmud (*Sukkah* 28b), "*teishvu ke'ein taduru*."

The Talmud (*Shabbos* 133b) speaks of fulfilling **all** *mitzvos* in an elegant fashion – an elegant *tallis*, an elegant pair of *tefillin*, etc. The same certainly applies to the *mitzva* of *sukkah* as well. In addition to that **general** *halacha*, making the *sukkah* fancy constitutes a **particular** enhancement of *mitzvas sukkah*, because of *teishvu ke'ein taduru*. We all add drapes, wallpaper, carpeting, etc. to our homes to beautify them and make them more comfortable, so the same ought to be provided to the *sukkah*.

In Yiddish folklore there is a common humorous saying that if one does not speak *lashon hara* at all in the *sukkah*, he has not fulfilled the *mitzva* because it is lacking *ke'ein taduru*, since at home we always speak *lashon hara*. This is the historical background of the comment in the *Mishna Berura* (639, note 2) that one must certainly be careful not to talk any *lashon hara* in the *sukkah*. The Talmud (*Sukkah* 9a) derives a *din deOraisa*

Originally published on TorahWeb.org in 2010

from a *pasuk* that just as a *korban chagiga* has *kedusha*, so too the *sukkah* has *kedusha*. According to the Ramban, this *pasuk* is the source of the principle that any religious article (e.g., an *esrog* or *tzitzis*) becomes *huktza lemitzvaso* for the duration of the *mitzva*. Because of the sanctity of the *sukkah*, one should avoid discussing *divrei chol*, and certainly *lashon hara*. The *lashon hara* belongs neither in our homes nor in our *sukkos*.

After one has finished eating, it is considered disrespectful to the sanctity of the *sukkah* to leave the dirty utensils which one no longer plans to use (*Sukkah* 29a). Some *poskim* write that is disrespectful to bring an infant into the *sukkah* who may dirty his diaper.

Toward the end of *Parashas Re'eh* (*Devarim* 16:13), the *Chumash* records the *mitzva* to celebrate the *Yom Tov* of *Sukkos* for seven days during the gathering season: "You shall make for yourself the holiday (*chag*) of *Sukkos* when you gather in your produce …." All summer long it does not rain in *Eretz Yisrael*, and only after *Sukkos*, when we expect the rains to begin, do we gather in the produce from the fields. This is the literal meaning of the *pasuk*'s reference to the gathering season.

The Talmud (*Sanhedrin* 34a) has a tradition that *Hashem* dictated the Torah to Moshe *Rabbeinu* in such a way that any given *pasuk* may have more than one level of interpretation: "*Achas dibber Elokim, shtayim zu shamati*," "God spoke one thing; I heard two" (*Tehillim* 62:12). The *Torah Shebe'al Peh* has an additional level of interpretation on the aforementioned *pasuk* in *Re'eh*, which is that we should construct our *sukkos* in such a way that they should be sturdy enough to last for the duration of the seven days of *Yom Tov*, and the *sechach* which we use as the roof should consist of the branches, leaves and chaff that were separated from the produce (i.e., something that grew from the ground, which is now detached, and which is not edible for humans, hence not *mekabel tuma*). This additional level of interpretation fits in to all the words of the *pasuk* except for "*chag*," which means "a holiday." How, then, can the *Torah Shebe'al peh* interpret the *pasuk* to refer to the construction of a *sukkah*?

The Talmud explains (*Sukkah* 9a) that only *Pesach, Shavuos* and *Sukkos* are referred to in the *Chumash* as "*chag*," because "*chag*" indicates an obligation to bring a *korban chagiga*, which exists only on these three *Yomim Tovim*. "*Chag haSukkos*," therefore, refers not to the holiday, but to the construction of the *sukkah*, which is compared to a *korban chagiga*. Just as the *korban chagiga* is sacred, so the *sukkah* is endowed with sanctity after we sit in it to fulfill our *mitzva*. Because of that sanctity, we must treat the *sukkah* with proper respect.

Active Prayer
RABBI YAAKOV HABER

The waving of the *arba'a minim* (the four species) – the *na'anuim* – serves as a focal point of the *tefillos* of *Chag HaSukkos*. Interestingly, though, one can fulfill his minimal obligation by merely picking up the *arba'a minim* (see *Sukkah* 42a). However, the clear implication of many *Rishonim* is that *na'anuim* are a *lechatechila deOraisa* – a biblically mandated ideal enhancement to the performance of the *mitzva* (see Rambam, *Hilchos Lulav* 7:9; also *Tosafos* and Ritva to *Sukkah* 37b, who rule stringently in case of doubt, presumably following the rule *sefeika deOraisa lechumra*). Indeed, the *Mishna* in *Masseches Sukkah* (29b; see Rashi there) indicates that unlike the *hadas* (myrtle) and *arava* (willow), whose minimum size is three *tefachim* (handbreadths), the *lulav* requires four *tefachim*. The extra *tefach*, as the *Mishna* explains, is necessary "*kedei lenanei'a bo*" – "in order to wave it." Although the *Ba'al HaIttur* and Meiri maintain that this requirement for the fourth *tefach* is only *miderabbanan*, the overwhelming majority of *Rishonim* and subsequent *poskim* maintain that four *tefachim* is an absolute requirement, which would seem to indicate its biblical origin. Even though the *na'anuim* are only *lechatechila*, the *lulav* must at least be fit for waving.

What is signified by this biblically mandated waving? Furthermore, it is clear from the *Mishna* (37b) that the four species are to be waved

Originally published on TorahWeb.org in 1999

at two places in the *Hallel*, once at "הודו לה' כי טוב -Give praise to God for He is good," and once at "אנא ה' הושיעה נא -Please God, save us now!" These expressions contain drastically different themes. "*Hodu*" is a call to praise *Hashem* for His everlasting kindness. "*Ana*" is a heartfelt prayer for salvation. How does the waving of the *arba'a minim* enhance these diverse prayers?

What clearly emerges is that the waving of the *arba'a minim* serves as both a *tefilla* of *bakasha* (request) and a song of *hoda'a* (praise). But how does the *lulav* accomplish both tasks? The *Mishna* in *Rosh Hashana* (16a) relates that "*bechag nidonin al hamayim*," on *Sukkos* the world is judged concerning the amount of rainfall for that year. The four species all require additional watering aside from rainfall to survive. The Torah even refers to *aravos* as "*arvei nachal*," willows that grow near a river. There is even a minority position in *Tosafos* (*Sukkah* 34a) that the *aravos* must grow near a river to be valid. Even though we do not follow this position [see *Shulchan Aruch* (647:1) and *Mishna Berura* (3)], certainly the Torah highlights the role of water in the *arba'a minim*. Indeed, one of the textual proofs that the biblical "*pri eitz hadar*" (*Vayikra* 23:40) is a citron is that the word "*hadar*" is etymologically related to the Greek "hydro," meaning water (*Sukkah* 35a). Hence, the Torah refers to a fruit that needs much additional watering to survive. The waving of the species, then, is a form of *tefilla* for rain. Besides the *tefilla* for rain on *Shemini Atzeres*, we pray every day of *Sukkos* for rain in the *Hallel* by waving the *arba'a minim* at "*ana*."

But the waving of the *arba'a minim* symbolizes more than *bakasha* alone. The Torah refers to *Sukkos* as the "*Chag Ha'asif*" (*Shemos* 23:16) – the festival of ingathering. The beginning of the fall ushers in the period of gathering the produce from the fields into the silos and warehouses. The long, arduous task of carefully sowing, watering, harvesting and drying is over. The Jewish farmer can finally partake of his bounty. Herein lies the danger of the farmer attributing his material success to his own efforts alone. "כוחי ועוצם ידי עשה לי את החיל הזה - My strength alone brought about this abundance of wealth" (*Devarim* 8:17). By waving the *arba'a minim* – the more prominent and beautiful of the crops – in the *Hallel* at "*hodu*," the farmer turns heavenward and declares to the *Mashgiach al hakol* (Provider for all): "I thank You, *Hashem*, for your kindness to me. I am fully cognizant that it is You הנותן כח לעשות חיל, Who crowns my efforts with success, and without Whom there would be no crops to celebrate."

This, then, can be the underlying meaning of the statement by R. Yochanan (*Sukkah* 37b) that we wave back and forth to the Creator of the four corners of the world, and we wave up and down to the Creator of heaven and earth. R. Yochanan underscores the role of the *na'anuim* as an expression of praise and thanksgiving. R. Yose bar R. Chanina states (ibid.) that we wave back and forth to stop harmful winds, and up and down to prevent harmful precipitation. R. Yose emphasizes the *bakasha* nature of the waving.

The underlying themes of prayer and thanksgiving through *mitzvos* other than oral *tefilla* itself appear in other *mitzvos* as well. Rav Joseph B. Soloveitchik *zt"l*, based on earlier sources, explains the blowing of the *shofar* as a form of prayer without words; a cry symbolically emanating from the heart of the *mispallel* (petitioner) (see *Yemei Zikaron*). Similarly, the Gemara (*Megilla* 4a) derives the requirement of the dual reading of the *Megilla*, once at night and once during the day, from two sources. One is the passage in *Tehillim* (30:13) "למען יזמרך כבוד ולא ידם ה' א-לקי לעולם אודך - in order that my soul sing to You and not be silent, *Hashem*, my God, forever I will thank You." The second is from *Tehillim* (22:3) "א-לקי אקרא יומם ולא תענה ולילה ולא דומיה לי - My God, I call to you by day and you do not answer, and at night and I am not silent." Rav Betzalel Zolty *zt"l* points out that the two sources apparently indicate that *mikra Megilla* contains the same dual nature as we find regarding the waving of the *lulav*. First, it serves as a paean to the *Ribbono Shel Olam* who foiled Haman's plot to decimate the Jewish people. Indeed, the *Gemara* (*Megilla* 14a) even suggests that *Hallel* need not be recited on *Purim* since the *Megilla* itself serves as the *Hallel*. However, the reading of the *Megilla* also serves as a *tefilla* of *bakasha*. By reading the narrative of how *Hashem* has saved us in the past, we implicitly beseech Him that He redeem us from our present exile as well.

The theme of prayer through the performance of *mitzvos ma'asiyos* – active commandments – highlights the recurrent theme of the *Sefer Hachinuch*. "*Acharei hapeulos nimshachim halevavos*," the mind follows the actions. Praying to *Hashem* and praising Him through words alone does not suffice. We must make use of the *kol shofar*, the *na'anuim*, and *mikra Megilla* to enhance our communication with the *Shomei'a tefillos*. Together with the words of our *tefillos*, these *mitzvos* help stir our emotions in a way that oral prayer alone cannot do. Ultimately, though, the goal is the "*avoda shebaleiv – zo tefilla*," the service of the heart, which is prayer. The *mispallel* with the *shofar*, the *lulav* and *Megilla* is urged to elicit in himself an outpouring of his heart and soul to the Source of all, coupled with the recognition of his utter dependence on his Creator, Who is his only true source of help. May all of our various forms of *tefilla* this *Sukkos* and throughout the whole year be answered *letova*.

Sukkos: Universal Holiday?
RABBI YAAKOV HABER

The *haftaros* for both the first day of *Sukkos* (from *Zecharia* chapter 14), and *Shabbos shebesoch hamoed* (from *Yechezkel* chapters 38-39) describe the wars of Gog and Magog, the battles preceding the advent of the messianic era. These battles revolve around Jerusalem, with the chief combatants being Edom and Yishmael (see Malbim to *Yechezkel* 38:2). Certainly the recent tragic events, once again pitting Christian countries (the traditional inheritors of the Edom dynasty) against Muslim countries (descendants of Yishmael), are frightening reminders of the eventual fulfillment of these prophecies.

Zecharia prophesies that after the battle, all the nations of the world will be called upon to celebrate the festival of *Sukkos*, with dire consequences for those refusing to do so. Presumably building on this concept, the Talmud (*Avoda Zara* 2a-3b) relates that in the future, *Hashem* will prepare the reward for those who were faithful to the Torah and its precepts throughout history. The nations of the world will advance various claims as to why they should receive reward even though they rejected the Torah and did not fulfill its commandments. Finally, *Hashem* grants them a last opportunity for merit by commanding them to build *sukkos* and dwell in

---

Originally published on TorahWeb.org in 2001

them. After the nations build their *sukkos*, *Hashem* shines the sun in full force, making the heat intolerable, after which the frustrated nations leave the *sukkah* and kick the *sukkah* during their hasty exit. God then laughs at the nations' insincerity. The Talmud questions why this should be held against the nations since, after all, even Jews are exempt from this *mitzva* when it is uncomfortable (*mitztaer*) to remain in the *sukkah*. The answer given is that at least the Jews do not kick the *sukkah* when leaving.

Perhaps we can offer a deeper explanation as to why the *mitzva* of *sukkah* is singled out as the test for the nations of the world, and why their refusal to fulfill it leads to such great punishment. Divine commandments, the *mitzvos*, can be fulfilled in one of two ways: (1) as necessary burdens, albeit beneficial, lofty ones; (2) as welcome opportunities to serve the Master of the world. The former is symptomatic of only a king-servant relationship with *Hashem*; the latter adds to this the loving father-son relationship. Indeed, God is referred to as "*Avinu Malkeinu*" – "Our Father; Our King." On the one hand, we have no choice but to fulfill the *devar Hashem*, the word of God, as transgression will lead to severe punishment and fulfillment to immense reward. But on the other hand, we rejoice at the opportunity to please our Heavenly Father. (See *Mishna Avos* 1:3 and commentaries there.) How a person reacts when faced with difficulties while performing *mitzvos*, even those hardships exempting him from their fulfillment, demonstrates his underlying attitude toward the commandments. One who views *mitzvos* as burdens is pleased with the exemption and even resents the hardship leading to the exemption, it being indicative of an increased burden associated with the commandment. By contrast, the *oheiv* is saddened by the missed opportunity to please his Creator. Hence, the *ummos ha'olam* (nations of the world) kick the *sukkah* while leaving it due to discomfort, indicative of a purely pragmatic approach to commandments. The Jews leave as well, but reluctantly (see Rama (639:7), demonstrating their love of God and His commandments.

These are the contrasting attitudes between *Klal Yisrael* and the *ummos ha'olam*. *Klal Yisrael* jubilantly declared "*na'aseh venishma*," "we will do and we will listen" (*Shemos* 24:7), to accept the Torah at *Har Sinai*. The other nations, after discovering that the Torah's precepts would be difficult to keep, rejected it. *Klal Yisrael* yearns for more opportunities for *mitzvos*; the *ummos ha'olam* rejoice when the burden is lifted. Specifically, the *mitzva* of *sukkah* readily emphasizes this point. *Sukkah* is one of the few *mitzvos* that encompass the entire body and all life activities. Eating and sleeping, as well as learning and prayer, all are complementary aspects of this *mitzva*. Indeed, the *poskim* (decisors) rule that even regular conversation with acquaintances should take place in the *sukkah*. Thus, all apparently mundane activities can become acts of Divine service. One who views *mitzvos* as all-pervasive opportunities for elevating every aspect of life will also perform them with love and enthusiasm. The nations reject this *sukkah* concept, of life revolving around the Divine command. Hence, they reject the entire message of the Torah and are not worthy of special Divine reward in the End of Days.

Indeed, unique *korbanos* are brought during the first seven days of *Sukkos* on behalf of the seventy nations of the world, as our Torah concerns itself with the benefit of all of mankind and looks toward the day when all the nations of the world will recognize God's oneness (see second half of *Aleinu* prayer). However, the inner meaning of *Sukkos* ultimately remains the special treasure of the Jewish people. Hence, on the last day of the holiday, *Shemini Atzeres*, *korbanos* are offered on behalf of only *Klal Yisrael*, as *Hashem*, requesting that His beloved children who serve Him with love stay another day, states: "קשה עלי פרידתכם - Your leaving is difficult for Me."

This aspect of *ahava* in the performance of *mitzvos* is further highlighted by the intense, extra joy accompanying the celebration of *Sukkos* (see Rabbi Rosensweig, "The Link between *Yom Kippur* and *Sukkos*," in this volume). In addition, the *mitzva* of *nisuch hamayim* (water pouring) on the *mizbeach* has been explained as an allusion to the verse in *Shir Hashirim* (8:7): "מים רבים לא יוכלו לכבות את האהבה - a multitude of water cannot extinguish the love [between *Klal Yisrael* and God]."

May the merit of our increased enthusiastic devotion to *Hashem*'s commandments out of love allow us to be spared from the great wars of Gog and Magog, and merit to dwell in the heavenly *oro shel Livyasan*!

Chag HaSukkos: The Festival of Divine Providence

RABBI YAAKOV HABER

The upcoming holiday of *Sukkos* overflows with underlying themes. Prayerful motifs accentuated by the waving of the *arba'a minim* and the *Tefillas Geshem* on *Shemini Atzeres*; faith and trust in God highlighted by the dwelling in a temporary structure, the *sukkah*; joyous exuberance demonstrated by the celebration of the *zeicher lesimchas beis hashoeiva*; ecstatic dancing on *Simchas Torah*, together with the messianic yearnings expressed by the prayer of meriting the *sukkas oro shel Livyasan* and the *haftaros'* focus on the final apocalyptic battle of Gog and Magog which will usher in the long-awaited blessed era of redemption, all blend together to form what can be described as a whirlwind of spiritually elevating activities crowning the intense period of repentance immediately preceding this festival. Here, we focus on but one aspect of one *mitzva* of the manifold ideas inherent in each of the observances of the festival: the *mitzva* of dwelling in the *sukkah*.

Many have noted that the main, but by no means the only, theme

---

Originally published on TorahWeb.org in 2003

taught by the *sukkah* is that of Divine providence and protection. Both R. Akiva's position that the *sukkah* reminds us of the actual booths built by our ancestors in the Sinai Desert, and R. Eliezer's position that it recalls the miraculous clouds of glory which surrounded and protected *Bnei Yisrael* in the *midbar* (see *Sukkah* 11b) serve to underscore God's supreme role as protector through natural means and through supernatural intervention.

We may suggest that the three core fundamental religious beliefs as delineated by Rav Yosef Albo in his *Sefer HaIkkarim*, those of (1) belief in God, (2) revelation of Torah and (3) reward and punishment through Divine Providence (*Sefer HaIkkarim* notes that each of Rambam's 13 principles can be categorized under one of these three), are each highlighted in turn by one of the *Shalosh Regalim* (Three Festivals). *Pesach* commemorates the miraculous Exodus from Egypt, which removed any doubts as to the existence of an all-powerful Creator, Who, not subject to the laws of nature, can manipulate them at will (see Ramban, end of *Parashas Bo*, and Omissions of *Minyan HaMitzvos laRambam – Mitzvos Asei*, no. 1). *Shavuos* of course is the festival commemorating revelation and the giving of the Torah. *Sukkos* completes the cycle by stressing Divine providence and protection. The Exodus was not a one-time Divine intervention in the affairs of man, but was evidence of the ongoing relationship that *Hashem* has with His creations, as manifested by His revealed protection of the Jewish people in the desert for a full 40 years. Our trust in this protection even in periods where God's hand is not openly revealed is based on the foundation of the *midbar* experience. Indeed, at a later point in history, when the Jews questioned *Hashem's* ability to provide for their needs to enable them to pursue Torah study, the prophet Yirmiyahu showed them the sample of the *mann* stored as a remembrance, in order to demonstrate that just as *Hashem* provided for their ancestors in the desert, so too does He continue to provide for them throughout history (see *Mechilta, Beshalach* 16).

The theme of constant Divine providence is also stressed in *Tefillas*

Arvis (the evening prayer). Questioning the interlocution of the blessing of "*hashkiveinu*" between the blessing of "*ga'al Yisrael*" and *Shemoneh Esrei*, in seeming violation of the principle of סמיכת גאולה לתפילה (juxtaposing the blessing of גאל ישראל to the *Amida*), the Talmud (*Berachos* 4b) answers that the blessing of "*hashkiveinu*" is part of a גאולה אריכתא, one long praise concerning the redemption. Maharal (*Nesivos Olam, Nesiv Hatefilla* 7, s.v. *veda od*) explains that "*ga'al Yisrael*" praises God for the one-time Exodus from Mitzrayim. "*Hashkiveinu*" continues to praise and pray to Him for His continued protection of the Jewish people after that Exodus, for redemption without subsequent protection is incomplete. Based on this idea, it is readily understandable why the *beracha* includes the phrase "ופרוש עלינו סוכת שלומך- and spread forth upon us the **sukkah** of Your peace," and on *Shabbosos* and *Yamim Tovim* we substitute the normal ending of the *beracha* with the phrase "ברוך אתה ה' הפורש סוכת שלום עלינו ועל כל עמו ישראל ועל ירושלים - Blessed are You *Hashem*, Who spreads forth the **sukkah of peace** upon us and upon His entire nation and on Jerusalem." The "*sukkah*," with its underlying motif of Divine providence and protection, blends in readily with the main theme of the blessing.

The *halacha* mandating that the *sechach* consist of material grown from the ground which has not been shaped into any kind of utensil can also be explained in accordance with this theme. On the one hand, man is charged to "conquer the world," "*vekivshuha*" (*Bereishis* 1:28), to utilize its resources and the laws existent within the cosmos to discover the wisdom of its Creator and channel its blessings to better and ease the human condition through advances in science and technology. On the other hand, man must never lose sight of the Grantor of these gifts and never cease to thank Him and serve Him in order to elevate man's true self by cleaving to his Creator. On the festival of providence, we use precisely as our roof, symbolic of protection, those elements which are clearly directly from God's blessings, natural materials unfashioned by human hands. This underscores the idea that all of the tools and inventions of mankind are also ultimately results of Divine gifts bestowed with love upon His creations. Rav Samson Raphael Hirsch notes that Gog, king of Magog, the archenemy of the Jewish people about whom we read in the *haftaros* of *Sukkos*, whose name and country are derived etymologically from "permanent roof," is the antithesis of the *sukkah*-Jew. The Jew is charged to view even his permanent structures fundamentally as *sukkos*, flimsy and always in need of Divine protection; Gog views everything as an object of his own accomplishment with no need for any Divine intervention. (See also "On *Makkot* and Scientific Endeavors," http://www.torahweb.org/torah/2000/parsha/rhab_bo.html)

In our current world of uncertainty, when future world history hangs in the balance, let us all incorporate into our essential world-outlook this theme of *sukkah* – that of our essential need for Divine protection and assistance for all the blessings of existence and all of human endeavor. As a result, may we merit the fulfillment of the *beracha* of the *Sukkas Shalom* of *Hashem Yisbarach*.

Chag HaSukkos:
The Tishrei Connection
RABBI YAAKOV HABER

Tur (*Orach Chaim* 625) raises a famous question concerning the commandment to celebrate the festival of *Sukkos* in the Jewish month of *Tishrei*. If, as the Torah indicates (*Vayikra* 23:43), the *mitzva* of dwelling in a *sukkah* reminds us of the fact that *Hashem* – both miraculously through clouds of glory (the position of R. Eliezer, *Sukkah* 11b), and through natural means via man-made actual huts in a previously uninhabited desert (R. Akiva, ibid.) – protected us in the *midbar*, the festival should take place in *Nisan*, the month of the Exodus, when *Bnei Yisrael* first entered the *midbar* and received this protection.

Ibn Ezra (*Vayikra* 23:43) answers that the *Bnei Yisrael* only found it necessary to construct actual huts, or *sukkos*, from *Tishrei* onward, to protect themselves from the cold. The *ananei hakavod* provided shelter from the sun during the summer months.

Tur himself suggests that *Hashem* delayed the celebration from the spring to the fall so that our dwelling in the *sukkos* should be noticeable as a *mitzva* performance in the not-always-pleasant fall weather, and not be interpreted as a relaxing stay outdoors, unrelated to Divine ser-

---

Originally published on TorahWeb.org in 2004

vice, in the balmy spring weather.

The Vilna Gaon offers an alternative explanation. Since the *sukkos* commemorate the *ananei hakavod*, we celebrate the date that they **remained** with us throughout our stay in the desert. After the *cheit ha'eigel*, the clouds of glory left as a punishment for this grave sin. Only after *Klal Yisrael* started work on the construction the *Mishkan*, which served as an atonement for this sin, did the clouds return. This occurred on the fifteenth of *Tishrei*, exactly the date of *Sukkos*, soon after *Yom Kippur*, when Moshe descended with the second *luchos* and informed the Jews of the commandment to build the *Mishkan*.

Bina LaIttim by R. Azaria Figo (quoted in *Talelei Orot*), offers a novel explanation. *Hashem's* involvement in the world manifests itself in two ways: first, through the natural order, the fixed rules of creation; second, through Divine providence overriding the regular rules of nature. The goal of creation was that mankind, through their connecting to God by fulfilling His will, would merit the second, transcendent level of Divine intervention in the world. This was to be realized through *Bnei Yisrael*, who committed to fulfilling *Hashem's* mission for the world as embodied in His Torah. Malbim (*Bereishis*) explains the concept of the *Avos* being the "Divine Chariot" as meaning that they were the ones who caused this second, more intense level of Divine intervention to occur in the world, hence fulfilling the goal of Creation. The ancient Egyptians were steeped in the belief of the power and absolute supremacy of the "*ma'areches hakochavim*," the order of the constellations, or the natural order. Hence, Pharaoh warns Moshe, based on the statements of his astrologers, that "evil" is "in the stars" for the Jewish people in the desert (*Shemos* 10:10). Through His miraculous overriding of the laws of nature both in Mitzrayim and subsequently by protecting the Jewish people in the desert by sending supernatural, Divine clouds of glory to shield *Klal Yisrael*, *Hashem* indicated

Originally published on TorahWeb.org in 2005

that He intervenes in nature, shattering the myth of the supreme rule of "natural law" and underscoring His intense intervention in the world for the purpose of guiding the destiny of His beloved people, descendants of the Patriarchs who originally merited this level of Divine intervention. It is for this reason that *Sukkos*, which commemorates this manifestation of Divine intervention, occurs in *Tishrei*, the month of the creation of the world, thus reminding us that the Creator of the natural order overrides it at will for those who cleave to Him. (See also Defying Human Nature and Divine Miracles, http://www.torahweb.org/torah/2001/parasha/rhab_vayeishev.html, 2001.)

In the *Hallel* which we joyfully recite throughout the entire holiday, we state: "רם על כל גוים ה'. מי כה' א-לוקינו המגביהי לשבת, המשפילי לראות בשמים ובארץ - God is exalted above all of the Nations. Who is like **our** God who dwells on High, but who lowers Himself to see in the heavens and the earth? Who raises up the downtrodden from the dust …" (*Tehillim* 113:4-7). Malbim interprets this series of *pesukim* in a manner which highlights the above-mentioned theme. For the "nations of the world," God is the Creator alone, exalted in His Majesty, not concerned with the actions of mankind. The Jewish people, by contrast, recognize "**our** God" as One who, despite His exaltedness, interestedly observes and intervenes in the affairs of mankind, guiding them toward their destiny. (Also see *Lonely Man of Faith*, chapter 2, by Rav Joseph B. Soloveitchik *zt"l*.)

May the holiday of *Sukkos* serve as an impetus for all of us to recommit ourselves to *Hakadosh Baruch Hu*'s mission for us in the world, and thereby merit His constant, miraculous protection.

Kerias Shema and the Festivals of Tishrei
RABBI YAAKOV HABER

Often we find that central religious themes, which are expressed in an abbreviated form regularly, are more fully expressed on a particular occasion. Thus, the commemoration and celebration of *Yetzias Mitzrayim* (the Exodus from Egypt) which finds its full expression on *Pesach*, is remembered twice daily through the *mitzva* of *zechiras Yetzias Mitzrayim*, fulfilled through a brief recitation at the end of *kerias Shema* and in the blessing of *"ga'al Yisrael."* Similarly, the intense grief felt over the absence of the *Beis Hamikdash* and *Hashem's* revealed *Shechina* (Divine Presence) on *Tisha Be'Av* is more briefly experienced through the blessings focusing on the return of Temple service in the *Shemoneh Esrei* and *Birkas Hamazon*, the introductory paragraph of *"Al Naharos Bavel"* before *Birkas Hamazon* and the *Tikkun Chatzos* recited by many at midnight. It can be suggested that the same type of relationship exists between the twice-daily recitation of *kerias Shema* and the three festivals of *Rosh Hashana, Yom HaKippurim* and *Sukkos*.

One of the primary themes of *Rosh Hashana* is clearly *kabbalas ol malchus Shamayim*, acceptance of Divine sovereignty, over every aspect of our individual and collective lives. From the majestic coronation tunes

Originally published on TorahWeb.org in 2005

sung at the introductory "*Barechu*" of the evening prayer, to the frightful declaration of "*Hamelech!*" before *Shacharis*, to the dominant theme of "*Melech al kol ha'aretz*" in the *Shemoneh Esrei*, the *Rosh Hashana* experience is clearly suffused with the theme of God's majesty. Mention of repentance and our faults is hardly present at all. Several Jewish thinkers have suggested that before focusing on our individual faults, we must first realign ourselves with our unique mission in life – to subjugate our will to the will of our Creator, the Master of all, who placed us into existence; only then can we properly attempt to redirect our energies toward that lofty goal.

Yom HaKippurim, with its heavy emphasis on our faults, both in our fulfillment of the positive and negative commandments through the *viduy* (confession) and our embarrassment and regret at not performing them properly, stresses the fact that it is insufficient to merely accept Divine sovereignty; we must recommit ourselves to the totality of *avodas Hashem* (Divine service). Nothing less than perfection in every aspect of Divine service is our eventual, hopeful goal.

Rounding out the *Tishrei* cycle of festivals, *Sukkos* stresses, in an extreme way, the actual **performance** of *mitzvos*. From the preparations before the holiday – the building of the *sukkah* and the search for and purchase of the four species, combined with the regular hectic *Yom Tov* preparations – to the celebration of *Sukkos* itself – through living in the *sukkah*, augmenting our prayers with the joyous singing of *Hallel* and the intense recital of *Hoshanos*, coupled with the taking of the four species, culminating in the longer *tefillos* and *teshuva* themes of *Hoshana Rabba*, *Tefillas Geshem* on *Shemini Atzeres* and the jubilant, ecstatic celebration of *Simchas Torah* – the Jew is totally immersed in the preparation for and the actual performance of *mitzvos*. Indeed the *mitzva* of dwelling in the *sukkah* itself encompasses the entire body and most human activities. The four species also represent the various parts of the human body all being utilized for Divine service, as described in a well-known *midrash*.

These same three themes – acceptance of Divine sovereignty, acceptance of all of the Divine commandments, and the actual performance of them – are expressed in a compacted form every day in the *kerias Shema*. The *Mishna* in *Masseches Berachos* (13a) cites R. Yehoshua ben Karcha who explains the reason that we recite the three sections of the *kerias Shema* in the order that we follow. The first *parasha* of *"Shema"* is recited before the second *parasha* of *"Vehaya"* in order that we first be *"mekabel ol malchus Shamayim"* (accept the yoke of Heaven), and only afterward accept *"ol mitzvos"* (the yoke of commandments). *Maharal* (*Nesivos Olam, Nesiv Ha'avoda* 8) elaborates on this *Mishna*, emphasizing the fact that the true servant of God must fully accept both the belief in God as ruler and commit himself fully to the totality of His legislation. The *Maharal* concludes by noting that the third *parasha*, that of *tzitzis*, is symbolic of the actual performance of *mitzvos*. *Tzitzis* is chosen as a prototype *mitzva* because it is a commandment that encompasses the entire body. It is insufficient to theoretically accept *ol mitzvos*, the yoke of Divine commandments; one must translate the commitment into action through his whole being. This action is symbolized by *tzitzis*.

According to the above analysis, it is precisely this progression which we follow in a more magnified and focused manner throughout the the three festivals of *chodesh Tishrei*. We start by recommitting ourselves in theory to *Hashem* and His Torah during the festivals of *Rosh Hashana* and *Yom HaKippurim*; we then translate this commitment immediately into action through the *mitzva*-filled celebration of *Sukkos*, whose main commandments themselves symbolize total dedication of all aspects of our existence to Divine service. After the last *hakafa* on *Simchas Torah*, we are hopefully then able to apply this new twofold theoretical and active commitment to the rest of the year, with the attitude of *"ana avda deKudsha Berich Hu"* – "I am a servant of the Holy One, Blessed is He!"

Sukkos: Two Types of Divine Providence[48]
RABBI YAKOV HABER

"In order that all your generations should know that I caused the Children of Israel to dwell in booths when I took them out of Egypt" (Vayikra 23:43). In a well-known debate (Sukkah 11b), R. Eliezer maintains that the booths refer to the clouds of glory. R. Akiva holds that they were actual huts set up at the various stops on the way to Eretz Yisrael. Surprisingly, Tur follows the position of R. Eliezer, even though the halacha normally follows R. Akiva over R. Eliezer. Aruch LaNeir notes that in several places in the midreshei halacha, the positions are presented switched. R. Akiva maintains that we commemorate the clouds of glory and R. Eliezer holds that we recall the actual booths. The Tur, then, does follow the accepted position of R. Akiva. Perhaps we can propose another approach based on other sources related to the celebration of Sukkos.

The lulav is waved not only at the time of the beracha, but also during the Hallel. All agree that it is waved not only during the recital of "hodu laShem ki tov," but also at "ana Hashem" (Sukkah 37b). Beis Sham-

---

[48] The core of the ideas outlined here concerning the debate between R. Eliezer and R. Akiva is based on concepts delivered by my esteemed father-in-law, Rabbi Yitzchak Handel shlita, at the bris of his first child, now my brother-in-law. Here the ideas are presented with expansions.

Originally published on TorahWeb.org in 2015

mai maintain that we wave at "ana Hashem hatzlicha na." Beis Hillel hold that we only wave at "ana Hashem hoshia na." The halacha follows this latter view. What is the root of their debate?

The two aforementioned verses beginning with "ana" both plead with Hashem for help, but in two different ways. "Ana Hashem hoshia na" asks for a "yeshua," a salvation. This word is used when God saves in a situation where those whom He is saving are not actively participating in their salvation. A classic example is the Splitting of the Sea. Moshe tells Bnei Yisrael, "התיצבו וראו את ישועת ה'" - Stand and observe the salvation of Hashem" (Shemos 14:13). You are not able to save yourselves at all; God will miraculously do so.[49] If someone, chas veshalom, is terminally ill and the doctors have given up hope of medical intervention, the family will oftentimes say, "He needs a yeshua," i.e., only Hashem can save him now; human beings cannot do anything.

"Ana Hashem hatzlicha na" requests "hatzlacha," success. Asking for success addresses a situation where the one praying is acting to bring about the result in a natural way, but, realizing that no human effort can succeed without Divine assistance, he prays for it. A classic example of this is Shlomo Hamelech's declaration "אם ה' לא יבנה בית שוא עמלו בוניו בו -If God does not build a house, its builders have toiled in vain" (Tehillim 127:1). The builders are engaging in acts of building. Hashem created a natural order in which gathering building blocks and adhesives leads to the rising of an edifice. But, Shlomo teaches us, that this too needs the Divine blessing of "hatzlacha." When a person is about to take a test or engage in a new business we bless him: "have hatzlacha," not "have a yeshua" (unless he hasn't studied or has no business kup!)

These two ideas represent two different forms of Divine provi-

---

[49] True, the Jews were commanded to enter the Sea, but this was a demonstration of faith in God that He would save them, the merit of which caused the salvation. It was clearly not an act that would naturally cause the Sea to split.

dence. Throughout our lives we actively engage in beneficial physical activities, such as producing food, construction, pursuit of a livelihood or seeking a spouse. We also pursue spiritual activities such as praying, studying Torah, performing mitzvos and engaging in chesed. Judaism teaches us generally to be active and not just passively await Divine salvation.[50] Sifrei (Re'eh 123:18) on the promised blessing of "[Hashem] will bless you in all of your handiwork," comments, "I would think one should be idle (and God will supernaturally bless him), therefore the verse states 'in all of your handiwork.'" But we recognize that we always still need Divine blessing, otherwise, no activity can succeed. Therefore we pray for "hatzlacha."

But there is another form of Divine providence – "yeshua." At times, we have no choice but to rely on miracles.[51] Oftentimes there are situations in which no human intervention or activity can, by natural means, bring about the desired salvation. At these times, knowing that nothing is impossible for God we plead, "Hoshia na!"

It would appear that the debate between Beis Shammai and Beis Hillel revolves around the focus of the Sukkos holiday. Many have noted that the main theme of Sukkos is celebrating and inculcating into our religious mindset the concept of Divine providence and protection. (See "Chag HaSukkos: The Festival of Divine Providence," in this volume.) Divine providence expresses itself in two ways: within the natural order and transcending it. Most of the time, God operates in a hidden way, seamlessly maneuvering within His natural system to bring about His desired result. Whether a person finds his or her spouse, gets the healing (s)he

---

[50] Much has been written and said about the appropriate blend of *hishtadlus* and *bitachon* and how active one should be in pursuing *parnasa*, especially for those engaged in full-time Torah study. See the debate in *Berachos* (35b) between R. Shimon bar Yochai and R. Yishmael, and the insightful series on yutorah.org by Rabbi Daniel Stein on *emunah* and *bitachon*. Here, we are discussing regular situations.
[51] Even David ben Gurion, the former Prime Minister of Israel, not coming from a Torah-observant perspective of belief, famously stated concerning events revolving around the State of Israel, "In Israel, in order to be a realist you must believe in miracles."

needs, connects with the right employer or the right yeshiva, he is experiencing the first, "natural" type of providence. But sometimes Hashem intervenes in a way that defies the normal rules. Sometimes there are unexplainable medical miracles or unexpected and ultimately not understandable military victories. These belong to the second category of Divine providence. Which type of Divine providence is recalled, commemorated and incorporated into our service of God? Beis Shammai, by focusing on hatzlacha, seems to view the first type as the primary one commemorated, perhaps since this is more common and hence more relevant. Beis Hillel seems to hold that the second, the supernatural, unexplainable, yeshua-type of providence is being recalled and re-enacted. On a simple plane, this is because the miracles of the Exodus and subsequent stay in the desert were supernatural, and hence this aspect should be highlighted. Below we will propose a different explanation of Beis Hillel's view.

Upon reflection, we can perhaps suggest that this debate is rooted in different approaches that the progenitors of these two great yeshivos followed. The Talmud (Beitza 16a) teaches us that Shammai would "live Shabbos" all week. Every time he found a choice delicacy, he would put it away for Shabbos. If he found an even better one, he would consume the first and put away the second. This way, Shabbos was always on his mind, in fulfillment of the simple meaning of "zachor es yom haShabbos lekadesho." But Hillel is described as "midda acheres haisa bo," "he had a different characteristic." He followed the thrust of the verse "Baruch Hashem yom, yom," "praise Hashem every day for its blessings" (Tehillim 68:20). Therefore, he would immediately partake of whatever came his way, trusting that the One who provided it for him that day would provide an even nicer item for Shabbos. The Gemara then records that their respective schools taught in accordance with their Rosh HaYeshiva. What is the root of this debate?

The poskim rule in this debate in accordance with Shammai,[52] and

---

[52] See *Mishna Berura* to 250:2, and end of *seif kattan* 42:4.

explain that this is not a classic debate which would apply to all people. As the Talmud states concerning Hillel, "midda acheres haisa bo." Everyone in their life blends together the two middos of hishtadlus, physical effort at achieving a goal, with bitachon, trust in God and recognizing that ultimately all efforts are futile without Divine blessing. For Shammai, since he prepared for other aspects of his life as well, he had to do so for Shabbos. To rely solely on Hashem to provide for Shabbos would be a slight to kavod Shabbos by not actively preparing for it. Hillel apparently operated with less effort and more reliance on providence in his other efforts as well, and therefore, consistent with this attitude, was able to rely totally on Hashem to provide for Shabbos as well.[53] In essence, then, Shammai puts more emphasis on human hishtadlus creating the "utensil" for the Divine blessing to occur. Put differently, he trusted that Hashem would cause him to be "matzliach" – give success to his endeavors. Hillel put his trust in God that he would somehow bring about what he needed without any effort on his behalf, i.e., that He would send a "yeshua." It seems apparent that Shammai had greatly developed his midda of bitachon as well, but that his bitachon expressed itself in the hatzlacha rather than the yeshua model. Their conduct the whole year, then, is consistent with their view concerning where the lulav is waved in the Hallel.

Based on the above, perhaps we can answer why the Tur followed R. Eliezer's view. Since the halacha follows Beis Hillel that we wave the lulav at "hoshia na," this indicates that the main emphasis of Sukkos is the second type of hashgacha peratis, the yeshua model, even if year-round we generally follow the hatzlacha model. To create consistency between the theme of lulav and sukkah, the Tur ruled that the sukkos commemorate the ananei hakavod, clearly an open miracle, a yeshua.[54]

---

[53] In the language of Rav Soloveitchik *zt"l* (as heard from *Mori veRabi* Rav Schachter *shlita*), "We are all 'Shammai-niks.' We all buy insurance!" Also see the *Mishna Berura* referenced in previous footnote, who has a somewhat different formulation.

[54] It would be anomalous, though, that R. Eliezer who was a member of *Beis* Shammai, would break this pattern. Perhaps this is a further proof to the version of the *midreshei*

At first glance, the view of Hillel and his yeshiva is only relevant to the supernatural, historical event of the midbar experience or the select few who are granted that level of Divine providence. But perhaps the message of the emphasis on yeshua on Sukkos is that even hatzlacha assumes yeshua as well. Every human endeavor, thought or action is itself based on a reoccurring Divine will. It is only God Who creates and recreates "nature," constantly allowing it to function. Ideas themselves often are implanted within our minds by God without our even knowing it (see Targum Onkelos to Devarim 8:18). Hence, according to Beis Hillel, the holiday celebrating Divine providence highlights that ultimately everything in the world comes from Divine salvation.

May our fulfillment of the mitzvos of sukkah and lulav help us live our lives fully cognizant of, and in a manner consistent with, our realization of the pervasive role of Hashem's guidance in our individual and communal lives.

---

halacha quoted above, which switches the positions.

The Sukkah: The Key to True Happiness

RABBI ELIAKIM KOENIGSBERG

"בסוכות תשבו שבעת ימים" - *Basukkos teishvu shivas yamim*," "You shall live in booths for seven days" (*Vayikra* 23:42). *Chazal* explain (*Sukkah* 2a) that the Torah is saying, "Leave your *diras keva*, your permanent dwelling, your home, and live in a *diras arai*, a temporary dwelling, for seven days." What is the purpose of living in a *diras arai* for seven days? And why are we commanded to do so specifically at this time of the year?

One answer might be that during *Sukkos*, the *Chag Ha'asif*, which celebrates the new harvest, there is a concern that one might get carried away with his financial success. He might mistakenly perceive that "*kochi ve'otzem yadi asa li es hachayil hazeh*," "my strength and the power of my own hand made me successful" (*Devarim* 8:17). The Torah, therefore, commands us to leave our comfortable, protective homes and enter into the *sukkah*, a temporary, flimsy dwelling that is open to the sky, to reinforce the notion that man is constantly dependent on *rachamei Shamayim*, Divine assistance, to achieve anything in life. Whether we sit in a *sukkah* to commemorate how *Bnei Yisrael* in the *midbar* were protected by the clouds of glory or to commemorate that they sat in actual huts (*Sukkah* 11b), the lesson is the same, namely that just as *Hashem* protected *Bnei Yisrael* in the

Originally published on TorahWeb.org in 2015

midbar, so too He is the One who protects and provides for each one of us.

The Chida (*Simchas Haregel, Sukkos*) adds that there is a second important message that living in the *diras arai* of the *sukkah* is meant to highlight, and that is that our existence in *olam hazeh* is only temporary, that all the pleasures of the physical world are ephemeral and insignificant. Lasting, eternal pleasure can only be achieved through our involvement in *talmud Torah*, *mitzvos* and *ma'asim tovim*. By commanding us to sit in the *sukkah* right after the *Yamim Noraim*, the Torah wants to remind us how important it is to have the proper sense of priorities if we want to follow through on our *teshuva* resolutions, to effect meaningful change in our lives.

This, writes the Chida, is the idea that Yaakov *Avinu* tried to convey after his encounter with Esav. The *pasuk* says, "And Yaakov traveled to *Sukkos*, and he built for himself a home (*bayis*), and for his cattle he made huts; therefore he called the name of the place *Sukkos*" (*Bereishis* 33:17). Why did he name the place *Sukkos*? He should have named it "*Bayis*" after the home he built. The Chida explains that by building huts for his cattle (*lemikneihu*) and naming the place *Sukkos*, Yaakov *Avinu* wanted to express the idea that all worldly possessions (*mikneh*) are only temporary, so they do not deserve to be stored in a permanent structure.

The Chida's comment can shed light on the statement of the *Tur* (*Orach Chaim*, 417) that the *mitzva* of *sukkah* was given to *Bnei Yisrael* in the merit of Yaakov *Avinu*, who built *sukkos* for his cattle. What is the connection between the *sukkos* of Yaakov *Avinu* and the *mitzva* of *sukkah*? The answer is that the purpose of living in the *diras arai* of the *sukkah* is to help us develop the perspective of Yaakov *Avinu*, that material possessions are insignificant, and that one should focus his attention in this world on spiritual pursuits which have lasting value.

This can also be the reason why we read *Koheles* on *Chol Hamoed Sukkos*: to remind us how temporary, frustrating and unfulfilling life in this world can be. The only accomplishments which have lasting value are spiritual ones. The bottom line is what Koheles writes in his conclusion, "In the end, when all is considered, fear God and keep His *mitzvos*, for that is the whole purpose of man" (12:13). The message of *Koheles* is that to achieve real success in this world, one must have an appreciation of what is primary and what is secondary, what is temporary and what has lasting value.

Rav Shmuel Aharon Yudelevitch, a son-in-law of the famed *tzaddik* Rav Aryeh Levin *zt"l*, once suggested (see *Me'ilo Shel Shmuel*, p. 264) that perhaps this is why *Sukkos* is called *zeman simchaseinu*, because the *sukkah* is a vehicle which can teach us how to be truly happy. The message of the *sukkah* is that life in this world is *arai* – it is only temporary. All physical pleasure is fleeting. The older a person gets, the more he appreciates that the endless pursuit of physical pleasure does not really satisfy a person. The only way to achieve real happiness is by connecting oneself to the *Ribbono Shel Olam* – by studying His Torah and observing His *mitzvos*, by focusing on spiritual matters. The *Yom Tov* of *Sukkos* teaches us how to live a more satisfying and meaningful life. It helps keep the fire of the *Yamim Noraim* burning inside us throughout the winter. It reveals the key to true happiness.

Sukkos and Shemini Atzeres: Hashem's Expression of Love

RABBI ELIAKIM KOENIGSBERG

On *Shabbos Chol Hamoed Sukkos* we read from *Parashas Ki Sisa*. The simple reason that this portion was chosen is that it mentions the *Shalosh Regalim*. But the *kerias haTorah* also discusses the second *luchos*, the Thirteen Attributes of Divine Mercy, and the dialogue between *Hashem* and Moshe *Rabbeinu* about whether a *malach* or *Hashem* himself will lead *Klal Yisrael*. What do these other topics have to do with the *Yom Tov* of *Sukkos*?

The *Tur* (*Orach Chaim* 625) asks a famous question. If we sit in *sukkos* to remind ourselves of the clouds of glory that surrounded *Klal Yisrael* when they left Mitzrayim, then why do we celebrate the *Yom Tov* of *Sukkos* in the month of *Tishrei*? Since *Klal Yisrael* left Mitzrayim during *Nisan*, we should celebrate *Sukkos* then.

The Vilna Gaon (*Shir Hashirim* 1:4) answers that on *Sukkos* we are not commemorating the clouds of glory that enveloped *Klal Yisrael* when they first left Mitzrayim, because those clouds disappeared after *cheit ha'eigel*. But after *Hashem* forgave *Klal Yisrael* for *cheit ha'eigel* on *Yom*

Originally published on TorahWeb.org in 2016

Kippur, they received the command to build the *Mishkan*, and when they started building the *Mishkan* on the fifteenth of *Tishrei*, the clouds of glory returned. It is this return of the clouds of glory that we commemorate by sitting in *sukkos*, because this showed that *Hashem* had forgiven *Klal Yisrael* for *cheit ha'eigel* and He was willing to rest His *Shechina* on them once again. Since the clouds returned during the month of *Tishrei*, we celebrate *Sukkos* specifically at this time.

This idea can help explain why we read *Parashas Ki Sisa* on *Shabbos Chol Hamoed Sukkos*. At the beginning of the *keria*, Moshe *Rabbeinu* asks *Hashem* not to rest His *Shechina* on any nation except *Klal Yisrael*, "ונפלינו אני ועמך מכל העם אשר על פני האדמה" - And I and your people will be distinct from all other nations of the world (*Shemos* 33:16). Later, after *Hashem* teaches Moshe the Thirteen Attributes of Mercy, Moshe once again asks, "*Yeilech na Hashem bekirbeinu*," "Let *Hashem* go in our midst" (*Shemos* 34:9), and *Hashem* responds, "I will establish a covenant [with you]; I will make distinctions (*e'eseh niflaos*) with your people." Rashi interprets that here *Hashem* finally agrees to Moshe's request that *Klal Yisrael* should be different (*veniflinu*) from all other nations, in that *Hashem* should rest His *Shechina* only on them.

These *pesukim* are especially appropriate for the *Yom Tov* of *Sukkos* because, as the Vilna *Gaon* explains, it was on *Yom Kippur* that *Hashem* forgave *Klal Yisrael* and agreed to rest His *Shechina* on them, and then on *Sukkos* He reaffirmed that commitment by returning the clouds of glory which represent the *Shechina*.

The return of the clouds of glory on *Sukkos* could be another reason why we refer to *Sukkos* as *zeman simchaseinu*, the time of our happiness. The simple explanation is that this refers to the happiness of the farmer who rejoices in the new harvest. Others explain that *Sukkos* is a time when we feel *simcha* for the atonement we achieved on *Yom Kippur*.

But in light of the Vilna Gaon's comment, it would seem that *Sukkos* could be called *zeman simchaseinu* because the fifteenth of *Tishrei* is the time that *Klal Yisrael* saw *Hashem*'s intense love for them, when He returned the clouds of glory and established a covenant to rest His *Shechina* only on them. This realization that we enjoy such a special relationship with *Hakadosh Baruch Hu* is a source of great *simcha*, and it transforms *Sukkos* into *zman simchaseinu*.

The expression of love between *Hakadosh Baruch Hu* and *Klal Yisrael* reaches a climax on *Shemini Atzeres* and *Simchas Torah*. On *Sukkos* we sacrifice a total of seventy bulls, but on *Shemini Atzeres* we sacrifice only one bull. Rashi (*Bemidbar* 29:35-36) quotes the *Midrash*, which explains that the seventy bulls we sacrifice on *Sukkos* correspond to the seventy nations of the world, while the one bull we sacrifice on *Shemini Atzeres* represents *Klal Yisrael*. Why do we bring *korbanos* corresponding to the nations of the world only on *Sukkos*? The answer is that the *korbanos* of *Sukkos* and *Shemini Atzeres* demonstrate the unique bond between *Hashem* and *Klal Yisrael*. The reality is that *Hashem* sustains the entire world and, in truth, the *Yom Tov* of *Sukkos* which celebrates the new harvest is relevant to all of the nations. But *Hashem* has a special relationship with *Klal Yisrael* that is expressed by the private feast that *Klal Yisrael* enjoys with Him on *Shemini Atzeres* (see Rashi, *Bemidbar* 29:36).

Shemini Atzeres is the culmination of the *Yom Tov* of *Sukkos* because it serves as a contrast to the universal *Yom Tov* of *Sukkos*. *Shemini Atzeres* is *Hashem*'s expression of love for *Klal Yisrael*. It shows the unique relationship that *Klal Yisrael* has with Him. There are no special *mitzvos* on *Shemini Atzeres* because the *simcha* of *Shemini Atzeres* comes from simply feeling a sense of closeness to *Hakadosh Baruch Hu*. On *Shemini Atzeres* we don't need a *simcha shel mitzva* to help us express our joy because we are overcome by a feeling of "- נגילה ונשמחה בך we will rejoice and be happy with You" (*Shir Hashirim* 1:4).

And that is why *Simchas Torah* is linked to *Shemini Atzeres*. When *Hakadosh Baruch Hu* forgave *Klal Yisrael* on *Yom Kippur*, He gave them the second *luchos*, the gift of Torah, to demonstrate his love for them. On *Shemini Atzeres* this love is expressed once again when *Hakadosh Baruch Hu* asks of *Klal Yisrael* to be His special guest for one last day of *Yom Tov*. We reciprocate by rejoicing with the Torah and showing how much we appreciate His gift and His expressions of love for us.

Shemini Atzeres: Living in Hashem's Presence

RABBI ELIAKIM KOENIGSBERG

Shemini Atzeres and *Simchas Torah* are the conclusion of the *Yom Tov* season which begins with *Rosh Hashana*. How are these days an appropriate finale to the *Yamim Noraim*? The *tefillos* of *Rosh Hashana* focus on expressing our desire that *Hakadosh Baruch Hu*'s kingship over the world be recognized by all. The *beracha* of *kedushas hayom* begins, "Rule over the entire world in Your glory ... let everything created by You know that You are its Maker." Even on *Yom Kippur*, the theme of *kabbalas malchus Shamayim*, accepting *Hashem*'s kingship and praying for the day when all recognize *Hashem*'s strength and power, remains a primary motif. And yet, the main focus of *Yom Kippur* is *teshuva*. Why is discussing *malchus Shamayim* so important in the process of *teshuva*?

The answer is that sin is possible only when a person forgets that he is constantly in the presence of the *Ribbono Shel Olam*. Our *tefillos* express a desire that all people recognize *Hashem*'s kingship, and included in that request is that we ourselves constantly live with an awareness of *Hashem*'s presence, that we evaluate all of our actions through the prism of the To-

Originally published on TorahWeb.org in 2017

rah, and that our goal should be not to satisfy our own desires, but to carry out *Hashem*'s agenda for ourselves and for the world at large. Dedicating ourselves to *malchus Shamayim* is not extraneous to the *teshuva* process at all, but rather it is a prerequisite for *teshuva*.

On *Shemini Atzeres*, our allegiance to *Hashem* and His Torah reaches its pinnacle. We leave the *sukkah* and put down the *daled minim*. We have no special *mitzvos* on this *Yom Tov*. Rather, our sole focus is celebrating with *Hashem* and His Torah. The *Midrash* (*Yalkut Shimoni, Pinchas* 782) comments that on *Shemini Atzeres*, the Jewish people declare, "זה היום עשה ה' נגילה ונשמחה בו - This is the day that *Hashem* made, we will rejoice and be happy *bo*." Asks the *Midrash*, "What does *bo* mean? 'With it' (meaning the *Yom Tov* of *Shemini Atzeres*) or 'with Him' (meaning *Hashem*)? Comes the *pasuk* and explains, "נגילה ונשמחה בך - we will rejoice and be happy with You," (*Shir Hashirim* 1:4) – "*bach beTorascha, bach biyshuascha* – with You in your Torah, with You in Your salvation."

Shemini Atzeres is the day when we declare that ultimate happiness can be felt only when a person connects to *Hakadosh Baruch Hu* and His Torah, when one recognizes that his strength and his success come only from *Hashem*. On *Simchas Torah*, we circle around the Torah to demonstrate that we want to subordinate ourselves to the spirit of the Torah and to live by the dictates and agenda of the Torah. Our exuberance and joy when dancing with the Torah are expressions of our heartfelt desire to take with us the *tefilla* of the *Yamim Noraim* that *Hashem*'s kingship be recognized by all, including ourselves.

The message of *Shemini Atzeres* is an appropriate prelude to *Parashas Bereishis*. The *pasuk* says that when *Hashem* created *Adam Harishon*, He declared, "Let us make man in our image, in our form" (*Bereishis* 1:26). Rashi comments that although the angels did not assist *Hakadosh Baruch Hu* in the creation of man, nevertheless the Torah uses the plural verb *na'aseh* in order to teach the trait of humility by implying that *Hashem* consulted with the angels, even though by doing so, the Torah makes it easier for heretics to claim that multiple gods were involved in the process of man's creation.

The question is, why is it worth taking the risk that someone might err in his beliefs just to teach a proper character trait? Rav Chaim Friedlander (*Sifsei Chaim, Moadim* 1, pp. 185-186) suggests that the Torah goes out of its way to teach the importance of humility because specifically this *midda* can prevent a person from making a mistake in his beliefs in the first place. If a person humbles himself and accepts *malchus Shamayim*, he will not make a mistake in *hashkafa*. As the *pasuk* says, "And you will become haughty, and you will forget *Hashem*" (*Devarim* 8:14). Having the proper perspective on life is often not a function of a person's intelligence, but rather of his *middos*. If a person develops a sense of humility, that will prevent him from making a mistake in his beliefs.

The truth is that all negative character traits stem from the same basic source, and that is a person's drive for self-satisfaction. The Rambam writes (*Hilchos Teshuva* 7:3) that one is obligated to do *teshuva* not only for improper actions, but even for inappropriate character traits such as anger, jealousy, competition and chasing after money, honor and physical pleasure. Why is this a part of *teshuva*? The answer is that improper character traits can lead a person to sin, because if a person is focused on satisfying himself, he will not be able to exercise self-control. To do a complete *teshuva*, it is not enough to regret the actions a person has done. He must also uproot the negative attitudes and *middos* which caused his *aveiros*, because without doing so, his *teshuva* will only be temporary.

The first two *aveiros* recorded by the Torah are the sin of eating from the *eitz hada'as* and the killing of Hevel. Each of these was caused not by a heretical belief, but by an improper *midda*. Chava ate from the *eitz hadaas* because the tree "was a delight to the eyes and it was desirable as a means for wisdom" (*Bereishis* 3:6). Chava wanted, "to be like God knowing good and bad" (*Bereishis* 3:5), and she did not control herself. Similarly, after Hevel's *korban* is accepted and Kayin's is rejected, Kayin kills Hevel. Once again, it was Kayin's jealousy, not a heretical belief, which caused him to kill his brother. These two sins highlight the insight of the Rambam that to do a complete *teshuva*, a person must uproot his negative character traits, because often a person's *middos* determine how he thinks and acts.

What can motivate a person to want to change his *middos*? A sincere desire to sacrifice his own interests for the sake of *kevod Shamayim*, to subordinate his own will to that of *Hakadosh Baruch Hu*. That is the message of the *Yamim Noraim* and *Shemini Atzeres* – to search for happiness not in the pursuit of physical pleasure and personal satisfaction, but in accepting *malchus Shamayim* and fulfilling the will of *Hashem*. "*Nagila venismecha bach*"; may we rejoice and find happiness in our connection to *Hakadosh Baruch Hu*, because that is the ultimate delight.

Simchas Torah: In Anticipation

RABBI YAAKOV NEUBURGER

The excitement generated by the successful completion of studying the entire *Torah Shebichsav* – as individuals preparing the text with *Targum* and *mefarshim*, and as a community listening to the *leining* and participating in public study – has its roots in several sources. The Ramban in his commentary to *Parashas Mishpatim* (*Shemos* 24:11) relates our annual dancing and perhaps any *siyum* to the recorded celebration of our leaders upon receiving the Torah at Sinai. He writes, "… and they [the nobility] ate and drank; they celebrated and made a *Yom Tov*, for one is obligated to celebrate the receiving of Torah." The Ramban parallels these occasions to the feast that Shlomo *Hamelech* celebrated in Yerushalayim after being granted unsurpassed intellectual gifts (*Divrei Hayamim II* 1:12 with *Melachim* I 3:15) and to Dovid *Hamelech*'s great feast marking the preparations to establish the first *Beis Hamikdash* (*Divrei Hayamim I* 29:21).

At first blush, these events and seeming precedents for our *Simchas Torah* are not similar at all. The festivities of *Matan Torah* and of Dovid and Shlomo *Hamelech* celebrated the anticipation of horizons of spirituality and knowledge that had just been unlocked and laid out for them. They correctly perceived that they had been catapulted beyond the boundaries

---

Originally published on TorahWeb.org in 1999

that hemmed in the most talented people of all times, and what a passionate *simcha* they must have experienced. Isn't the annual completion of *Vezos Haberacha* quite different? Are we not expressing our happiness and gratitude for the privilege of accomplishing the understanding of part of *Hashem*'s instruction?

Perhaps the Ramban wants us to understand that every *siyum*, be it of a *massechta* or the entire *Torah Shebichsav*, is celebrating not the accomplishment, but rather the anticipation of applying all of one's knowledge to future studies and situations. Indeed, that is why at every *siyum* we focus on the "*Hadrans*," praying and promising that we will return to the *massechta* at hand and that the *massechta* has become an active and alive part of our consciousness. Thus, the *simcha* has its roots in *kabbalas haTorah* and the joy of Shlomo *Hamelech* upon his receiving the gates of all knowledge.

In similar fashion we can appreciate the explanation offered by the Avudraham for our rush to start *Bereishis* as soon as we have completed *Sefer Devarim*. He refers us to a challenge that the Satan raises in an attempt to deride *Klal Yisrael*. He claims that now that we have completed the study of the entire Torah, we will be putting it away and presumably going on to other masterpieces, *lehavdil*. Upon hearing the beginning of *Bereishis* immediately after *chazak chazak*, *Hashem*'s confidence in us and our knowledge of the absolute singularity of Torah and its place in our lives, is vindicated. Perhaps the *Midrash* is also pointing out that *Klal Yisrael* sees the successful completion of one cycle not as an end but rather as a new rung in the ladder on which to penetrate the texts ever more deeply the next time around. Our *simcha* on this *Yom Tov* celebrates our well-founded expectation that we will always find new insights in the Torah, and the blessing that we have as Torah and life continuously illuminate one another.

Bezos Ani Boteach
RABBI YAAKOV NEUBURGER

As we conclude another round of the twice daily recitation of *Tehillim* 27, "*LeDovid Hashem Ori*," at a time when our *Yom Tov* spirit is so dampened, we probably identified with many of the sentiments expressed by Dovid *Hamelech* more so than in other years. The *pasuk* that associates this *perek* with *Sukkos* certainly expresses the prayer in all our hearts throughout the *Yomim Tovim*, "Indeed He will protect me in His [*sukkah*] shelter on the day of evil; He will conceal me in the recesses of His tent; He will lift me up on a rock."

In fact, in an altogether different context, the *Yalkut* in *Parashas Emor* says that the *zechus* of the *mitzva* of *sukkah* will bring us Divine protection. Why the *mitzva* of *sukkah* more than any other *mitzva*? The *Kesav Sofer* explains that through the *mitzva* of *sukkah*, one expresses one's *bitachon* in *Hashem*'s protection, and one who is so keenly aware of *Hashem*'s protection and open to appreciating it will certainly merit it.

At the same time, our experiences this *Yom Tov* must strengthen one of the age-old difficulties in understanding the central request of this *perek*, "One thing I asked from *Hashem* and that I shall seek – that I dwell in the House of *Hashem* all the days of my life, to behold the sweetness of *Hashem* and contemplate in His sanctuary." Should this really be the one request uppermost in Dovid *Hamelech*'s mind – the leader of all Israel?

Especially at times of war, would we not expect that the one responsible for the physical and spiritual welfare of our people would plead with all his strength for our security and wellbeing? Isn't yearning to be personally found in *Beis Hamikdash* tantamount to neglecting his duties to the people for whom he was appointed?

Harav Chaim Friedlander, in his widely acclaimed *sefer*, *Sifsei Chaim*, explains that certainly Dovid *Hamelech*'s primary concerns were the responsibilities of his leadership, the security and spiritual and physical prosperity of his people. It is precisely for this that Dovid *Hamelech* is praying in his request to find himself in the House of *Hashem*. Indeed, Dovid *Hamelech* wants to be continuously aware of *Hashem* and appreciative of His constant protection and guidance and is begging not only for physical sustenance, but for protection from the hubris that affects so many successful leaders as well. That is the "*beis Hashem*" in which he wants to travel at all times, be it in on the battlefield or in the palace courts.

This interpretation sheds light on another very difficult passage in the *perek*, "Though an army would besiege me, my heart would not fear; though war would arise against me, in this [*bezos*] I trust." In exactly what is Dovid *Hamelech* placing his trust? Many of the *mefarshim* have pondered this, suggesting various references in the surrounding *pesukim*. Perhaps we are to see "*bezos*" as referring to the entire sequence of *pesukim* that follow: "Indeed He will protect me in His [*sukkah*] shelter on the day of evil; He will conceal me in the recesses of His tent; He will lift me up on a rock. Now my head is raised above my enemies around me and I will slaughter offerings in His Tent, accompanied by joyous song; I will sing praise to *Hashem*." Dovid *Hamelech* places his trust in the *zechus* that he will always see himself in the "*beis Hashem*," so that every moment of salvation that he experiences will give him opportunity to express his recognition of *Hashem*'s protective wings. Similar to Yaakov *Avinu* as he found himself in his most difficult time and defined for all time how we react *be'eis tzara*

(*Bereishis* 28:20-21), Dovid *Hamelech* promises that he will attribute any success to *Hashem*'s mercy and love for him and for *Klal Yisrael*.

In the *zechus* of our observance of the *mitzva* of *sukkah* and all that it entails, may we be speedily be *zocheh* to joyously express our gratitude for His protection during this *eis tzara*.

Grass-Roots Ownership of the Torah

RABBI YAAKOV NEUBURGER

Probably one of the great surprise endings of Torah literature is Rashi's closing comment to the Torah *Shebichsav*, which concludes with *Hashem*'s *hesped* (eulogy) for Moshe *Rabbeinu*. The *hesped* explicitly refers to the unsurpassed level of prophecy which Moshe achieved and to the role that Moshe had in performing the miracles of our redemption from Mitzrayim. Yet it concludes with a vague reference to the "mighty hand and most awesome acts that Moshe did for all to the Jews to see" (*Devarim* 34:12). Obviously, this needs Rashi.

Rather surprisingly, Rashi interprets that this refers to the shattering of the first tablets of the Ten Commandments. Thus the final verse of *Hashem*'s tribute to Moshe, and especially its climax, bring us back to what must have been one of the most painful events of Moshe's career. Furthermore, Rashi seems to place this grand disappointment on par with Moshe's unique status as a prophet, peerless in clarity and understanding. Moreover, it is at first blush quite difficult to see how a moment of desperation and failure should figure together with Moshe's majesty as he orchestrated the miracles of the Exodus and *Yam Suf*. Where are the references to the many items we would expect to see in the *hesped* for Moshe: feeding

Originally published on TorahWeb.org in 2009

millions with the miraculous manna and the traveling wellspring, arguing with God in defense of His people, silencing the powerful and popular rebellion of Korach, building the *Mishkan* and the superhuman efforts in climbing *Har Sinai* and the ensuing lifetime of teaching Torah?

Simply glancing at the last two *pesukim* of the Torah, one can readily see what was bothering Rashi. Reading them together, we understand that *Hashem* distinguishes between the mighty miracles that Moshe did as an agent of *Hashem* (ibid. 34:11), and the awesome event that Moshe himself publicly performed for the entirety of our people (ibid. 34:12). Indeed, it would be hard to find a better fit. What other event aside from the throwing down of the *luchos* was witnessed by all the Jews and shows Moshe's unparalleled independence, as he clearly was not acting as an agent of *Hashem*? This independence is emphasized by Rashi, who also quotes the passage in the *Gemara* (*Shabbos* 87a) that records *Hashem*'s consent and praise for Moshe and his actions.

Nevertheless, we still need to understand why the culmination of *Hashem*'s homage to Moshe should include what seems to be a moment of grave and enduring failure.

It would seem to me that though the frustration and disillusionment of Moshe's descent from *Har Sinai* were enormous, the shattering the *luchos* turned into the consummate expression of his acquisition and ownership over *Hashem*'s greatest gift to us. No teaching or observance, no legislation or appropriate change, expresses our title to the Torah as the decision to withhold and even ruin its Divinely determined form. Pondering that moment will forever remind us that we have been entrusted with *Hashem*'s Torah not only to observe it and teach it, but to treat it as our own and interpret it, take responsibility for transmitting it and legislate based on our understanding of it.

Thus the climax of *Hashem*'s words about Moshe described a defining moment of Moshe's life, one which would never be surpassed by mortal man and one which would forever inspire us to care for our *mesora* and its study with depth and rigor, with passion and concern.

Perhaps that is also communicated in the manner in which we celebrate *Simchas Torah*. This most joyous celebration of Torah study is marked almost entirely by customs that our people have conjured up over centuries. The *hakafos* and dancing; the *chasanim* and their *berachos*; the unending *aliyos* and the *kol ne'arim*, to name a few, are all "grass-roots" expressions of our joy, even as they celebrate the privilege and responsibility of the ownership of our tradition.

The Majesty at Hand: The Torah Readings of Yom Kippur and Sukkos

RABBI YAAKOV NEUBURGER

It should certainly not surprise us that *Chazal* would emphasize our responsibilities to the poor even as we celebrate our *Yomim Tovim*; after all, it is inconceivable for us celebrate in an uplifting manner without sharing our joy with the less fortunate (Rambam, *Hilchos Yom Tov perek* 6). At first glance, that explains why *Chazal* expanded the reading of *Shemini Atzeres*, the final reading before we resume the regularly scheduled conclusion of *Devarim*, to include a section that addresses our obligations to those in need. The central part of the reading focuses on *aliya laregel*, the mandated ascent to Yerushalayim every *Yom Tov*, but it is expanded to include the laws of tithing for the poor and leaving them with some provisions in our fields.

Nevertheless, it is surprising to find embedded in the talmudic passage that records the readings for *Rosh Hashana* through *Simchas Torah* the oft-quoted passage of Rav Yochanan, "Wherever you find the greatness of *Hashem*, there you will find His humility as well" (*Megilla* 31a). Whether Rav Yochanan is quoted to introduce the *Yom Tov* readings of *Sukkos* and

---

Originally published on TorahWeb.org in 2014

Shemini Atzeres or as commentary to the *haftara* of *Yom Kippur* morning is open to interpretation, but incorporating his teaching as a bridge between the *Yomim Tovim* of this season should pique our curiosity in any event.

How does Rav Yochanan's observation deepen our understanding of the *Yom Kippur* and *Sukkos* readings? How is he commenting on Yeshayahu's stinging rebuke of a fast day that is superficial, that stresses our communications with *Hashem* without inspiring a commitment to be more empathetic and giving? "Can such be the fast I choose, a day when man afflicts himself? ... Surely this is the fast I choose ... Share your bread with the hungry, and bring the terribly downcast to your home, when you see the naked, give him clothes ..." (*Yeshayahu* 58:5-7).

Additionally, every *motzaei Shabbos* we complete *Ma'ariv* with a quick review of this passage. At that time, we recite the teaching in its entirety, as Rav Yochanan continues to record three proof texts, one from each part of *Tanach*, establishing at once the depth of this teaching and the relevance and meaningfulness that he attached to it.

Yet the proof texts quoted to uphold the principle focus on *Hashem's* benevolence rather than His humility, and in fact relate His charity, rather than His modesty, to His immanence. "It is written in the Torah (*Devarim* 10:17-18) 'For *Hashem* is a great, mighty and awe-inspiring God ... He upholds the cause of the orphan and widow, loves the stranger, giving him food and clothing.' It is repeated in the *Nevi'im* (*Yeshayahu* 57:15) '... I live in a high and holy place ... to revive the spirit of the lowly and to revive the heart of the contrite.' It is stated a third time in the *Kesuvim*, (*Tehillim* 68:5) '... extoll He who rides the cloud...'; immediately afterward (*Tehillim* 68:6) it is written, 'Father of the fatherless and judge of widows is *Hashem* ...'"

Thus it would be more accurate to translate Rav Yochanan's tradition as teaching us that we find *Hashem's* benevolence juxtaposed to the descriptions of His majesty.

Consequently, Rav Yochanan reminds us that even though days after the spiritual high of a *Yom Kippur* we find ourselves us at a distance from the "great and mighty," and this could be frustrating, we can still emulate Him in our efforts on behalf of the orphan and the defenseless. We are certainly far from "His high place," and imitating His ways seems far out of reach, but that should not deter us from trying to cheer up the hearts of the lonely and bereft. *Hashem* encompasses majesty and benevolence, as emphasized by Rav Yochanan, and being God like in our benevolence is far more accessible to us than the majesty that oft can only be observed from afar.

That lesson may not only be recorded explicitly at the end of our weekly appointment with the spirituality of *Shabbos*, but may give meaning to a phrase in "*Nishmas*," recited *Shabbos* morning, as well.

How jarring it is that we praise *Hashem* for saving the poor from those who rob them and the weak from those who overpower, instead of thanking Him for reducing the thieves and bullies to begin with. Whereas the answer to the question in our hearts is well beyond our grasp, the words that roll from our lips remind us that the opportunity for us to act in a God-like fashion is readily at hand.

This idea may give meaning to a phrase in *Hallel*, "Their idols are silver and gold, made by human hands. They have mouths but cannot speak, eyes but cannot see … Their manufacturers should become like them" (*Tehillim* 115:4-8). Rashi and Radak both explain that we are praying for the diminution of idol worshipers – they should become as lifeless and uninfluential as the idols they serve. Yet one could also translate the phrase to teach that those who fashion and worship unresponsiveness will themselves develop ears and eyes that will not hear or see the pain of others, and will not have the hands or legs that try to lighten those loads.

Thus, at the close of the *Yom Tov* season, and even at the close of *Shabbos*, with its many moments filled with *Hashem*'s majesty, Rav Yochanan reminds us that some of that majesty can indeed become ours.

The Link between Yom Kippur and Sukkos
RABBI MICHAEL ROSENSWEIG

The period of *teshuva* ushered in by *Rosh Hashana* appears to end dramatically with the blowing of the *shofar* at the culmination of *Yom Kippur*. The holiday of *Sukkos* that follows appears to be independent of the days that precede it. Indeed, *Sukkos* presents quite a sharp contrast to *Yom Kippur*. Rambam characterizes *Yom Kippur* as a day lacking in "*simcha yeseira*" (*Hilchos Chanuka* 3:6), while he depicts *Sukkos* precisely as a time of "*simcha yeseira*" (*Hilchos Sukkah* 8:12). However, the fact is that according to many halachic sources, the final "*gemar*" with respect to man's status is not until *Hoshana Rabba*, the conclusion of *Sukkos*. Moreover, compelling parallels bind *Yom Kippur* and *Sukkos*, and there are strong indications that the intervening period is not merely a bridge between them but constitutes a significant period by virtue of the link between them.

In *Sefer Devarim*, *Tehillim*, and elsewhere we find references to *avodas Hashem beyira*, particularly accented by *Yom Kippur*, as well as to *avoda besimcha*, projected by *Sukkos*. The *Midrash* in *Tehillim*, commenting on these distinctive approaches reflected in *Tehillim* chapters 2 and 100, questions the relationship between them: "אם בשמחה איך ביראה ואם ביראה איך בשמחה?" - if with joy, how with fear, and if with fear, how with joy?"

Originally published on TorahWeb.org in 2001

One view in the *Midrash* perceives the "*yira*" as a method employed in this world to achieve the ultimate reward of "*simcha*" in the World to Come. Others argue that "*yira*" and "*simcha*" are simply distinctive approaches to man's relationship with *Hashem*. However, *Tanna DeBei Eliyahu* (no. 3) projects a mutually enhancing impact: "אמר דוד המלך, 'יראתי מתוך שמחתי, ושמחתי מתוך יראתי' - King David said, 'I feared from within my joy, and rejoiced from within my fear.'" It is possible that this approach also characterizes the relationship between *Yom Kippur*, the holiday of *yira*, and *Sukkos*, the festival of *simcha*.

A careful reading of *Parashas Emor* reveals several parallels between these two *moadim*. The term "*ach*" (*Vayikra* 23:27, 39), connoting something different or exclusive, is used only regarding these two holidays. The term "*mikra kodesh*," which is the common theme of all the holidays delineated in the *parasha*, is treated in an unusual manner with respect to *Yom Kippur*, as it does not connect to the general prohibition to do work on a festival, as with other *moadim*, but to the specific expression of fasting on this day. *Sukkos*'s treatment in *Emor* is also unique. The Torah records a second account of this holiday, which includes reference to the *lulav* but omits the term "*mikra kodesh*." In both *Yom Kippur* (*Vayikra* 23:28 – "כי יום כפורים הוא לכפר עליכם" - for it is a day of atonement, for you to gain atonement") and *Sukkos* (23:43 – "למען ידעו דורותיכם כי בסכות הושבתי את בני ישראל בהוציאי אותם מארץ מצרים" - in order that your generations should know that I had the children of Israel live in booths when I took them out of the land of Egypt"), the Torah feels the need to justify the holiday. The term, "לפני ה' א-לקיכם" "Before *Hashem*, your God" (23:28, 40)) appears in connection with each of these events. Ibn Ezra and Seforno allude to the apparent link between *Yom Kippur* and *Sukkos* rooted in some aspects of their unusual treatments.

It is possible that the Torah conveys by means of some of these parallels that the themes of "*yira*" and "*simcha*" are each critical components of a comprehensive *avodas Hashem*, and that each enhances the other when implemented properly. The role of *yira* as preceding wisdom and Torah knowledge is well documented. *Simcha*, too, is critical for the study of Torah ("משמחי ... 'פקודי ה - the laws of *Hashem* ... cause the heart to rejoice" [*Tehillim* 19:9]), for the attainment of prophecy (*Shabbos* 30b), and it plays a role in many other halachic norms, as well.

Yom Kippur and *Sukkos* contrast in ways that accent the parallels between them. On *Sukkos*, the exemption of *mitztaer*, the expanded role of *Hallel*, and the motif of "*teishvu ke'ein taduru*," for example, reflect an extreme manifestation of *simcha*. The motif of *inuy*, a full complement of *issur melacha*, and a rejection of *Hallel* accentuate the *yira* of *Yom Kippur*. Each extreme plays an important role in the overall balance represented by the different *moadim*, reflecting the broad spiritual ambition of halachic life itself.

The *Rishonim* questioned why *Sukkos* is not celebrated in context of *Yetzias Mizrayim*, which it celebrates? The Ramban (*Emor*, ad loc.) and *Tur* (begining of *Hilchos Sukkah*) address this question. They posit that weather conditions during the period of *Nisan* would not have properly accented the normative aspect of *sukkah*. However, the *Tzeror Hamor* and *Aruch Hashulchan* suggest that the Torah deliberately linked *Sukkos* with *Yom Kippur* for thematic reasons!

The *Shulchan Aruch* rules that *Tachanun* is not to be recited in the period between *Yom Kippur* and *Sukkos*. The *Beis Yosef* (no. 131) explains that this is the period in which the *Beis Hamikdash* will be completed. The *Aruch Hashulchan* (524:7), however, posits that this ruling is connected to the period of *simcha* that follows the aftermath of *Yom Kippur*, and characterizes the entire intervening period until *Sukkos* as "*yemei simcha*." One may speculate that the appropriate time to complete the *mikdash* is in this period precisely because of this status, particularly if this period symbolizes the integration of *simcha-yira* which is especially indispensable to the proper functioning of the *Beis Hamikdash*.

The obligation to begin the process of building the *sukkah* immediately after *Yom Kippur* is formulated twice in the *Shulchan Aruch*: in the last *halacha* of *Hilchos Yom Kippur* and again in the first *halacha* of *Hilchos Sukkah*. While the commentators struggle to explain the differences between the two contiguous formulations, it remains difficult to fathom why this law (or laws) could not be articulated in one place. In light of our brief analysis of the complementary relationship between the two extreme manifestations of *yira* and *simcha*, we can perhaps further appreciate the precision of these formulations. *Yom Kippur* is significantly enhanced by anticipating the upcoming festival of "*usemachtem lifnei Hashem Elokeichem shivas yamim*." Immediate involvement with the *sukkah* is, indeed, a most fitting culmination to *Hilchos Yom Kippur*. At the same time, the themes of *Sukkos* take on greater meaning against the framework of "*ki Yom Kippurim hu lechaper aleicheim lifnei Hashem Elokeichem*." Thus, *Hilchos Sukkah* itself demands that the process of building the *sukkah* be initiated in the immediate afterglow of *teshuva, selicha, kappara* and *yira*.

Vehayisa Ach Sameach: The Joy of *Shemini Atzeres*

RABBI MICHAEL ROSENSWEIG

The *Mishna* (*Sukkah* 48a) determines that while one should not completely dismantle the *sukkah* on the seventh day of *Sukkos* in advance of *Shemini Atzeres*, one should begin transferring out the utensils that established the *sukkah* as the primary residence during the week of *Sukkos*. The Rambam (*Hilchos Sukkah* 6:11, 14) codifies this *halacha*. The Ra'avad speculates that this preliminary evacuation of the *sukkah* is limited to circumstances in which one will be eating in the structure on *Shemini Atzeres*, and is designed to preclude the prohibition of *bal tosif*. However, the *Mishna* and Rambam make no allusion to these conditions. It seems that departing from the *sukkah* in anticipation of *Shemini Atzeres* ("*mipnei kevod Yom Tov ha'acharon*") is an important element in the transition from *Sukkos* to *Shemini Atzeres*! A brief analysis of some of the salient features of *Shemini Atzeres* may serve to clarify this prerequisite.

It is evident from the *pesukim* in *Parashas Emor* and *Parashas Pinchas* that *Shemini Atzeres* is both a continuation and culmination of *Sukkos*, as well as an independent *chag*. This dual status is reflected by the totally

Originally published on TorahWeb.org in 2006

different configuration of the *korbanos* and by the unique *halachos* signified by the acronym "PZRKShV" (*Sukkah* 48a) that govern this day. While *Shemini Atzeres* is ideally referred to by its own designation – "*haShemini chag ha'Atzeres hazeh,*" many *poskim* conclude that the designation "*chag haSukkos*" is also effective, obviating the need to repeat the *Shemoneh Esrei* or *Birkas Hamazon*. *Shemini Atzeres* certainly serves as part of the extended period for the *korban chagiga* of *Sukkos*. It appears that *Shemini Atzeres*, precisely because of its singular character, is the perfect conclusion to *Sukkos*!

The Seforno notes that the transition to *Shemini Atzeres* is particularly striking, as the holiday in which there are two distinct *mitzvos* – *lulav* and *sukkah* – is followed by or even concludes with a *Yom Tov* which focuses exclusively on *tefilla* and *talmud Torah*, the staples of year-round halachic observance. It is also significant that the *kerias haTorah* of *Shemini Atzeres* (*Parashas Re'eh*) only obliquely alludes to *Shemini Atzeres* ("*vehayisa ach sameach*" [*Devarim* 16:15], as understood by *Sukkah* 48a). The reading concentrates on the *mitzvos* of *tzedaka*, etc. that apply all year. Only the *Shalosh Regalim* are explicated in these sections. Perhaps it is precisely the concentration on year-round themes, and the de-emphasis of particular festival themes on this unique day, that qualify *Shemini Atzeres* as the perfect culmination of *Sukkos* and the entire period that begins with *Rosh Hashana*.

After the intense religious experiences of *Rosh Hashana* and *Yom Kippur*, it is inconceivable that one could simply revert to routine life. Moreover, the charged environment and process of introspection engendered by the *Yamim Noraim* provide an opportunity for further spiritual advancement that should be capitalized upon. And yet, the ultimate goal is to integrate the impact of the *Yamim Noraim* experience into an upgraded daily halachic life. (See also Maharsha, conclusion of *Masseches Megilla*.) Thus, one ideally begins to build the *sukkah* immediately after *Yom Kippur*. It is important to take the experience of the *Kodesh Hakodashim* and to apply it to one's own dwelling, but this requires a more vulnerable and temporary structure that is evidently reliant upon *Hashem's hashgacha* (Divine providence). Many of the dimensions of the *sukkah* are patterned on the *Beis Hamikdash* itself, and at least the *sechach* is *muktza lemitzvaso* (used exclusively for the *mitzva*) for the entire holiday.

The first *halacha* recorded in the *Shulchan Aruch* regarding *Sukkos* is the disqualification of a *sukkah* under the roof of one's home. The Taz explains that there should be nothing intervening between the *sukkah* and the heavens, undoubtedly symbolizing the direct relationship and reliance upon *Hashem*. The *Magen Avraham* emphasizes that the very objective of the *sukkah* is the departure from one's permanent home. The fact that the *sukkah* ideally is a seven-day structure meant to house all major activities of the week – eating, sleeping, social interactions etc., reflects the importance of this total relocation. The Rama notes that one should conduct oneself in the *sukkah* in a manner befitting a *mitzva*, although the range of activities should parallel one's real home. The *poskim* explain that one should avoid anger or idle gossip and increase Torah study. The *sukkah* should be a real home, but one in which idealized standards are practiced, as befitting post-*Yamim Noraim* developments!

And yet, one must ultimately return to one's permanent abode and routine. Moreover, the goal of the holidays of *Tishrei* is not to escape and abandon daily life, but to inspire and secure its elevation. After seven days of intense additional *avodas Hashem* highlighted by both the *sukkah* and *arba'a minim*, one is sufficiently fortified and spiritually revitalized for a triumphant reintegration with the challenges of daily life.

Shemini Atzeres is the appropriate culmination to *Sukkos* precisely because it is finally time to relinquish the *lulav* and *sukkah* and to give full concentration to the spiritual staples of *talmud Torah* and *tefilla*. Thus, this day is both an indispensable component of *Sukkos* and an independent

---

Originally published on TorahWeb.org in 2011

chag. Anticipating the transition to *Shemini Atzeres*, we already begin to dismantle parts of the environment of the *sukkah*, declaring that we have successfully assimilated the idealized framework of that structure and are confidently poised to return to our more permanent structure, having achieved spiritual renewal and reinforcement. The Torah reading only alludes to *Shemini Atzeres*, instead focusing on *tzedaka* and other year-round challenges that are, ironically, more relevant to this decompression from *Sukkos* and significant transition to the rest of the year. The commemoration of *Simchas Torah*, in which we conclude and renew the Torah cycle, accentuates this theme as well. The theme and method of observance of *Shemini Atzeres* are simple and straightforward. However, the significance of this day as the culmination of the *Yomim Noraim* and *Sukkos* and as the transition to the rest of the year is profound and ambitious. For this reason, *Shemini Atzeres* is a day of unvarnished *simcha*: "*vehayisa ach sameach.*"

Shemini Atzeres: The Contrast, Complement and Culmination of Sukkos

RABBI MICHAEL ROSENSWEIG

The *mishna* in *Masseches Sukkah* (48a) purports to depict or crystallize the seven-day holiday of *Sukkos* ("*sukkah shiva keitzad*"). Surprisingly, the *mishna* focuses not on the salient characteristics of the festival itself, as one would have anticipated, but on the appropriate method of concluding *Sukkos* and transitioning into *Shemini Atzeres*. While this alone is puzzling, the mystery is compounded by the *mishna*'s complex prescription that one may not yet dismantle the *sukkah*, but that one should begin to evacuate some of its utensils in order to convey anticipation and respect for the upcoming *Shemini Atzeres*. Although respectful preparation for *Yom Tov* is a typical requirement, its application here, seemingly at the expense of the prevailing *chag*, is hardly self-evident. Elsewhere ("*Vehayisa Ach Sameach*: The Joy of *Shemini Atzeres*," in this volume), we have noted that the Rambam (*Hilchos Sukkah* 6:11, 14), in contrast to the Ra'avad and *Shulchan Aruch* (*Orach Chaim* 666), requires this as an act of closure per se (rather than as a necessary practical facilitation of *Shemini Atzeres*), per-

---

Originally published on TorahWeb.org in 2011

ceiving it as an important dimension of the transition between the two holidays. This is particularly intriguing considering that the *Gemara* (*Sukkah* 28b), and especially the Rambam (*Hilchos Sukkah* 6:5), project the presence of special utensils in the *sukkah* that reflect a tangible symbolic relocation from one's home as a central feature of the *mitzva* of *sukkah*. The fact that the *mishna* in this context designates *Shemini Atzeres*, typically defined as an independent *chag* (*Sukkah* 48a), as "*Yom Tov acharon shel chag*" – "the last *Yom Tov* of *chag haSukkos*" is also noteworthy.

These phenomena may be explained (see also "*Vehayisa Ach Sameach*: The Joy of *Shemini Atzeres*") when *Sukkos* is perceived within the framework of the rest of the *moadim* that surround it, as part of a process that renews and reinvigorates the spiritual persona and spurs greater religious observance and commitment. Several *chachmei Ashkenaz* (Maharil, *Hilchos Sukkah*; *Tzeror Hamor, Parashas Emor*) respond to the Ramban's (*Emor*) query regarding the *Tishrei*-timing of *Sukkos* by positing that the Torah intended for various reasons to link *zeman simchaseinu* (time of joy) and the principle of *diras arai* (temporary dwelling) with the *Yomim Noraim*. *Sukkos* is thus perceived as eschewing the apparent security and priority of physical permanence and protection, and as reflecting an acute recognition of our dependence upon *Hashem*, the omnipresence of His *hashgacha*, and the need to disengage periodically from a more intense physical focus on life. *Sukkos* absorbs the lessons of the *Yomim Noraim* precisely by channeling them in the very different, even opposite, manner of *simcha yeseira* (excessive joy). The *halachos* of *Hoshana Rabba* revisit the emphasis of the *Yomim Noraim* within *Sukkos*, as numerous *Yom Kippur* themes resonate precisely at the juncture in which *Sukkos* transitions into *Shemini Atzeres*.

The capacity of *Shemini Atzeres*, absent the *sukkah* and four *minim*, to achieve a continuity of *avoda besimcha* that is still consistent with the *Yom Kippur* themes absorbed into *Sukkos* constitutes a significant further stage in the progression towards internalizing all of *Tishrei*'s themes in a manner that profoundly impacts upon halachic life throughout the entire year. From this perspective, the *mishna*'s depiction of the essence of seven-day *Sukkos* by highlighting the method of transition between the *chagim* of *Sukkos* and *Shemini Atzeres* is impressively precise. While the *sukkah* must remain intact until the very end of the *Sukkos* period, as the themes of dependence and vulnerability continue to prevail, it is entirely appropriate even from *Sukkos*'s vantage point to anticipate and prepare for the transition. This acknowledgment of the next phase is not a concession, but a fulfillment of *Sukkos*'s own *telos*. In this context, the *mishna* specifically refers to *Shemini Atzeres* as "*Yom Tov acharon shel chag*" because it is this sense of continuity, notwithstanding the very acute contrast in substance and style, that justifies the application of "*kavod hachag*" as an internal factor in *Sukkos* itself.

This analysis highlights the fact that *Sukkos*'s immediate proximity to *Shemini Atzeres* is intentional. The very designation of "*atzeres*" demonstrates this, as *Chazal* frequently note. The Torah conjoined the two celebrations to accentuate the dialectic of their simultaneous independence-dependence. *Sukkos* and *Shemini Atzeres* are independent, even contrasting, *chagim* with respect to the method and motif of their celebration, but that very contrast reflects the spiritual development and progression that constitutes a single *kiyum*. For this reason, the evidence on *Shemini Atzeres*'s dual status vis-a-vis *Sukkos* is intentionally conflicting, both in the written Torah and in halachic literature. [I hope to demonstrate in the future that this complex relationship is crucial for understanding both *Sukkos* and *Shemini Atzeres*, and especially the interaction between them in issues such as *bal tosif*, *Yom Tov sheni shel galuyos*, and *tosefes Yom Tov*.]

It is possible that this perspective underpins the controversial formulation in *Tefilla* and *Birkas Hamazon* of *Shemini Atzeres* as "*Shemini hachag ha'Atzeres hazeh." This designation, found already in *Seder Rav Amram Gaon* and recorded in the *Shulchan Aruch* (666), is criticized by some *poskim* from several perspectives. Some note the absence in the Torah of the term "*chag*" in connection with *Shemini Atzeres*. They posit that the day should be referred to simply as "*yom Shemini Atzeres hazeh.*" Others express discomfort with the interposing of "*chag*" between the two words which the Torah invokes regarding this holiday. Upon reflection, however, this ancient designation powerfully captures the dialectical character of this *chag*. *Shemini Atzeres* is precisely a continuation-holdover celebration of *Sukkos*, the ultimate and default "*chag*," despite but especially because of its divergent character. It is, indeed, an eighth day that is simultaneously part of the "*chag*" and independent, as its own parallel and culmination "*chag*," truly a "*chag ha'Atzeres.*"

Chag HaSukkos: Avodas Hashem in the Aftermath of the Yomim Noraim

RABBI MICHAEL ROSENSWEIG

The Torah's presentation of *Chag haSukkos* in *Parashas Emor* in two different sections (*Vayikra* 23:33-36; 23:39-43) conveys *Sukkos*'s distinctiveness, as well as its substantive link to the *Yomim Noraim*, particularly to *Yom Kippur*. Several *mefarshim* (see Netziv) note the Torah's emphasis of *"lachodesh hashevi'i hazeh"* (23:27, 34) regarding both *Yom Kippur* and *Sukkos*. The extra word (*"hazeh"*) implies a connection, probably a progression, between the three *moadim* of *Tishrei*. Moreover, the Torah's introduction of its second discussion of *Sukkos* in *Emor* (23:39) invokes the qualifying word *"ach,"* paralleling the previous introduction to *Yom Kippur* (23:27). [See Ibn Ezra and Rashbam who underscore this link. Seforno, on the other hand, only accentuates the distinctiveness of *Sukkos*.] The expression *"Shabboson"* in *Emor* is applied exclusively (beyond *Shabbos* itself in 23:3) to the *moadim* of *Tishrei*: *Rosh Hashana* (23:23), *Yom Kippur* (23:32) and *Sukkos* (23:39). Only *Yom Kippur* (23:28) and *Sukkos* (23:40) emphasize the festival aspiration and experience of *"lifnei Hashem Elokeichem."*

Originally published on TorahWeb.org in 2013

Only these holidays explicate a broader spiritual agenda (23:28 –"כי יום כפו־ רים הוא לכפר עליכם", "for it is a day of atonement, for you to gain atonement"; 23:43 – "למען ידעו דורותיכם כי בסכות הושבתי את בני ישראל בהוציאי אותם מארץ מצרים", "in order that your generations should know that I had the children of Israel live in booths when I took them out of the land of Egypt") binding them together.

The *Tzeror Hamor* (ad loc.; see also Netziv, *Ha'amek Davar*) attributes *Sukkos*'s special status as a *moed*, also reflected by other unusual manifestations that are exclusive to this *chag*, precisely to this link to the *Yomim Noraim* experience. Having successfully confronted the challenges of *din* by attaining *kappara*, *Klal Yisrael* achieved a level of *sheleimus* hitherto unattained, even at *Yetzias Mitzrayim*, and unsurpassed, even during *Matan Torah*. He argues that these achievements are symbolized by the *mitzvos* of *lulav* (an expression of victory and success) and *sukkah* (underscoring the transition from anxiety, even panic, to total self-confidence in *Hashem*'s *hashgacha*), establishing *Sukkos* as the premier *moed*, worthy of a double treatment in *Parashas Emor* and of unprecedented daily *Hallel* throughout the whole *chag*.

While this perspective accounts for a number of *Sukkos*'s special manifestations, it does not fully explain what appears to be a special emphasis on the role of *mitzvos* as the premium expression of *avodas Hashem* in this holiday. In addition to the exceptional fact that there are two distinct *mitzvos* on this *chag*, it is noteworthy that each of these *mitzvos* – *lulav* and *sukkah* – also particularly accentuates the concept of the special stature of *hechsher mitzva* (the steps needed to prepare for and enable a *mitzva*), and of *cheftza shel mitzva* (an object used in *mitzvos*), as well as promoting the consequential notion of *hiddur mitzva*.

Sefer Hachinuch (no. 325) formulates this emphasis without elaborating on its foundation in the *Sukkos* holiday. However, the halachic perspective on the significance of building the *sukkah* (see *Kesuvos* 86a; *Shavuos* 29a; *Sukkah* 46a and *Tosafos* s.v. *ha'oseh* and s.v. *nichnas*; and see Netziv, *Ha'amek Davar,* and especially in his commentary on the *Sheiltos*) and even regarding the integration of the diverse *minim* exemplifies this point. The concept of *muktza lemitzvaso* (*Sukkah* 9a – "כשם שחל שם שמים על החגיגה כך חל שם שמים על הסוכה - just as the name of Heaven takes effect upon the festival offering [*chagiga*], so does the name of Heaven take effect upon the *sukkah*"), which determines that the *sukkah* materials can be utilized exclusively for the *mitzva*, and the parallel concept with respect to the use of the four *minim*, project the prominence of *mitzva* objects. The special role of "*hadar*," the esthetic quality of the *esrog* and other *minim*, and the status of *sukkah* decorations ("*noy sukkah*") constitute a definite motif of *chivuv hamitzvos* during *Sukkos*.

It is unsurprising, given this pattern of emphasis, that some *poskim* (Bach, Taz, etc.; see also *Rabbeinu* Chananel, *Sukkah* 2b) understood the Torah's charge – "*lema'an yeidu doroseichem ki basukkos hoshavti es Bnei Yisrael …*"; "in order that your generations should know that I had the children of Israel live in booths …" as demanding a special awareness of the *mitzva* of *sukkah* and possibly even its rationale or objective. In part, this concentrated focus on the two special *mitzvos* of the holiday, and by extension, the general attitude toward *mitzvos*, reflect a clean slate in the aftermath of the attainment of *kappara* during the *Yomim Noraim*. Indeed, the *Midrash* (*Vayikra Rabba* 30:7), commenting on the use of the term " ולקח-) ביום הראשון (חתם לכם - (you should take for yourselves) on the first day" (*Vayikra* 23:40), concludes that מין הכא נחל חושבנא (the record of merits and transgressions begins anew from *Sukkos*).

However, the accentuation of *mitzvos* at this juncture also reflects upon the sincerity of the *teshuva* attained during the *Yomim Noraim*, as well as the sensitivity to spiritual life and opportunity which ideally underlies that process. (Indeed, Rambam [*Hilchos Teshuva* 3:3, 4] rules that *mitzvos* are a mechanism of *teshuva*, distinct from the spiritual credit they provide.) In this light, the broader perspective on *mitzvos* as a preeminent expression of *avodas Hashem* assumes particular importance at this spiritual juncture. We can readily appreciate that the *Midrash* (*Vayikra Rabba* 30:7) perceives that the *mitzva* preparation itself in the interim period between *Yom Kippur* and *Sukkos* constitutes a significant spiritual involvement ("*eisek haTorah*").

Finally, *Sukkos* magnificently conveys and embodies the necessary temporal transition from *kabbalas ol malchus Shamayim* to *kabbalas ol mitzvos*. The *Yomim Noraim*, particularly *Yom Kippur*, reaffirm the indispensable principle of *kabbalas ol malchus Shamayim* in many of its facets. Indeed, the *Neilah* prayer (in the Ashkenazic tradition) concludes with a ringing articulation of the *Shema* and *yichud Hashem*. As the *Mishna* (*Berachos* 13a) notes, this foundational but abstract commitment always demands the follow-through of *kabbalas ol mitzvos*, the ideal vehicle for *avodas Hashem*. In this respect, *Sukkos*, with its dual *mitzvos*, each of which particularly embodies the broader perspective and parameters of *mitzvos* as the ideal avenue to *avodas Hashem*, perfectly follows, reinforces and completes the singular holiday cycle of "*ha-chodesh hashevi'i hazeh*," the foundation for Torah life year-round.

Simchas Sukkos: An Expression of Avoda and Hashra'as HaShechina

RABBI MICHAEL ROSENSWEIG

The Torah presents the holiday of *Sukkos* in *Parashas Emor* in a most singular fashion. The Torah first (*Vayikra* 23:33-36) delineates *Sukkos* in typical fashion (*mikra kodesh*, etc.) as the chronological conclusion of the festival cycle. The comprehensive survey then (23:37-38) appears to terminate with an appropriate (albeit not necessarily anticipated) reference to the *musaf korbanos* (detailed in *Parashas Pinchas*) that are brought on every *chag*. However, the Torah then (23:39-44) surprisingly returns to the subject of *Sukkos*, initiating this supplementary section with the jarring word "*ach*" (used in parallel only with respect to *Yom Kippur*, the other equally exceptional presentation in the *Emor* survey), introducing the obligation of the four *minim* that was omitted in the previous section, and expanding on the obligation of *simcha* in the *mikdash* during this seven-day holiday: "*Usemachtem lifnei Hashem Elokeichem shivas yamim*," "and you shall rejoice before *Hashem* your God for seven days" (*Vayikra* 23:40). The striking omission of the ubiquitous "*mikra kodesh*" phrase that unifies the

Originally published on TorahWeb.org in 2016

wide-ranging presentation of all the *moadim* in the main exposition reinforces the impression that this supplement is intended to accentuate a dimension that is unique to this holiday. The fact that *Sukkos* is the only one of the *moadim* that warrants a double treatment sufficiently commands our attention. The other facets in this second rendition need to be accounted for as well.

Previously ("*Chag HaSukkos: Avodas Hashem* in the Aftermath of the *Yomim Noraim*," and "The Link between *Yom Kippur* and *Sukkos*," in this volume), we have addressed the link between *Yom Kippur* and *Sukkos*, and have proposed that this additional emphasis on *Sukkos* is related to the contrast-complement that *Sukkos* embodies in the aftermath of the inimitable, all-consuming *Yom Kippur* experience. We may further develop and apply this theme particularly in light of the *Chasam Sofer*'s (*Parashas Haazinu*, "*lechag haSukkos*") explication of the "*ach*" that introduces this section. He suggests that this exclusionary usage qualifies the previous verse which identifies *avodos-korbanos* beyond the festival *musaf* as only *matanos, nedarim* or *nedavos*. The Torah qualifies this characterization by declaring that the four *minim*, which registers as a central theme on *Sukkos* only in these added verses, is an exception to this rule, as it constitutes a kind of *korban-avoda* celebrating the successful attainment of *kappara* on *Yom Kippur*. He further proposes that the coveted *teshuva mei'ahava* (*Yoma* 85b) that transforms sins into merits, is actually attained in conjunction with the *mitzva-avoda* of the four *minim*!

The notion that the *mitzva* of *lulav*/four *minim* evokes *avoda* and *korban* is articulated by the *Midrash* (*Yalkut Shimoni, Emor*) and by the Talmud. The *Gemara* (*Sukkah* 45a) interprets the verse (*Tehillim* 118:27), "*isru chag ba'avosim ad karnos hamizbeach*" as a reference to the *mitzva* of the four *minim*, which is equated with the construction of the *mizbeach* and the bringing of a *korban*: "כל הנוטל לולב באגודה והדס בעבותו מעלה עליו הכתוב כאילו בנה מזבח והקריב עליו קרבן" - Anyone who takes a *lulav* in its binding and a myrtle in its thickness is considered as though he built an altar and offered a sacrifice on it."

This perspective certainly accounts for the additional dimension and experience of joy on *Sukkos* (*usemachtem*), particularly in the *mikdash* (*lifnei Hashem Elokeichem*), and especially for the unusual seven-day celebration of the four *minim* specifically in the *mikdash*. Moreover, the fact that the *mitzva* of four *minim* applies on the first day of *Sukkos* even outside the precincts of the *mikdash*, even in the diaspora, assumes great significance.

In this respect, as well, *Yom Kippur* and *Sukkos* constitute an important contrast-complement. It is evident that *Yom Kippur* is an extremely *mikdash* and *avoda*-centric *moed*. Although the *Kohen Gadol* is the almost exclusive participant in the intricate *avoda*, the gripping drama of the *Kohen Gadol*'s odyssey into the *Kodesh Hakodashim* (*lifnai velifnim*) as the representative of *Klal Yisrael* dominates not only our *Musaf* prayers, but actually embodies and crystallizes the central themes of this *Shabbos Shabboson*, the most singular, most relevant ("*achas bashana*" [*Vayikra* 16:34; *Shemos* 30:10]), and most sanctified day of the year. Indeed, the Rambam (*Hilchos Avodas Yom HaKippurim* 1:1, *Hilchos Klei Hamikdash* 5:10) feels the need to integrate the universal obligation to fast on this singular day into the *avoda-mikdash* structure by repeatedly referring to the day as "*yom hatzom*." Certainly, the aspirations and attainments of the *Kohen Gadol* as the vehicle for *Klal Yisrael* are difficult to match, seemingly impossible to supersede.

Yet, *Sukkos* is emphatically no spiritual derogation or compression. It is an authentic and spiritually ambitious successor to *Yom HaKippurim*, as numerous *mefarshim* discern from the otherwise superfluous emphasis of "*lachodesh hashevi'i hazeh*" (23:34). Indeed, some propose that *Sukkos* was integrated into the *Tishrei* cycle, although it naturally should have been celebrated in the aftermath of *Yetzias Mitzrayim*, not only because the miracle was more discernable during *Tishrei*, but because it is the appropriate continuation and complement to *Yom Kippur* and the *yemei teshuva* of *Tishrei*.

This certainly is acutely manifest in the *yira-simcha* dialectic (see "The Link between *Yom Kippur* and *Sukkos*," in this volume), but it also is exhibited in the respective manifestations of *avoda-mikdash*. In the aftermath of structured and *Kohen-Gadol*-focused *avodas hayom*, *Sukkos* involves all of *Klal Yisrael*, and even simulates a quasi-*avoda* in the form of the *simcha* of the four-*minim* obligation. It is noteworthy that some Tosafists (see *Tosafos Rabbeinu Peretz* and Ramban, *Pesachim* 36a; Ritva *Sukkah* 9a, 30a) argue that the Talmud *Bavli* disqualifies only the *mitzvos* of *lulav* and *korban* on the basis of *mitzva haba'a be'aveira* (a *mitzva* enabled by an illegal transgression), as *ritzuy*, an idealistic *korban*-esque requirement that is indispensable to both, cannot abide this offensive taint. While the Talmud *Bavli* (*Arachin* 10a) identifies *ribuy korbanos* (distinctive *korbanos* configurations on each day of the festival) as the basis for an independent obligation to recite *Hallel* each day of *Sukkos* (in contrast to *Pesach*), it is interesting that the *Yerushalmi* (*Sukkos* 5:1) attributes this phenomenon to the obligation to rejoice with the four *minim* in the *mikdash* on each of the seven days. Numerous other sources reinforce the notion that the *mitzva* of *lulav* parallels or is perceived as a dimension of *avoda-korban*.

The *korban-avoda-mikdash* motif is equally evident with respect to the other prominent *mitzva* that defines this *chag*, *sukkah*. The dimensions of the *sukkah* are linked to the dimensions of the *Mishkan* in the first chapter of Tractate *Sukkah*. The *sukkah* is designated and defined in the *Sifrei* as an entity that is consequentially invested and suffused with the stature of *Hashem*'s Divine name (*sheim Shamayim chal aleha*) stemming from the sanctity and *hashra'as haShechina* that models the *mikdash*. Indeed, the *geonim* discuss whether the prohibition of *kapandarya* (use as a short-cut) that originates in the sanctified status of the *mikdash* applies also to the *sukkah*. *Poskim* debate the parameters of appropriate conduct in the *sukkah* in light of the dialectic of sanctity, on the one hand, and ubiquitous presence and familiar use based on the principle of *teishvu ke'ein taduru*, on the other.

It is perhaps consistent with this perspective on the symmetrical relationship between *Yom Kippur* and *Sukkos* that the Rambam, who was impelled to reiterate the *tzom* motif in the *avodas Yom HaKippurim*, also strikingly identifies and projects the *mikdash* experience as an integral part of *Hilchos Lulav* and *Sukkah*. In the *koseres* to *Hilchos Lulav* and in his *Sefer haMitzvos*, he emphasizes the seven-day *mikdash* obligation of *lulav*, although most of the Jewish world only fulfills this biblical obligation on the first day! It is evident that he perceives the extended obligation not as an independent *kiyum* in the *mikdash*, but as the most ideal expression of the core one-day *mitzva*, as well. [This may be the case notwithstanding some differences in the details of implementation, an issue that is debated by the *Rishonim*. I hope to address this in an expanded treatment of these topics.] This position underscores the singular character of *Sukkos* as a manifestation of *hashra'as haShechina*, and an outpost of the *mikdash* and *avoda*. The very existence of a form of *ritzuy* and *avoda* outside of the typical formal confines and structures is a remarkable phenomenon and reflection of the singular character this *mitzva*, albeit one that is even more powerfully expressed in the *mikdash* itself.

Toward the conclusion of *Hilchos Lulav* (8:12), the Rambam invokes the verse that is the focal point of the second presentation of *Sukkos* and the source of the *mikdash* extension of the *mitzva* of *lulav* (that he cites as relevant in the *koseres* and *Sefer haMitzvot*, as noted) "'ושמחתם לפני ה' א-לקיכם שבעת ימים- and you shall rejoice before *Hashem* your God for seven days" (*Vayikra* 23:40) – to support his view that the nightly *mikdash* celebrations of *simchas beis hashoeiva* distinguish *Sukkos* as a unique festival of "*simcha yeseira*." Rav Soloveitchik zt"l (*Kovetz Chiddushei Torah*) notes that the Rambam evidently does not associate *simchas beis hashoeiva* as a special *mikdash* manifestation of *nisuch hamayim*. Had this been the case, he would have codified these *halachos* in *Sefer Avoda* in that alternative context. He concludes that the Rambam believed that *simchas beis hashoeiva*, and the charge of "*usemachtem*," was a singular expression of *simchas Yom Tov* that was reserved for and confined to the celebration of *Yom Tov* in the *mikdash*.

However, the fact is that the Rambam formulates this position in *Hilchos Lulav*. Moreover, he cites *simchas beis hashoeiva* in his *Sefer haMitzvos* (*aseh* 55) in a broader discussion of *simchas Yom Tov*. In light of his integration of the *mikdash* celebration of *lulav*, based on the same verse, as a more intense application of the more universal *lulav* obligation, we might modify this conclusion. Near the conclusion of his discussion of *Sukkos*, the Rambam articulated the idea that the Torah itself subtly formulated, by adding a supplementary treatment of this remarkable *chag*, the idea that unique among the *chagim*, and possibly against the backdrop of the *Yom Kippur* experience, the intense *mikdash* motifs of *Sukkos* highlight the capacity to bring even some dimensions of *ritzuy*, *avoda* and *hashraas haShechina* into our *sukkos*-homes. This capacity and its expression within the framework of *Yom Tov* is, indeed, worthy of "*simcha yeseira*."

The Song of Life
RABBI ZVI SOBOLOFSKY

In *Masseches Arachin* 10b, we are taught that we are obligated to say *Hallel* on all *Yomim Tovim*, but on *Sukkos*, there is an additional unique requirement to say *Hallel* every day. Thus, the recitation of *Hallel* on *Sukkos* has a dual role in *halacha*.

There is a definite link between between the *mitzva* of *daled minim* and *kerias Hallel*. The incorporation of shaking the *lulav* within the context of *Hallel* clearly demonstrates that there is a connection between these two *mitzvos*.

Chazal teach us that there is another occasion when a *mitzva* is performed together with the recitation of *Hallel*. The *Mishna* in *Masseches Pesachim* teaches us that in the time of the *Beis Hamikdash*, the *korban Pesach* was offered simultaneously with the singing of *Hallel*. Why are the *mitzvos* of *daled minim* and *korban Pesach* singled out as *mitzvos* to be performed in conjunction with *Hallel*?

The *Gemara*, in *Masseches Megilla*, relates that at the time of the miracle of *Purim*, *Chazal* were unsure as to how to commemorate the event appropriately. They wanted to institute the reading of the *Megilla* as an eternal commemoration of the miraculous events that had transpired, but were concerned with this being considered an "addition to the Torah."

Originally published on TorahWeb.org in 2000

Ultimately, they delved into the Torah itself to find a source obligating the commemoration of a miracle. *Chazal* concluded that just as the Jewish people celebrated the culmination of *Yetzias Mitzrayim* by praising *Hashem* at *Kerias Yam Suf* with the singing of "*Az Yashir*," so too the events of *Purim* should be celebrated by praising *Hashem*, with the *Megilla* acting as the vehicle of praise. It is this requirement of praising *Hashem* following deliverance from slavery that obligates us to recite *Hallel* as we offer the *korban Pesach* – the *korban* that transformed us from being slaves to being free men.

Chazal noted that there is a greater cause for celebration following the miracle of *Purim*. At *Kerias Yam Suf* it was freedom that was at stake; at *Purim* it was life itself that was threatened. They concluded that the occurrence of a miracle requires us to respond by praising *Hashem*. A miracle that ensures our freedom warrants celebration; how much more so for one that saves our very lives.

The obligation to celebrate our being saved from death is also at the root of our *Hallel* as we take the *lulav* on *Sukkos*. On *Rosh Hashana* and *Yom Kippur* we did not say *Hallel*. *Chazal* explain that as we are being judged and our lives are hanging in the balance, it is inappropriate to sing the words of *Hallel*. Following *Yom Kippur*, when we believe that we have been sealed in the *sefer hachaim*, we have indeed been delivered from the brink of death. The *Midrash* compares the Jew who shakes a *lulav* on *Sukkos* to the warrior returning home victorious, waving his spear to indicate that he has returned safely. As we lift our *lulav* in celebration of the gift of life we were granted on *Yom Kippur*, our entire being bursts forth in song, praising *Hashem* who has delivered us from death to life.

The Secret of Shemini Atzeres

RABBI ZVI SOBOLOFSKY

After celebrating seven days of *Sukkos*, the *Yom Tov* of *Shemini Atzeres* arrives. *Chazal* offer the famous parable of a father who invites his children to visit him. When the time comes for them to leave, the father begs them to stay one more day, as it is difficult for him to part from them. Having spent a week with the Jewish people during *Sukkos*, *Hashem* asks us to remain for one more day to celebrate *Shemini Atzeres* together.

The additional day of *Yom Tov* spent with *Hashem* does not appear to solve the problem of making our departure from *Hashem* any easier. On the contrary, the longer we spend in *Hashem*'s presence, the more difficult it is to leave. What is it about *Shemini Atzeres* that enables us to leave without the sadness that would have otherwise been present at our departure?

Shemini Atzeres is different from the other *Yomim Tovim* of *Tishrei* in that it lacks a particular *mitzva* to focus on. *Rosh Hashana* centers around the *shofar*; fasting and *teshuva* are the themes of *Yom Kippur*; *Sukkos* is celebrated with the *mitzvos* of *sukkah* and *arba'a minim*. The essence of *Shmini Atzeres* is the very fact that there is no *mitzva* unique to it. How do we come close to *Hashem* on a *Yom Tov* which lacks a vehicle to connect with *Hashem*?

Originally published on TorahWeb.org in 2003

On *Shemini Atzeres* our connection to *Hashem* is only through *talmud Torah*. After having completed a month full of *shofar*, fasting, *sukkah* and *lulav*, we realize that our closest relationship to *Hashem* is through the Torah itself. This is why *Simchas Torah* has become the celebration of *Shemini Atzeres*, in Israel on the same day and outside Israel as the second day of the *Yom Tov* of *Shemini Atzeres*. There is no more appropriate time than the conclusion of the *Yomim Tovim* of *Tishrei* to celebrate our overwhelming love for the Torah.

Chazal compare a *mitzva* to a small candle and learning Torah to a great light. A candle lights up a very small corner, whereas a light illuminates an entire area. A *mitzva* is limited in that it provides spiritual light only while the *mitzva* is being performed. The study of Torah continues to radiate forever. *Mitzvos* are limited to specific times, places and circumstances, whereas *talmud Torah* has no bounds.

As we come to the end of a month of *mitzvos*, we sense our relationship with *Hashem* being diminished. There will not be a *shofar*, *sukkah* or *lulav* for an entire year. The level of spirituality achieved on *Yom Kippur* will not be reached again until next year. We are saddened and so is *Hashem*, as it is difficult to say goodbye. Enters *Shemini Atzeres* and lifts our spirits, informing us that we can continue to remain close to *Hashem* for the entire year through *talmud Torah*. There is no need to say goodbye because we have discovered the secret of remaining with *Hashem* under all circumstances. We don't need a *shofar* or a *sukkah* for the next twelve months to keep us in contact with *Hashem*. We have His Torah to study. As *Tishrei* draws to a close, let us focus on *talmud Torah* as the secret of *Shemini Atzeres* that will accompany us throughout the year.

The Harvest Festival: A Spiritual Perspective
RABBI ZVI SOBOLOFSKY

The celebration of *Sukkos* is a culmination of several cycles that occur every year. It is the last of the *Shalosh Regalim*; *Hashem* now rests His Divine Presence on us, completing the process of *Yetzias Mitzrayim* and *kabbalas haTorah*. *Sukkos* is also referred to in the Torah as the *Chag Ha'asif*, the harvest festival, thereby completing the agricultural year that had begun during the previous planting season. We also conclude the month of *Tishrei*, with its spiritual highs of *Rosh Hashana* and *Yom Kippur*, by celebrating *Sukkos*.

It appears that the agricultural aspect of *Sukkos* is merely physical in nature, and yet when analyzed more carefully, there is a spiritual dimension even to the harvest festival. This celebration is closely linked to the post-*Rosh Hashana* and *Yom Kippur* aspect of *Sukkos*. The Rambam (*Hilchos Teshuva, perek* 9) elaborates on the relationship between blessing and success in this world and our ultimate reward for *mitzva* observance. True reward for performance of *mitzvos* cannot take place in this world; the benefits of *mitzva* observance are spiritual and thus are only appropriate in the spiritual setting of the next world. If so, why does the Torah elaborate upon physical things, such as bountiful harvests, as a reward for

Originally published on TorahWeb.org in 2014

mitzva performance? The Rambam explains that the promises are not as a reward, but rather as a mechanism to further *mitzva* observance. We cannot serve *Hashem* properly without the physical blessings bestowed on us. These blessings are only significant because they enable us to continue in our performance of *mitzvos*.

Based on this Rambam, we can understand an otherwise strange *tefilla* recited by the *Kohen Gadol* on *Yom Kippur*. After experiencing the most intense spiritual encounter with *Hashem*, as he leaves the *Kodesh Hakodashim*, the *Kohen Gadol* offers a fervent prayer. We would have expected this prayer to be spiritual in nature, and yet he prays for seemingly very materialistic blessings. Requests for bountiful crops and economic prosperity seem out of touch with the spiritual dimension of the day. However, if we understand the role of physical blessing as the enabler for future spiritual success, this prayer fits perfectly into the tone of the day.

The celebration of *Sukkos* as the harvest festival is not just about physical produce. By marking the bountiful harvest on the heels of the *Yamin Noraim*, we are confirming our belief as to why *Hashem* grants us these seemingly materialistic blessings: our harvest is only meaningful if it furthers the spiritual goals attained during the weeks preceding *Sukkos*.

Today, most of us are not directly involved in the world of agriculture, and it is difficult for us to relate to the notion of a harvest festival. Yet, the message of the role of physical bounty in the service of the spiritual is as true today as it was for our forefathers. As we celebrate *Sukkos* and express our thanks to *Hashem* for our bountiful physical "harvest," let us focus on its true worth as a way of enabling us to attain the spiritual "harvest" of Torah and *mitzvos*. With this mindset, the celebration of *Sukkos* is truly fitting as the culmination of the *Rosh Hashana* and *Yom Kippur* experience.

The Unity of the Sukkah and the Daled Minim

RABBI DANIEL STEIN

According to *Chazal*, both of the *mitzvos* that we perform on the holiday of *Sukkos*, taking the *daled minim* (the four species) as well as dwelling in the *sukkah*, represent *achdus* (unity). The *Midrash* compares the *esrog*, which has an appetizing taste and a pleasing aroma, to Jews who possess both Torah learning and the performance of *mitzvos*; the *lulav*, the date palm, which has a positive flavor but no fragrance, to those Jews who have Torah learning but lack good deeds; the *hadasim*, the myrtle, which has fragrance but no taste, to Jews who perform *mitzvos* but lack the learning of Torah; and the *aravos*, the willow, to those Jews who lack both Torah learning and good deeds. During *Sukkos*, we bind all of these species together to underscore the necessity of uniting all Jews together under the mutual banner of serving the *Ribbono Shel Olam*. Similarly, the *Gemara* (*Sukkah* 27b) derives from the *pasuk*, "Every citizen in Yisrael shall dwell in *sukkos*" (*Vaykira* 23:42), that all of the people of Israel could theoretically dwell in one *sukkah*, for the *sukkah* need not be owned by those sitting within it. Undoubtedly, all of *Klal Yisrael* inhabiting one *sukkah*, coexisting under the same roof for seven consecutive days, would be a powerful statement of unity and *achdus*.

Originally published on TorahWeb.org in 2017

However, in actuality these two symbols of *achdus* correspond to two distinct forms of unity. In *Parashas Vayechi*, Yaakov *Avinu* twice summons all of his children before his death: "Gather, and I will tell you what will happen to you at the end of days. Gather and listen, sons of Yaakov, and listen to Yisrael, your father" (*Bereishis* 49:1-2). The *Sefas Emes* explains that Yaakov beseeched his children to gather together in a show of unity two times, corresponding to two discrete types of *achdus*. There is the *achdus* of individuals who don't necessarily enjoy each other inherently, but who share a common goal and agenda, which breeds a bond born out of convenience and expediency (much like siblings who gather sparingly only to honor their parents). This is the unity being described in Yaakov's latter plea: "Gather and listen, sons of Yaakov, and listen to Yisrael your father." However, in Yaakov's first call for *achdus*, which provided no further context other than a directive to "gather," he was hoping for a deeper and more profound kind of unity, which is the aspiration of every parent. He was yearning for the genuine *achdus* of loving siblings, who sincerely like each other, and for whom honoring their parents is not an anchor, but a pretext, or an excuse to see and spend time with each other.

The *Chafetz Chaim* observes that even though the *daled minim* signify the virtue of *achdus*, the *esrog* is not tied together with the other *minim* and is generally held in a different hand from the other species. It only joins with the other species in order to perform and fulfill the *mitzva* of *daled minim*. Therefore, while the *mitzva* of *daled minim* represents unity, it is the type of *achdus* generated by those who possess a shared and collective goal and unite expressly for that purpose. The *achdus* of the *sukkah*, however, is entirely different. All of *Klal Yisrael* can theoretically sit in one *sukkah*, but there is certainly no *mitzva* to do so. When many Jews choose to sit in the same *sukkah* together, they are bound together not by a communal obligation or common objective, but rather by a mutual fondness for one another. Rav Dov Weinberger (*Shemen Hatov*) suggests that the Arizal and the Shelah *Hakadosh* advised taking the *daled minim* in the *sukkah* each morning of *Sukkos* in an attempt to fuse these two notions of *achdus* together.[55] While we long to forge an honest and adoring relationship with one another, we also desire for that relationship to be grounded in a unified vision, mission and purpose. Even the most loving relationships that are not founded in substance and shared beliefs can become temperamental and indecisive. We aspire to engender a genuine affection among all Jews and to reinforce that friendship with a harmonious resolve and determination to serve *Hashem*.

Despite the fact that both the *sukkah* and the *daled minim* remind us of the different strands of *achdus*, neither *mitzva* calls for absolute uniformity; in fact, they both allow and even lobby for diversity. Within the *achdus* of the *daled minim* there seems to be a pecking order, and each species has its own assigned seat. The *esrog* is held in the right hand, while all of the other species are in the left hand. The *lulav* is in the center and rises above the rest. The *hadasim* are positioned on the right of the *lulav*, but must be shorter than the *lulav* and taller than the *aravos*. The *aravos* should be on the left of the *lulav* and cut to be the shortest species in the bundle. How can a symbol of unity and togetherness be so rigidly segregated? Moreover, the *Gemara* (*Sukkah* 28a) derives from the very same *pasuk* which previously emphasized the universality of the *sukkah*, "Every citizen in Yisrael shall dwell in *sukkos*" (*Vaykira* 23:42), that women are exempt from the *mitzva* of *sukkah*. How can the *sukkah*, which is purported to be a bold symbol of inclusivity, have exceptions or exclusions? Rav Yitzchok Menachem Weinberg, the Talner Rebbe (*Heima Yenachamuni*), explains that the *sukkah* and the *daled minim* teach us that true *achdus* must never come at the expense of legitimate diversity, but rather demands that we find common ground and build relationships despite our differences.

---

[55] See, however, Rav Tzvi Pesach Frank, Mikraei Kodesh (Sukkos vol. 2, sec. 20-21) and Rav Hershel Schachter, Nefesh HaRav (p. 217), who raise certain objections to this practice.

In fact, Yaakov *Avinu* seems to undermine his own impassioned appeal for unity amongst his children by subsequently blessing each one of his children differently, as the *pasuk* states "each man according to his blessing he blessed them" (*Bereishis* 49:28), potentially sowing the seeds of jealously and resentment in the future. For this reason, the *pasuk* concludes, "he blessed them," which according to Rashi was meant to convey that all of the children were included in each one of the blessings. What then was the purpose of giving each his own individualized *beracha* in the first place? The *Imrei Emes* cites the *Chiddushei Harim* who suggests that Yaakov was training his children to realize that accentuating their individual roles and abilities should never be an obstacle to unity, but the very foundation upon which genuine *achdus* must be built. Only when we appreciate and celebrate the differences that inherently exist between us can we begin to form the bonds of true *achdus* and join together properly in the service of *Hakadosh Baruch Hu*!

Sukkos: A Time for Teshuva

RABBI MAYER TWERSKY

With *Elul* and *Yomim Noraim* behind us, we are ready to shift focus. For the past forty days, the focus has been on *teshuva*. *Cheshbon hanefesh* and *teshuva* have been the *mitzvos hayom*. Now we are ready for change. What are the *mitzvos hayom* as we move forward?

One of the *mitzvos hayom* may come as a surprise. It is *teshuva*. The days after *Yom Kippur* are a time for *teshuva* – in fact, an optimal time for *teshuva*.

Two perspectives will help illumine this surprising answer. The first perspective is provided by the Maharsha. The *Gemara* at the end of *Masseches Megilla* teaches that Moshe *Rabbeinu* instituted that we should study the *halachos* of each *Yom Tov* on that *Yom Tov* – the *halachos* of *Pesach* on *Pesach*, *Shavuos* on *Shavuos*, and *Sukkos* on *Sukkos*. The Maharsha comments on the omission of *Rosh Hashana* and *Yom Kippur* from the list of *Yomim Tovim*. He explains that *Rosh Hashana* and *Yom Kippur* are not mentioned because the dominant *mitzva* of these days is *teshuva*, and it is ALWAYS a *mitzva* to do *teshuva*. The *mitzvos* of *chametz* and *matza* are limited to *Pesach*, *shetei halechem* to *Shavuos*, etc. Hence, there is a special

---

Originally published on TorahWeb.org in 2007

obligation to study *Hilchos Chametz Umatza* on *Pesach*, etc. But *mitzvas teshuva* is perennial, and hence our preoccupation with *teshuva* ought to be constant. Accordingly, the days after *Yom Kippur* – as all days of the year – are a time for *teshuva*.

It is difficult to exaggerate the importance of this perspective. I am not sure how much we think about *teshuva* during the year between *motzaei Yom Kippur* and the following *Rosh Chodesh Elul*. I am, however, sure about one thing. We do no think enough about *teshuva*. *Mesillas Yesharim* recommends that a person make a *cheshbon hanefesh* daily. Consider the following *mashal*. If the captain of a ship checks the ship's course daily, it can not veer too far off course. But if he neglects to check daily, the ship can veer far off course, and the necessary corrections become increasingly difficult. The analogue to this *mashal* and its relevance to out lives are obvious. And thus *teshuva* and *cheshbon hanefesh* are perennial, not seasonal.

There is a second perspective as well. This latter perspective is, *inter alia*, expounded upon in *sifrei chasidus*. *Sukkos*, in particular, is a time for *teshuva mei'ahava*. The *teshuva* of the *Yamim Noraim* was most likely a *teshuva miyira*. Sullied by our sins, our *teshuva* was most likely inspired by the awe and dread of the *yemei hadin*. Having been granted atonement by *Hakadosh Baruch Hu* on *Yom Kippur*, we, in our newly attained state of *tahara*, have an enhanced capacity for *teshuva mei'ahava*, a *teshuva* inspired by love of *Hakadosh Baruch Hu*.

May we merit to be *chozer beteshuva sheleima lefanav mei'ahava*.

Sukkos:
A Call to Teshuva
RABBI MAYER TWERSKY

As the sound of the final blast of the *shofar* signifying the end of *Yom Kippur* fades, we shift gears. No longer preoccupied with the judgment of *Rosh Hashana* and *Yom Kippur*, we prepare for *Chag HaSukkos, zeman simchaseinu*. The *kittel* is returned to the closet, the *Yom Kippur machzor* and Rambam *Hilchos Teshuva* to their respective spots on the bookshelf. We hasten to put the finishing touches on our *sukkos*, procure *daled minim* and cook for *Sukkos*.

In transitioning to *Chag HaSukkos* in the manner described above, we are making a major error. Allow the Maharsha and Malbim to explain.

The final lines of *Masseches Megilla* read as follows: "Moshe decreed for Israel that they should inquire about and expound upon the matters of the day [i.e., the current festival]. The laws of *Pesach* on *Pesach*, the laws of *Shavuos* on *Shavuos*, the laws of *Sukkos* on *Sukkos*" (*Megillah* 32a; Artscroll Schottenstein translation slightly modified). Maharsha comments on the omission of *Rosh Hashana* and *Yom Kippur* from the Mosaic decree. He explains that the thrust of Moshe *Rabbeinu*'s decree is that the seasonal *mitzvos* associated with the festivals (*sukkah, matza*, abstaining

---

Originally published on TorahWeb.org in 2008

from *melacha* on *Yom Tov*, etc.) ought to command our attention on the festivals. The dominant *mitzva* on *Rosh Hashana* and *Yom Kippur* – *teshuva* – is not seasonal because "a person should be preoccupied with *teshuva* throughout the year" (Maharsha, *Chiddushei Aggados* to *Megilla* 32a).[56]

The *haftara* for *Shabbos Shuva* opens with the following verse from the book of *Hoshea*, "Return, O Israel, to *Hashem*, your God, for you have stumbled through your iniquity. Take words with you and return to *Hashem*, etc." (*Hoshea* 14:2-3; Artscroll Stone edition translation). The Malbim explains the double call to repentance. The initial exhortation is addressed to the Jewish people when they are distant from *Hashem*; return from afar to *Hashem*. Such repentance is likely to arise out of fear (*teshuva miyira*). The *navi* then renews his call for *teshuva*. He exhorts us to build upon the foundation of the *teshuva miyira*, and repent again. Return to *Hashem* again – this time out of love (*teshuva mei'ahava*). According to *Sefer Chasidim*, the progression urged by the *navi* Hoshea is precisely the progression from *Aseres Yemei Teshuva* to *Sukkos*. *Aseres Yemei Teshuva*, culminating in *Yom Kippur*, are a time of *teshuva miyira*, whereas *Sukkos*, building upon the foundation of *Aseres Yemei Teshuva*, is a time of *teshuva mei'ahava*. The way to capitalize on the *teshuva* of *Rosh Hashana* and *Yom Kippur* is by expanding upon that *teshuva* and repenting again, in a deeper, more profound manner.

And thus while the *kittel* is rightfully returned to the closet and the *machzor* to the bookcase, Rambam *Hilchos Teshuva* ought to play a dominant role in our preparation for and celebration of *Chag HaSukkos*.

---

[56] Rambam's *Hilchos Teshuva* – incorporated into *Sefer HaMadda*, not *Zemanim* – corroborates Maharsha's assertion. Of the sixty-nine *halachos* which comprise *Hilchos Teshuva*, only five of them touch upon *Rosh Hashana* and/or *Yom Kippur*.

Seeing Straight
RABBI MORDECHAI WILLIG

I

"*Hashem* made man straight (*yashar*), but they sought many calculations" (*Koheles* 7:29). Originally, man was a straightforward creature, who was intellectually inclined to avoid sin, irrespective of the consequences. Later, mankind pursued sweet pleasures and avoided unpleasant conditions. This resulted in many calculations and schemes which entice to sin (Seforno).

Harav Elchanan Wasserman (*Kovetz Ma'amarim, Emuna*) explains that faith in *Hashem* the Creator is obvious. Just as a garment bears witness to the weaver, a door to the carpenter and a house to the builder, so the world bears witness to *Hashem* Who created it (*midrash* cited in *Beis Hamidrash* I, 114). "The heavens declare the glory of *Hashem*" (*Tehillim* 19:2). Why, then, are there so many atheists, including brilliant philosophers?

The answer is in the Torah: "Bribery blinds the eyes of the wise" (*Devarim* 17:19). A person's desires for pleasure blind him. One strays after his heart into heresy if he strays after his eyes in a desire for immorality (*Berachos* 12b). "Israel served idols in order to allow flagrant immorality" (*Sanhedrin* 63b). These heretical calculations of a person blinded by desire derail him from the straight path of his original state.

Originally published on TorahWeb.org in 2012

II

The aforementioned *pasuk* in *Koheles* 7:29 speaks of one man (Adam), and concludes that "they" (plural) strayed. "They" includes Chava, and together they planned to sin (Rashi).

The serpent said to Chava "You will not surely die" (*Bereishis* 3:4). The serpent pushed Chava until she touched the tree. He said to her, "Just as there is no death by touching it, so there is no death by eating it" (Rashi). Chava accepted the serpent's argument and denied *Hashem*'s statement, "On the day you eat from it you will surely die" (*Bereishis* 2:17). Her sin was one of lack of faith. However, the Torah later attributes Chava's sin not to lack of faith, but to desire. "Chava saw that the tree was good for eating and desirable in her eyes" (*Bereishis* 3:6). *Harav* Yaakov Yisrael Kanievsky (a.k.a. the Steipler, in *Birkas Peretz* 3:4) resolves this apparent contradiction by explaining that if not for her desire, Chava would have realized that *Hashem*'s command not to eat from the tree did not prohibit touching it. Her lack of faith was *caused* by her desires.

III

"Yeshurun became fat and kicked" (*Devarim* 32:15). Yeshurun, a name of *Am Yisrael*, derives from the root *yashar*, straight. Some say that its root is "*ashurenu*" "I will see" (*Bemidbar* 24:17) (Ibn Ezra). The Seforno elaborates: "Even those who engage in analysis (*iyun*), called Yeshurun, as in 'I will see,' acted like animals who kick people who feed them. You, Yeshurun, those who engage in Torah and analysis, turned to physical pleasures, and became fat ("*shamanta*"). You then became thick ("*avisa*") and unable to understand the fine points (*dakus*) of the truth. You (i.e., your eyes) became covered ("*kasisa*"), as it says in *Yeshaya* 44:18, "Their eyes are smeared (prevented) from seeing, their hearts from comprehending."

The intelligentsia of *Am Yisrael* was blinded by the desire for physical pleasure. They could no longer see or understand properly. As a result, the masses abandoned *Hashem* their Creator (Seforno).

This is a recurring theme read this week in *Koheles*, next week in *Bereishis*, and last week in *Ha'azinu*. One's desires are a form of bribery that blind and lead to heretical miscalculations, rationalizations in violating *Hashem*'s command, and abandonment of *Hashem*. This affects all of mankind and all members of *Am Yisrael*, regardless of intellectual level.

Perhaps the two interpretations of Yeshurun are related. In order to see, a person must be straight, as he was created, and not overly involved in blinding physical pleasures. By avoiding the miscalculations caused by temptation, we can, and must, be straight and see straight.

Success Is in the Palm of Your Hand

RABBI BENJAMIN YUDIN

The Rambam often closes specific sections of *halacha* with an aggadic or moral teaching. Thus it is not surprising that at the conclusion of *Hilchos Lulav* (8:15) he does the same. What is surprising, however, is the specific teaching he chooses. The last halachic topic he deals with there is the special *simcha* that was present at the *simchas beis hashoeiva* celebrations in the *Beis Hamikdash* during *Sukkos*. The Rambam then teaches that the emotion with which one performs *mitzvos* is so significant that if the performance lacks happiness and joy, one is fit for Divine retribution, as it says, "because you did not serve *Hashem*, your God, amid gladness and goodness of heart" (*Devarim* 28:47). We would have expected that his final teaching in *Hilchos Lulav* would be related to *kabbalas penei haShechina* (greeting the Divine presence, as was done at the *simchas beis hashoeiva*), perhaps throughout the year in our synagogues and study halls, and we would have placed the lesson regarding the importance of performing *mitzvos* with enthusiasm earlier in *Hilchos De'os*, where Rambam discusses the overall character of man.

I heard from one of my teachers a fascinating explanation as to

Originally published on TorahWeb.org in 2007

why the Rambam ends *Hilchos Lulav* with the concept of *simcha shel mitzva*. The *Yalkut Shimoni* (*Tehillim* 102:19) explains the verse, "Let this be recorded for a later generation, so that the newborn people will praise God." Commenting on "*ve'am nivra yehallel Kah* – so that the newborn people will praise God," the Rabbis ask: is there a nation yet to be born? Rather, the verse refers to the generations that are "as dead" in their actions and *mitzvos*, who pray and beseech *Hashem* on *Rosh Hashana* and *Yom Kippur* and God recreates them, giving them another opportunity. What is this *am nivra* – this newly created nation – to do? They are to "*yehallel Kah*" – to take their *lulav* and *esrog* and praise *Hashem* therewith. Why specifically should they praise *Hashem* with the four species?

Rabbeinu Bechaye in his commentary on *Parashas Emor* and in his *Kad Hakemach* explains why the four *minim* were singled out for the *mitzva* on *Sukkos*. The essence of a living thing, he notes, is its moisture, as the text states (*Devarim* 12:25) "כי הדם הוא הנפש", "*ki hadam hu hanefesh*" – "for the blood, it is the life." Similarly in the world of vegetation, the moisture contained within the fruit comprises its life and freshness. The four species reflect the freshness endowed within them, and they are taken as a symbol of vibrancy and life with which to praise *Hashem* for His renewing us and giving us a second chance to serve Him.

The *halacha* is that a dry *lulav* is *pasul* (may not be used) for the *mitzva*. Though it is clearly recognizable as a *lulav*, the Ra'avad (*Hilchos Lulav*, 8:9) explains that a dried-out, i.e., dead, *lulav* cannot be used for serving *Hashem*, as the *pasuk* (*Tehillim* 115:17) says, "לא המתים יהללו קה" "*Lo hameisim yehallelu Kah*" – "the dead cannot praise God." Thus, the *lulav* and its components were chosen as the medium to thank *Hashem* for the opportunity to serve Him with excitement and enthusiasm, as they themselves bespeak life.

Regarding man, in *Parashas Bereishis* (2:7) we are taught, "*vay-*

ipach be'apav nishmas chaim," "He blew into his nostrils the soul of life." There is man with a soul, alive, energetic, with great and unlimited potential, and there is man without a soul, lifeless. Similarly, there are the *mitzvos* of man with and without a soul. A *mitzva* performed with *simcha* – happiness and joy – is a *mitzva* possessing a soul, and the same *mitzva* performed perfunctorily, out of habit and routine, is literally lifeless.

Many have the practice, based on the Arizal and Shelah *Hakadosh*, to fulfill the *mitzva* of picking up the four *minim* in the *sukkah*. Perhaps the message is that one needs the environment of the *sukkah*, which reminds the dweller that he has left his permanent residence to dwell in a temporary one, literally in *Hashem*'s home and presence, to enable him to perform *mitzvos* with excitement and the realization that one is in *Hashem*'s presence. Too often throughout the year we are so distracted that we fail to be cognizant of our performing *mitzvos* in the presence of, and praying literally to, *Hashem*. The *Chafetz Chaim zt"l* in his *Shem Olam* writes, "Tell me truthfully my brothers – do you consider the closeness and potential of man to God on a daily basis, weekly basis, monthly or even annual basis?" The Rambam writes that the *simcha* accompanying our *mitzvos* is to be there all the time, but we learn it from the life and vibrancy of the *lulav*. Hence the Rambam teaches the lesson of *simcha* in *Hilchos Lulav* and not in *Hilchos De'os*.

Weather Forecast for Sukkos: Cloudy
RABBI BENJAMIN YUDIN

"You shall live in booths for a seven day period; every citizen in Israel shall dwell in booths so that your generations will know that I had the children of Israel live in booths when I took them out of the land of Egypt; I am *Hashem*, your God" (*Vayikra* 23:42-43). Rashi, citing the *Gemara* (*Sukkah* 11b), understands the above in accordance with the teaching of Rabbi Eliezer, that *sukkos* are the annual commemoration of the *ananei hakavod*, the clouds of glory in which *Hashem* enveloped the Jewish nation during their forty-year trek in the desert. The "climate control" setting of these clouds provided air conditioning during the day and heat at night. It is no wonder we celebrate *Hashem's* Divine providence and protection. Yet one has to ask, given that Moshe, Aharon and Miriam, the three shepherds who led the Jewish nation, each contributed a major phenomenon – Moshe the *mann*, Miriam the *be'eir* and Aharon the *ananei hakavod* – why we have a *Yom Tov* to commemorate Aharon's gift, while the other two are seemingly neglected?

An answer to the above may be culled from the commentary of the Gra (Vilna Gaon) on the opening verses of *Shir Hashirim*, and his commentary *Aderes Eliyahu* on *Shemos* (34:10). The *Tur* (*Orach Chaim* 625)

Originally published on TorahWeb.org in 2008

writes that *Sukkos* is observed at the time when people are returning to their homes after the summer to clearly indicate that our exit from our homes is for the sake of the *mitzva*, as opposed to our personal comfort. The Gaon provides another reason why *Sukkos* is celebrated in the fall and not in the spring when we left Egypt. The Gra notes that the *Yom Tov* of *Sukkos* is to remember *Hashem*'s protective clouds, and the Jewish nation was first introduced to the clouds immediately after the Exodus, as the Torah informs us (*Shemos* 13:21): "*Hashem* went before them by day in a pillar of cloud to lead them on the way." Why then do we not celebrate *Sukkos* in the spring? We should conduct the *Pesach seder* in the *sukkah*!

The Gra answers that when *Bnei Yisrael* committed the sin of the golden calf (on the 17th of *Tammuz*) *Hashem* withdrew the clouds and His apparent benevolent protection from the people. It was only after *Hashem* pronounced "סלחתי כדבריך - I have forgiven according to your word" (*Bemidbar* 14:20) on *Yom Kippur*, and after the people responded enthusiastically and generously with their wealth and willingness to the commandment to construct the *Mishkan*, that the clouds returned.

What happened subsequently is most remarkable. The clouds did not only return, but they were of much greater magnitude. Whereas prior to the sin of the golden calf the clouds enveloped only the righteous members of the nation, they now provided protection and care to all. This is how the Gra understands the verses immediately following the Thirteen Attributes of *Hashem* and His forgiveness of the Jewish people for the sin of the golden calf. *Hashem* said: "Behold! I seal a covenant before your entire people. I shall make distinctions (wonders) such as have never been created in the entire world and among the nations, and the entire people in whose midst you are will see the work of *Hashem* – which is awesome – that I am about to do with you" (*Shemos* 34:10).

The wonders that the verse is referring to are the clouds that returned to envelop the entire nation. It is for this reason that *Sukkos* is celebrated in the fall, as we are reliving the experience of the second set of *ananei hakavod* that appeared in the fall, following *Yom Kippur*, not the first set that arrived in the spring.

A most exciting phenomenon emerges: The Jewish nation backslid and sinned; they commited the grave sin of the golden calf, and then Moshe led the nation in *teshuva*. Had *Hashem* restored the relationship to its prior state before their sin, *dayeinu* – that would have been sufficient. We would have celebrated the return of the *Shechina*, Divine presence. What happened was the extraordinary! The relationship between *Hashem* and the people was not only restored, but improved and enhanced.

The fact that *Sukkos* follows *Yom Kippur* is not accidental, nor coincidental, but is rather the actualization of one of the basic tenets of *Yom Kippur*. The latter not only has the capacity to atone, but as Resh Lakish teaches (*Yoma* 86b), *teshuva* that is performed *mei'ahava*, motivated by love of *Hashem*, has the ability to transform willful transgressions into merits! Thus *Sukkos* serves as an annual symbol and testimony of not only our renewed relationship with *Hashem*, but our improved one.

It is thus understandable why *Sukkos* enjoys the distinction of being the happiest *chag*. Its very reference and identification in the prayers is *zeman simchaseinu*. Moreover, every morning in the *beracha* prior to *Shema*, we proclaim "אהבה רבה אהבתנו - with abundant love You have loved us." The proof of that love is the next verse, "חמלה גדולה ויתרה חמלת עלינו - with exceedingly great pity have You pitied us." The Gra explains that this line refers to the great reversal that took place after the golden calf. Initially, *Hashem* said to Moshe, "I will destroy them and make a nation from you" (*Shemos* 32:10). After Moshe's prayers and the nation's *teshuva*, *Hashem* not only forgave *Bnei Yisrael*, but extended His Divine presence, which had been at Sinai for a brief period, to dwell permanently in their midst in the *Mishkan*. Not only a return of the *Shechina*, but an upgrade.

Finally, it is understandable why we have a holiday to celebrate Aharon's contribution of the clouds more than Miriam's well and Moshe's *mann*. The latter two were necessities. *Hashem* brought them into a desert, and thus He had to provide them with the basics of nourishment. But an improved all-weather comfort system for the entire nation that showed a special love and affection – that, we excitedly reciprocate and return on *Sukkos*.

Resolving the Sukkah Paradox

RABBI BENJAMIN YUDIN

Every Yom Tov has its own unique character. Regarding the holiday of Sukkos there appears to be a basic contradiction between two conflicting themes. On the one hand, the Maharil explains the reason that Sukkos comes following Yom Kippur is that if it was decreed that an individual or community go into galus (exile) as result of the judgment of Yom Kippur, they can serve this sentence by exiting their homes for a seven-day period, and reside in a temporary abode, the sukkah. This teaching is found earlier in the Midrash Yalkut Shimoni (Vayikra 653) in the name of Rebbe Eliezer bar Marnus, that if the Jewish nation were judged to be exiled, their going into their sukkos is considered On High as though they had gone to Bavel.

Moreover, this concept of uprooting oneself and moving into a temporary dwelling is found in *halacha*. The Talmud (*Sukkah* 8b) teaches that if one lives in a kosher *sukkah* all year long, he cannot fulfill the *mitzva* of *sukkah* by remaining in that *sukkah*, but must leave the permanent *sukkah* and, like all Israel, experience the phenomenon of relocation and enter another *sukkah*. This is codified in *Orach Chaim* (636:2). It is not sufficient that one resides in a kosher *sukkah*; one has to literally experience the move.

Originally published on TorahWeb.org in 2011

Yet, paradoxically, we find that *Sukkos* is defined as a most happy, joyous, festive holiday. The *Yalkut* (654) notes that the charge to be in a state of *simcha* is found three times in the Torah regarding the *Yom Tov* of *Sukkos*. Interestingly, regarding *Pesach* there is no biblical directive for *simcha*, and the holiday of *Shavuos* has *simcha* incorporated but once. The *Zohar* (*Parashas Emor*) ascribes some of the special *simcha* of *Sukkos* to the seven *ushpizin* – privileged guests who join us daily in the *sukkah*. What is perhaps most fascinating is the exception to the rule that exists regarding the *mitzva* of *sukkah*, namely that a *mitztaer* – one who is uncomfortable and pained by fulfilling the *mitzva* of residing in the *sukkah* – is exempt thereof. Regarding the observance of Jewish law, we are generally governed by *lefum tzara agra*, i.e., the reward is in proportion to the difficulty and exertion (*Avos* 5:26). If one does not enjoy eating *matza*, or when we had, and please God in the future will have, the *korban Pesach*, his lack of enjoyment is not an exemption. The *Yerushalmi* relates that some Rabbis endured a headache from *Pesach* to *Shavuos* as a result of drinking wine and not grape juice for the *mitzva* of *daled kosos*. Sitting in the *sukkah* is radically different. If one is troubled by extreme weather conditions under which he would not remain even in his own home, or troubled by unpleasant odors or disturbing insects, the *Shulchan Aruch* (*Orach Chaim* 640:4) rules that one is exempt from the *sukkah* (except for the first night, when even under those conditions one must eat a *kezayis* in the *sukkah*).

At first glance there appears to be a startling inconsistency whereby exile and leaving one's comfortable home usually denotes hardships and sufferings bereft of the conveniences of home, yet one who is *mitztaer* is exempt from *mitzvas sukkah*. In the *sukkah* we are mandated to merge these divergent motifs.

The Torah (*Vayikra* 23:43) teaches that we are to reside in *sukkos* "למען ידעו דורותיכם כי בסוכות הושבתי את בני ישראל בהוציאי אותם מארץ מצרים" - so that your generations will know that I had the children of Israel live in booths when I took them out of the land of Egypt." Rav Yosef Salant *zt"l*, in his *Be'eir Yosef*, notes that we are told to relive and reenact, not simply remember, the manner in which *Hashem* provided for us during our forty-year trek through the desert. The *ananei hakavod* (clouds of glory) provided millions of travelers in the desert with perfect climate control – air conditioning by day to protect them from the beating sun, and heat by night to dispel the chill. Moreover, these clouds worked overtime at night by providing fresh laundering and dry cleaning for their clothes. They were provided miraculously with manna from heaven satisfying their individual tastes and diets, and fresh drinking water was supplied in abundance despite their location being far from any oasis. In their travels and exile from Egypt to the land of Israel, *Hashem* provided them with all the comforts of home. It is for this reason, explains the *Be'eir Yosef*, that if one is *mitztaer*, uncomfortable in the *sukkah*, that one is exempt thereof, as this would negate the positive characteristic of *mitzvas sukkah*, reliving His abundant kindnesses. This understanding of our stay in the desert, after which our *mitzvas sukkah* is modeled, puts to rest the *sukkah* paradox: through the *mitzva* of *sukkah* we reenact our desert experience, which included being in a form of *galus* but also included *Hashem*'s infinite kindness in making that *galus* very comfortable.

> # *Appendix:*
> # *Excerpt from*
> # *"Chinuch:*
> # *Contemporary*
> # *& Timeless"*

Introduction

"כי ידעתיו למען אשר יצוה את בניו ואת ביתו אחריו ושמרו דרך ה'" - For I (Hashem) have loved him (Avraham *Avinu*), because he commands his children and his household after him that they keep the way of Hashem" (*Bereishis* 18:19.)

The transmission of our *masorah* has been a defining mission of *Klal Yisroel* since the time of Avraham *Avinu*, and continues to be a central focus in our individual and communal *avodas* Hashem. When trying to determine the best approach to *chinuch* for an individual or a community, at least three sets of factors must be carefully considered. The first set of factors is comprised of the timeless values and priorities established by the Torah and explicated by *Chazal*. An unwavering dedication to *masorah*, the primacy of *talmud* Torah, *emuna*, *chessed*, *kedusha*, and all other Torah truisms define our ultimate goals in *chinuch*, as they do in all aspects of life, and provide the lens through which the other two factors are viewed. In addition to our timeless Torah values, successful *chinuch* has to take into account the contemporary challenges that exist in each generation and community. Current realities and problems, such as egocentrism, the arrogant superiority of youth, substance abuse, a rising divorce rate among religious families, children at risk, child abusers, and the unfettered hedonism of our surrounding society must be fully understood, and our *chinuch* efforts must be properly calibrated to overcome these challenges. And last, but by no means least, as Shlomo *haMelech* instructs us, "חנוך לנער על פי דרכו - educate a child in accordance with his capabilities" (Mishlei 22:6.) *Chinuch* must be personalized for each child, and the best interests of the child must be the driving force, and litmus test, for all decisions.

"חנוך לנער על פי דרכו" can only realistically be accomplished by dedicated parents and educators who know the child, engage in heartfelt *tefillah*, and are blessed with *siyata deShmaya*. The customized approach of individualized *chinuch* can't realistically be captured in the generic, one size fits all format of a *sefer*. At the same time, those tailored decisions must be made by parents and educators who have done all they can to master the first two areas mentioned above, i.e. timeless Torah values and contemporary *chinuch* challenges. We hope, through this *sefer*, to assist such committed individuals to succeed in their *chinuch* efforts. In the pages of this *sefer* the reader will find both timeless discussions of *hashkofas haTorah* on *chinuch* as well as an unflinching examination of, and guidance regarding, the many jarring and sensitive contemporary issues that parents and educators must grapple with.

About TorahWeb and the Sources of this Book

The TorahWeb Foundation, a 501(c)(3) not-for-profit organization, was founded in 1999 at the initiative of members of our community. Its goal is to disseminate *divrei Torah* and *hashkafa*, with special attention to contemporary religious and social issues. TorahWeb's board consists of Rav Hershel Schachter, Rav Michael Rosensweig, Rav Mayer Twersky, and Rav Mordechai Willig. TorahWeb's primary projects have been publishing weekly *divrei Torah* on www.TorahWeb.org and our email list, and arranging for *leilei iyun* a number of times a year in various communities, the audio and video of which is available on TorahWeb.org as well. Neither the *rebbeim* nor other individuals involved in TorahWeb receive any financial compensation. In addition, shuls receive the *leil iyun* programming free of charge.

The "Essays" section of this book is based on *shiurim* given at our *leilei iyun*. Some of these essays were written by the *maggid shiur* (speaker) himself, while some were converted to writing by others and reviewed by the *maggid shiur*. A footnote at the beginning of each essay states when and where the original *shiur* was given, as well as the name of the editor(s) for those essays that were not written be the *maggid shiur* himself. The rest of this book is comprised of selected *divrei Torah* written by the *rebbeim* which originally appeared on TorahWeb. org. The realities of the time pressures with which these Torah leaders function on a daily basis result in the *divrei Torah* on the web site not being properly edited and often missing *mareh mekomos*. These shortcomings were addressed for the *divrei Torah* included in this volume.[1]

The proceeds of this book will go towards TorahWeb programming. Please send any suggestions, comments, or questions to TorahWeb@TorahWeb.org.

Acknowledgments

Publishing a high quality book involves a tremendous amount of work by a number of talented and dedicated people. Converting a spoken shiur into a well written essay is an *avoda kasha*, and we extend our heartfelt thanks to Rabbi Michoel Zylberman and Dr. Allan Weissman for their editing work. We would like to thank Rebbetzin Meira Mintz and Mrs. Tamar Schwartz for their copy editing and proofreading. And finally, we extend our deepest gratitude to Rebbetzin Rina Schachter for her extensive and tireless effort to ensure that our rebbeim's *chochma mefuara* is presented in a *kli mefuar*.

---

[1] On TorahWeb.org, though, they remain in their original, unedited form.

Table of Contents

Rav Hershel Schachter

    Masorah and Change 3

    Ma'aseh Avos Siman LaBanim 4

    Ego and Humility in Torah Study 7

    Straightening Out Our Priorities 10

    True Simcha 13

    True Freedom 15

    Rachel's Longing for Children 18

    Regarding Mesira 19

Rav Dr. Abraham J. Twerski

    Adam – A Unique Individual 25

    The Lesson of Noach 27

    "Do Not Sin Against The Child":
    Divorce Involving Children 29

    The Lessons of the Yosef Epic 32

    Reaching Old Age: Victory or Defeat? 36

    Kedoshim: Rashi vs. Ramban 42

    Are We Derelict in Teaching? 44

    Substance Abuse in Adolescents:
    Detection, Treatment, and Prevention 46

    Materialism 55

    Histapkus vs. Consumerism and Entitlement 60

    Glatt Kosher Is Not Enough 63

    Getting the Uninterested Child to Shul 67

Rav Yakov Haber

    A Surprising Aspect of the Count:
    The Jewish Family 73

    The Methodology of Kindness 77

Ben Sorer U'Moreh: The Child at Risk 79
The Commandment of Peru U'Revu:
An Example of the Dual Law System 83
Children of All Levels 86

Rav Yaakov Neuburger

Chesseducation 93
Two Tents of Education:
The Yeshiva and the Home 95
Beginnings 97
Guarding Our Safety and
Protecting Our Values 99

Rav Michael Rosensweig

Ya'akov's Final Spiritual
Bequest to His Children 103
An Approach to Formative Jewish Education 105
Ben Sorer U'Moreh: The Importance of
Cultivating a Religious Personality 109
Educating About the Elevated Standard of Halachic Man's
Human Interactions 112

Rav Yonason Sacks

Teaching Torah Values 117
VeHa'amidu Talmidim Harbeh 118

Rav Zvi Sobolofsky

Giving vs. Taking 125
Back to Yeshiva 126
Shavuos: Do Not Forget,
For Ourselves and Our Children 128

Rav Mayer Twersky

Emuna and Masorah 133
Consistency 135
Superseding Societal Conventions 139

Appendix

Rav Mordechai Willig
- VeHigadta LeVincha 145
- Raising Children 149
- Descendants and Deficiencies 152
- Jewish Education, Family, and Community 155
- Family First 159
- Youthful Hearts and Eyes 162
- Inheritance Without a Fight:
  Writing a Will in Modern Times 164

Rav Benjamin Yudin
- A Man's Work Is Never Done 171
- Parental Guidance Suggested 173
- Home Equity Insurance 176
- Show and Tell: We Had It First 179
- Do As I Do 181

Essays
- Rav Hershel Schachter: Jewish Parenting 187
- Rav Dr. Abraham J. Twerski:
  Alcohol, Drugs, and Morality Among Orthodox Teens 217
- Rav Yaakov Neuburger:
  Scholarship and Scholarships: Marketing and Messages 227
- Rav Michael Rosensweig:
  How to Pick a School for Your Child:
  Values and Priorities in Jewish Education 233
- Rav Mordechai Willig:
  Dress Down Shabbos? 261
- Rav Mordechai Willig:
  Drinking: Purim and Beyond 273
- Rav Benjamin Yudin:
  Bridging the Religious Generation Gap 281